# METHODS FOR CRITICAL THINKING
## 3rd Edition

## With Contributions by Donald Nute

Department of Philosophy
University of Georgia

Taken from

*Introduction to Logic*
Tenth Edition and Eleventh Edition
by Irving M. Copi and Carl Cohen

Cover Art: *Sky II*, by George Herman.

Excerpts taken from:

*Introduction to Logic*, Eleventh Edition
by Irving M. Copi and Carl Cohen
Copyright © 2002, 1998, 1994 by Pearson Education, Inc.
Published by Prentice-Hall, Inc.
Upper Saddle River, New Jersey 07458

*Introduction to Logic*, Tenth Edition
by Irving M. Copi and Carl Cohen
Copyright© 1998, 1994 by Pearson Education, Inc.
Published by Prentice-Hall, Inc.

Selected excerpts copyright © 2005, 2004, 2003 by Donald Nute.
All rights reserved.

This special edition published in cooperation with Pearson Custom Publishing.

Printed in the United States of America

10  9  8  7  6  5  4  3  2  1

ISBN 0-536-84475-5

2004500062

JC

Please visit our web site at *www.pearsoncustom.com*

PEARSON CUSTOM PUBLISHING
75 Arlington Street, Suite 300, Boston, MA 02116
A Pearson Education Company

# Contents

*Unit I*

# PART ONE

# LOGIC AND LANGUAGE

*All our lives we are giving and accepting reasons.*
*Reasons are the coin we pay for the beliefs we hold.*
——Edith Watson Schipper

*Come now, and let us reason together.*
——Isaiah 1:18

*. . . this we do affirm—that if truth is to be sought in every division of Philosophy, we must, before all else, possess trustworthy principles and methods for the discernment of truth. Now the Logical branch is that which includes the theory of criteria and of proofs; so it is with this that we ought to make our beginnings.*
*—Sextus Empiricus*

*. . . everyone knows the distinction of cogent reasoning from fallacy. The study of logic appeals to no criterion not already present in the learner's mind.*
*—C. I. Lewis*

# CHAPTER 1

# BASIC LOGICAL CONCEPTS

## 1.1 WHAT LOGIC IS

Logic is the study of the methods and principles used to distinguish correct reasoning from incorrect reasoning. There are objective criteria with which correct reasoning may be defined. If these criteria are not known, then they cannot be used. The aim of the study of logic is to discover and make available those criteria that can be used to test arguments, and to sort good arguments from bad ones.

The logician is concerned with reasoning on every subject: science and medicine, ethics and law, politics and commerce, sports and games, and even the simple affairs of everyday life. Very different kinds of reasoning may be used, and all are of interest to the logician. In this book arguments of many varieties, on very many topics, will be analyzed. Our concern throughout will be not with the subject matter of those arguments, but with their *form* and *quality*. Our aim is to learn how to test arguments and evaluate them.

It is not the thought processes called reasoning that are the logician's concern, but the outcomes of those processes, the *arguments* that are the products of reasoning, and that can be formulated in writing, examined, and analyzed. Each argument confronted raises this question for the logician: Does the conclusion reached *follow* from the premisses used or assumed? Do the premisses *provide good reasons* for accepting the conclusion drawn? If the premisses do provide adequate grounds for accepting the conclusion—that is, if asserting the premisses to be true does warrant asserting the conclusion also to be true— then the reasoning is correct. Otherwise it is incorrect.

It would be a mistake to suppose that only the student of logic can reason well or correctly, just as it would be wrong to suppose that only the athlete who studies physiology can run well. Athletes unaware of the processes going on in their bodies often perform excellently, and some advanced students of physiology, although knowing much about the way the body functions, nevertheless perform poorly on the athletic field. Similarly, the study of logic does not give assurance that one's reasoning will be correct.

But a person who has studied logic is more likely to reason correctly than one who has never thought about the principles involved in reasoning. Partly this is because the student of logic will acquire methods for testing the correctness of reasoning, and the more easily errors are detected, the less likely they are to be allowed to stand. Among the errors detected will be those common fallacies, or "natural" mistakes in reasoning, that can be readily avoided when fully understood.

The study of logic is likely to improve the quality of one's reasoning for another reason: It gives one the opportunity to *practice* the analysis of arguments and the construction of arguments of one's own. Reasoning is something we *do* as well as understand; it therefore is an art as well as a science, with skills to be developed and techniques to be mastered. To this end this book provides an abundant supply of exercises through which those skills and techniques may be strengthened.

There are affairs in human life that cannot be fully analyzed by the methods of logic, and issues that cannot be resolved by arguments, even good ones. The appeal to emotion sometimes is more persuasive than logical argument, and in some contexts it may be more appropriate as well. But where judgments that must be relied upon are to be made, correct reasoning will in the long run prove to be their most solid foundation. With the methods and techniques of logic we can distinguish efficiently between correct and incorrect reasoning. These methods and techniques are the subject matter of this book.

## **1.2** PROPOSITIONS AND SENTENCES

We begin by examining *propositions,* the building blocks of every argument. **A proposition is something that may be asserted or denied.** Propositions in this way are different from questions, commands, and exclamations. Neither questions, which can be asked, nor commands, which can be given, nor exclamations, which can be uttered, can possibly be asserted or denied. Only propositions assert that something is (or is not) the case, and therefore only they can be true or false. Truth and falsity do not apply to questions, commands, or exclamations.

Moreover, every proposition *is* either true or false—although we may not know the truth or falsity of some given proposition. The proposition that there is life on some other planet in our galaxy is one whose truth or falsity we do not know; but either it is true that there is such extraterrestrial life, or it is not true. In short, an essential feature of propositions is that they are either true or false.

It is customary to distinguish between propositions and the *sentences* by means of which they are asserted. Two sentences that consist of different words differently arranged may in the same context have the same meaning and be used to assert the same proposition. For example,

Leslie won the election.
The election was won by Leslie.

are plainly two different sentences, for the first contains four words and the second six, and they begin differently, and so on. Yet these two declarative sentences have exactly the same meaning. **We use the term *proposition* to refer to what declarative sentences are typically used to assert.**

A sentence, moreover, is always a sentence in a particular language, the language in which it is used. But propositions are not peculiar to any language; a given proposition may be asserted in many languages. The four sentences

It is raining.
Está lloviendo.
Il pleut.
Es regnet.

are certainly different, for they are in different languages: English, Spanish, French, and German. Yet they have a single meaning, and all may be uttered to assert the same proposition.

The same sentence can be used, in different contexts, to make very different statements. For example, the sentence

The largest state in the United States was once an independent republic.

would have been a true statement about Texas during the first half of the twentieth century, but it is now a false statement about Alaska. A change in the temporal context, plainly, may result in very different propositions, or statements, being asserted by the very same words. (The terms "proposition" and "statement" are not exact synonyms, but in the context of logical investigation they are used in much the same sense. Some writers on logic prefer "statement" to "proposition," although the latter has been more common in the history of logic. In this book, both terms are used.)

The propositions illustrated thus far have been simple: "Leslie won the election"; "It is raining"; and so on. But propositions are often *compound*, containing other propositions within themselves. Consider the following passage from an account of the last days of Hitler's Third Reich in 1945:

The Americans and Russians were driving swiftly to a junction on the Elbe. The British were at the gates of Hamburg and Bremen and threatening to cut off Germany from occupied Denmark. In Italy Bologna had fallen and Alexander's Allied forces were plunging into the valley of the Po. The Russians, having captured Vienna on April 13, were heading up the Danube.[1]

Several propositions contained in this paragraph are compound. "The British were at the gates of Hamburg and Bremen," for example, is the *conjunction* of two propositions: "The British were at the gates of Hamburg," and "The British were at the gates of Bremen." And that conjunctive proposition is itself one component of a larger conjunction, that "the British were at the gates of Hamburg and Bremen and [the British] were threatening to cut off Germany

---

[1]William L. Shirer, *The Rise and Fall of the Third Reich* (New York: Simon and Schuster, 1960).

from occupied Denmark." Every proposition in this passage is asserted; that is, it is stated as true. Asserting the conjunction of two propositions is equivalent to asserting each of the component propositions themselves.

But there are other kinds of compound propositions which do not assert the truth of their components. For example, in *alternative* (or *disjunctive*) propositions, such as

Circuit Courts are useful, or they are not useful.[2]

neither of the two components is asserted; only the compound "either-or" disjunctive proposition is asserted. If this disjunctive proposition is true, either of its components could be false. And in compound propositions that are *hypothetical* (or *conditional*), such as

If God did not exist, it would be necessary to invent him.[3]

again neither of the components is asserted. The proposition that "God does not exist" is not asserted here; nor is the proposition that "it is necessary to invent him." Only the "if-then" proposition is asserted by the hypothetical or conditional statement, and that conditional statement might be true even though both of its components were false.

In the course of this book we shall analyze the internal structure of many kinds of propositions, both simple and compound.

## 1.3 ARGUMENTS, PREMISSES, AND CONCLUSIONS

Propositions are the building blocks with which arguments are made. **The term *inference* refers to the process by which one proposition is arrived at and affirmed on the basis of one or more other propositions accepted as the starting point of the process.** To determine whether an inference is correct, the logician examines the propositions with which that process begins and ends, and the relations between them. This cluster of propositions constitutes an *argument*, and therefore there is an argument corresponding to every possible inference.

It is with arguments that logic is chiefly concerned. As logicians use the word **an *argument* is any group of propositions of which one is claimed to follow from the others, which are regarded as providing support or grounds for the truth of that one.** The word "argument" is often used in other senses also, of course, but in logic it has strictly the sense just explained.

In this strict sense, it is clear that an argument is not a mere collection of propositions; a passage may contain several related propositions and yet contain no *argument* at all. For an argument to be present, the cluster of propositions must have a structure. In describing this structure, the terms "premiss" and "conclusion" are commonly used. **The *conclusion* of an argument is the proposition that**

---

[2]Abraham Lincoln, annual message to Congress, 3 December 1861.

[3]Voltaire, *Épitre à l'Auteur du Livre des Trois Imposteurs*, 10 November 1770.

is affirmed on the basis of the other propositions of the argument, and these other propositions, which are affirmed (or assumed) as providing support or reasons for accepting the conclusion, are the *premisses* of that argument.

The simplest kind of argument consists of one premiss and a conclusion that is claimed to follow from it or be implied by it. The premiss and the conclusion, in that order, may each be stated in a separate sentence, as in this argument that appears on a sticker affixed to biology textbooks in the State of Alabama:

> No one was present when life first appeared on earth. Therefore any statement about life's origins should be considered as theory, not fact.

Or both the premiss and the conclusion may be stated in the same sentence, as in the following argument:

> Since it turns out that all humans are descended from a small number of African ancestors in our recent evolutionary past, believing in profound differences between the races is as ridiculous as believing in a flat earth.[4]

Even in simple arguments, the statement of the conclusion may *precede* the statement of the single premiss. When it does, the two propositions may appear in separate sentences or in the same sentence. An example of separate statements in which the conclusion is stated first is this:

> The Food and Drug Administration should stop all cigarette sales immediately. After all, cigarette smoking is the leading preventable cause of death.[5]

And an example of a combined statement in which the conclusion comes first is this:

> Every law is an evil, for every law is an infraction of liberty.[6]

Most arguments are much more complicated than these, and some arguments, containing compound propositions with several components, are exceedingly complicated, as we shall see. But every argument, whether simple or complex, consists of a group of propositions, of which one is the conclusion and the others are the premisses offered to support it.

Since an argument is made up of a group of propositions, no single proposition can, by itself, be an argument. But some compound propositions closely resemble arguments. Care must be taken not to confuse such propositions with arguments. Consider the following hypothetical proposition:

> If life evolved on Mars during an early period in its history when it had an atmosphere and climate similar to Earth's, then it is likely that life evolved on countless other planets that scientists now believe to exist in our galaxy.

---

[4]David Hayden, "Thy Neighbor, Thy Self," *New York Times,* 9 May 2000.
[5]"Ban Cigarettes," *Orlando Sentinel,* 27 February 1992.
[6]Jeremy Bentham, *Principles of Legislation,* 1802.

Neither the first component of this proposition—"life evolved on Mars during an early period in its history when it had an atmosphere and climate similar to Earth's"—nor the second component—"it is likely that life evolved on countless other planets that scientists now believe exist in our galaxy"—is asserted. The proposition asserts only that the former implies the latter, and both could very well be false. No inference is made in this passage, no conclusion is claimed to be true. This is a hypothetical proposition, not an argument. But now consider the following passage:

> It is likely that life evolved on countless other planets that scientists now believe exist in our galaxy, because life very probably evolved on Mars during an early period in its history when it had an atmosphere and climate similar to Earth's.[7]

In this case we *do* have an argument. The proposition that "life very probably evolved on Mars" is here asserted as a premiss, and the proposition that "life likely evolved on countless other planets" is here claimed to follow from that premiss and to be true. Thus, a hypothetical proposition may *look* very much like an argument, but it never can *be* an argument, and the two should not be confused. Recognizing arguments is a topic discussed below in section 1.5.

Finally, it should be emphasized that while every argument is a structured cluster of propositions, not every structured cluster of propositions is an argument. Consider this passage from a recent account of travel in Africa:

> Camels do not store water in their humps. They drink furiously, up to 28 gallons in a ten-minute session, then distribute the water evenly throughout their bodies. Afterward, they use the water stingily. They have viscous urine and dry feces. They breathe through their noses and keep their mouths shut. They do sweat, but only as a last resort....They can survive a water loss of up to one-third of their body weight, then drink up and feel fine.[8]

There is no argument here.

## Exercises

Identify the premisses and conclusions in the following passages, each of which contains only one argument.[9]

## Example:

1. A well regulated militia being necessary to the security of a free state, the right of the people to keep and bear arms shall not be infringed.

   —*The Constitution of the United States*, Amendment 2

---

[7]Richard Zare, "Big News for Earthlings," *New York Times*, 8 August 1996.

[8]William Langewiesche, *Sahara Unveiled: A Journey Across the Desert* (New York: Pantheon Books, 1996).

[9]Solutions to the starred exercises may be found at the back of the book.

**Solution:**

PREMISS: A well regulated militia is necessary for the security of a free state.

CONCLUSION: The right of the people to keep and bear arms shall not be infringed.

2. We can avert a majority of cancers by prevention efforts, even if we never get straight on the causes; more research on prevention and less on cure makes increasing sense.

> —Daniel Callahan, "Lab Games,"
> *New York Times Book Review*, 9 April 1995

3. Good sense is of all things in the world the most equally distributed, for everybody thinks himself so abundantly provided with it that even those most difficult to please in all other matters do not commonly desire more of it than they already possess.

> —René Descartes, *A Discourse on Method*, 1637

4. Of all our passions and appetites the love of power is of the most imperious and unsociable nature, since the pride of one man requires the submission of the multitude.

> —Edward Gibbon, *The Decline and*
> *Fall of the Roman Empire*, vol. 1, chap. IV

*5. Forbear to judge, for we are sinners all.

> —William Shakespeare, *Henry VI, Part II*, act 3, scene 3

6. In preparing for the national census of 2000, intense disagreement arose over whether the U.S. Constitution requires an actual head count of the population, or whether a sophisticated sampling technique might reasonably replace the head count. A letter to the *New York Times* on 6 September 1998 contained the following argument: With the "head count" method, the Census Bureau cannot succeed in counting all the people in the United States. Therefore the 'head count' system is itself a sampling method, in which the sample is the portion of the population that actually returns the questionnaire.

> —Keith Bradley, "What Did the Founders Expect
> From the Census?"

7. The essence of our admirable economic system is to create wants as fast as, or faster than it satisfies them. Thus the improvement of living conditions, meaning greater consumer satisfaction, is, by definition, impossible.

> —J. Maher, "Never Better," *New York Times*, 1 January 1993

8. Because they clear the way for pathogens bio-chemically, as well as giving them a free ride, ticks are among the most pernicious disease vectors in the world.

> —Cynthia Mills, "Blood Feud," *The Sciences*, April 1998

9. He that loveth not knoweth not God; for God is love.

—1 John 4:8

*10. Because light moves at a finite speed, looking at objects that are millions of miles away is actually looking at light that was emitted many years ago.

—D. Richstone, "University of Michigan
Joins Magellan Project," *Ann Arbor News*, 13 February 1996

11. What stops many people from photocopying a book and giving it to a pal is not integrity but logistics; it's easier and inexpensive to buy your friend a paperback copy.

—Randy Cohen, *New York Times Magazine*, 26 March 2000

12. Some live to 100 without ever contributing to the improvement of humankind. Some die young in an undertaking that improves humankind. So it is absurd simply to concentrate on some scientific means to extend longevity."

—William J. Cousins, "To a Long Life! But How Long?"
*New York Times*, 25 December 1999

13. The theoretical justification of our argument [that the legalization of abortion in the 1970s substantially reduced crime in the 1990s] rests on two simple assumptions: 1) Legalized abortion leads to fewer "unwanted" babies being born, and 2) unwanted babies are more likely to suffer abuse and neglect and are therefore more likely to be criminally involved in later life.

—Steven Levitt, *www.slate.com/dialogues/*, 23 August 1999

14. Today's first year college students have lived the external appearances of an adult life for many more years than their counterparts 50 years ago did. [Therefore], what we have traditionally associated with the intellectual awakening during the college years must now occur in the high school."

—Leon Botstein, *Jefferson's Children: Education and
the Promise of American Culture*, 1998

*15. The institution of public education thrives on its own failures. The more poorly its charges perform, the more money it asks for (and gets) from the public and the government. The more money it gets, the more it can grow itself.

—Ian Hamet, "School for Scandal,"
*The Weekly Standard*, 23 August 1999

16. The ideal audience [for the magician] is one comprising mathematicians, philosophers, and scientists, because a logical mind, receptive to a connection between each apparent cause and its ap-

parent effect, is more prone to surprise when an illusion reaches its 'illogical' climax.

> —Martyn Bedford, *The Houdini Girl*, Pantheon Books, 1999

17. Accusations [of sexual harassment] are based on "impact" not intention; therefore the accused is guilty if the accuser believes him to be guilty.

> —Herbert London, New York University Dean,
> quoted in Alan Kors and Harvey Silverglate,
> *The Shadow University*, The Free Press, 1998

18. It is wrong to tax people on the income they make while they are living and to double-tax them when they die and want to pass their life savings on to their children, grandchildren, or the charity of their choice. The death tax, otherwise called the estate tax, is unfair and should be abolished.

> —Representative Bill Archer,
> Chairman of the U.S. House Committee
> on Ways and Means, 3 July 1998

19. Standardized tests have a disparate racial and ethnic impact; white and Asian students score, on average, markedly higher than their black and Hispanic peers. This is true for fourth-grade tests, college entrance exams, and every other assessment on the books. If a racial gap is evidence of discrimination, then all tests discriminate.

> —Abigail Thernstrom, "Testing, the Easy Target,"
> *New York Times*, 15 January 2000

*20. Unquestionably, no more important goal exists in medical research today than the development of an AIDS vaccine. Last year (1998) AIDS, caused by HIV (Human Immunodeficiency Virus) was the infectious disease that killed the most people around the world, and the epidemic is not abating.

> —David Baltimore, President of the
> California Institute of Technology, in
> *The Chronicle of Higher Education*, 28 May 1999

## 1.4 ANALYZING ARGUMENTS

Many arguments are simple, but some are quite complex. The premises of an argument may support its conclusion in different ways. The number of premises and the order of the propositions in an argument may vary. We need techniques to analyze argumentative passages and clarify the relations of premises and conclusions within them.

Two techniques are common. We may *paraphrase* an argument, setting forth its propositions in clear language and logical order. We may also *diagram* an argument, exhibiting its structure using spatial relations in two dimensions. Both techniques can be useful; we choose the one that helps most in the context given.

## A.   Paraphrasing

Consider the following argument, in which there are more than two premisses and the conclusion is stated first:

> Upright walking therapods, the group that includes Tyrannosaurus rex, could not have evolved into modern birds, for three main reasons. The first is that most fossils of bird-like therapod dinosaurs originated 75 million years *after* the fossilized remains of the first bird....The second is that the ancestors of birds must have been suited for flight—and therapods are not. A third problem is that ... every therapod dinosaur has serrated teeth, but no bird has serrated teeth.[10]

To clarify it we may *paraphrase* it, listing each premiss, restating the conclusion, and simplifying the language for the sale of clarity:

1. Fossils of bird-like therapod dinosaurs originated long after the fossilized remains of the first bird.
2. The ancestors of birds must have been suited for flight, but therapod dinosaurs were not so suited.
3. Every therapod dinosaur has serrated teeth, but no bird has serrated teeth.
   Therefore therapod dinosaurs could not have evolved into modern birds.

Paraphrasing an argument often assists our understanding of it because in doing so we must bring to the surface what is assumed in the argument but is not fully or explicitly stated. The great mathematician G. H. Hardy argued thus:

> Archimedes will be remembered when Aeschylus is forgotten, because languages die and mathematical ideas do not.[11]

To paraphrase this argument fully we would spell out what it takes for granted:

1. Languages die.
2. The great plays of Aeschylus are in a language.
3. So the work of Aeschylus will eventually die.

---

[10]Adapted from Alan Feduccia, *The Origin and Evolution of Birds* (New Haven, CT: Yale University Press, 1996).

[11]G. H. Hardy, *A Mathematician's Apology* (Cambridge University Press, 1940).

4. Mathematical ideas do not die.

5. The great work of Archimedes was with mathematical ideas.

6. So the work of Archimedes will not die.
    Therefore Archimedes will be remembered when Aeschylus is forgotten.

The paraphrase enables us to see that several arguments, with disputable premisses, have been compressed into Hardy's one short sentence.

## B. Diagramming

Sometimes it is useful to *diagram* an argument to exhibit its structure. To do this we number each proposition in the order in which it appears, circling the numbers. We then exhibit the logical relations of premisses and conclusion using arrows between the numbers. This avoids the need to restate the premisses. Consider this argument:

> ① Contrary to what many people think, a positive test for HIV is not necessarily a death sentence. For one thing, ② the time from the development of antibodies to clinical symptoms averages nearly ten years. For another, ③ many reports are now suggesting that a significant number of people who test positive may never develop clinical AIDS.[12]

Without restating the propositions of this argument we can use the circled numbers to represent the propositions and diagram the argument as follows:

If an argument is straightforward, we may not need a diagram to understand it fully. But arguments often are not straightforward, and the diagramming technique[13] is helpful because it displays the structure of the argument *visually* in space. We place the conclusion in the space below the premisses, while the premisses of a given argument will all appear on the same horizontal level.

Unlike a paraphrase, a diagram can readily exhibit the *way* in which the premisses support the conclusion. In the argument above, for example, each of the premisses, (2) and (3), supports the conclusion (1)—that a positive test for HIV is not necessarily a death sentence—*independently*. That is, each premiss by itself supplies some reason for accepting that conclusion and gives such sup-

---

[12]R. S. Root-Bernstein, "Misleading Reliability," *The Sciences*, March 1990.

[13]The technique was first developed and perfected decades ago by several distinguished logicians: Monroe C. Beardsley, in *Practical Logic* (Prentice-Hall, 1950); Stephen N. Thomas, in *Practical Reasoning in Natural Language* (Prentice-Hall, 1973); and Michael Scriven, in *Reasoning* (McGraw-Hill, 1976). We follow their lead.

port even in the absence of the other premiss. This separate support is visually exhibited in the diagram.

But in some arguments the premisses serve their purpose only when combined. For example:

> ① If an action promotes the best interests of everyone concerned and violates no one's rights, then that action is morally acceptable. ② In at least some cases, active euthanasia promotes the best interests of everyone concerned, and violates no one's rights. Therefore ③ in at least some cases active euthanasia is morally acceptable.[14]

An accurate diagram of this argument will exhibit the fact that its premisses work only because they are *joined together*, thus:

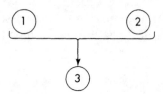

We bracket the premisses here because in this case neither premiss supports the conclusion independently. If the principle expressed in the first premiss were true, but there were no case in which active euthanasia promoted everyone's best interests, the conclusion would be given no support at all. And if there were cases in which active euthanasia did promote everyone's best interests, but the principle expressed in the first premise were not true, the conclusion would remain without support.

Diagrams are particularly useful when the argument has a complicated structure. What cannot be easily said can sometimes be easily shown. Consider the following argument:

> ① Desert mountaintops make good sites for astronomy. ② Being high, they sit above a portion of the atmosphere, enabling a star's light to reach a telescope without having to swim through the entire depths of the atmosphere. ③ Being dry, the desert is also relatively cloud-free. ④ The merest veil of haze or cloud can render a sky useless for many astronomical measures.[15]

In this argument proposition ① is plainly the conclusion, and the other three provide support for it—but they give that support in different ways. The single statement ② by itself supports the claim that mountaintops are good sites for telescopes. But statements ③ and ④ must work together to support the claim that *desert* mountaintops are good sites for telescopes. A diagram exhibits this relationship neatly:

---

[14]James Rachels, cited in T. A. Mappes and J. S. Zembaty, eds., *Social Ethics,* 3d ed. (McGraw-Hill, 1987).

[15]Blanchard Hiatt, University of Michigan Research News, September 1979.

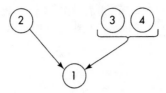

But some kinds of complications are revealed more efficiently using paraphrase. For example, when an argument has a premiss that is not explicitly stated, a paraphrase allows us to simply add the tacit premiss to the list. A diagram would require us both to formulate the tacit premiss and to represent it visually in some form—usually a broken circle—that indicates that it has been added to the original passage. Thus the argument

> [I]t is only when it is believed that I could have acted otherwise that I am held to be morally responsible for what I have done. For a man is not thought to be morally responsible for an action that it was not in his power to avoid.[16]

may be more readily clarified by paraphrase in which its tacit premiss is made explicit, thus:

**1.** A man is not thought to be morally responsible for an action that it was not in his power to avoid.

**2.** Only when I could have acted otherwise was the action one that was in my power to avoid.

Therefore only when it is believed that I could have acted otherwise am I held responsible for what I have done.

## C. Interwoven Arguments

When a passage contains two or more arguments and a number of propositions whose relations are not obvious, a diagram may prove particularly useful. Here, for example, is a passage from one of the letters of Karl Marx to Friedrich Engels:

> ① To hasten the social revolution in England is the most important object of the International Workingman's Association. ② The sole means of hastening it is to make Ireland independent. Hence ③ the task of the "International" is everywhere to put the conflict between England and Ireland in the foreground, and ④ everywhere to side openly with Ireland.[17]

The number of arguments in a passage is generally agreed to be determined by the number of conclusions. Thus, because there are two conclusions in this

---

[16]A. J. Ayer, "Freedom and Necessity," *Polemic*, no. 5.

[17]Karl Marx, Letter #141, 9 April 1870, *Karl Marx and Friedrich Engels Correspondence, 1846–1895* (International Publishers, 1936).

passage, it contains two arguments. Here, however, both conclusions are inferred from the same two premises. A diagram exhibits this structure nicely:

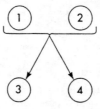

In some passages two conclusions, and hence two arguments, have a single stated premiss. Here is an example:

> Older women have less freedom to fight sexual harassment at their jobs or to leave a battering husband, because age discrimination means they won't easily find other ways of supporting themselves.[18]

The single premiss here is that older women cannot easily find alternative ways of supporting themselves. That premiss supports two conclusions: that older women have less freedom to fight sexual harassment at their jobs, and that older married women have less freedom to leave a battering husband. Ordinarily, by a "single argument" we mean an argument with a single conclusion, regardless of how many premises are adduced in its support.

When there are two or more premises in an argument, or two or more arguments in a passage, the order of appearance of premises and conclusions may need to be sorted out. The conclusion may be stated last, or first, or it may be sandwiched between the premises offered in its support, as in the following passage:

> The real and original source of inspiration for the Muslim thinkers was the Quran and the sayings of the Holy Prophet. It is therefore clear that the Muslim philosophy was not a carbon copy of Greek thought, as it concerned itself primarily and specifically with those problems which originated from and had relevance to Muslims.[19]

Here the conclusion, that "Muslim philosophy was not a carbon copy of Greek thought," appears after the first premise of the argument and before the second.

The same proposition that serves as a conclusion in one argument may serve as premiss in a different argument, just as the same person may be a commander in one context and a subordinate in another. This is well illustrated by a passage from the work of Thomas Aquinas. He argues

> Human law is framed for the multitude of human beings.
> The majority of human beings are not perfect in virtue.
> Therefore human laws do not forbid all vices.[20]

---

[18]Boston Women's Health Book Collective, *Our Bodies, Our Selves* (Simon and Schuster, 1984).
[19]C. A. Quadir, *Philosophy and Science in the Islamic World* (London: Croom Helm, 1988).
[20]Thomas Aquinas, *Summa Theologiae*, I, Question 96, Article 2, circa 1265.

The conclusion of this argument is used immediately thereafter as a premiss in another, quite different argument:

> Vicious acts are contrary to acts of virtue.
> But human law does not prohibit all vices....
> Therefore neither does it prescribe all acts of virtue.[21]

A cascade of arguments in which the conclusion of one serves as the premiss of another may be so compressed that a full paraphrase can be very helpful. Consider the following set of arguments:

> Because ① the greatest mitochondrial variations occurred in African people, scientists concluded that ② they had the longest evolutionary history, indicating ③ a probable African origin for modern humans.[22]

We might diagram the passage thus:

A paraphrase of the same cascade, though clumsier, is more complete:

1. The more mitochondrial variation in a people the longer its evolutionary history;
2. The greatest mitochondrial variations occurred in African people.
   Therefore African people have had the longest evolutionary history.

1. African people have had the longest evolutionary history.
2. Modern humans probably originated where people have had the longest evolutionary history.
   Therefore modern humans probably originated in Africa.

Such combinations make it evident that a proposition taken in isolation is neither a premiss nor a conclusion. It is a premiss where it occurs as an assumption in an argument. It is a conclusion where it is claimed to follow from other propositions assumed in an argument. In other words, "premiss" and "conclusion" are *relative* terms.

---

[21]*Ibid*, Article 3.
[22]From *Science*, 26 May 1995.

Multiple arguments may appear in forms other than cascades; they may be interwoven in unusual patterns that require thoughtful analysis. The diagramming technique is particularly well suited to such cases. For example, in John Locke's influential *Second Treatise of Government*, two arguments are combined in the following passage:

> It is not necessary—no, nor so much as convenient—that the legislative should be always in being; but absolutely necessary that the executive power should, because there is not always need of new laws to be made, but always need of execution of the laws that are made.

The component propositions may be numbered thus: ①It is not necessary or convenient that the legislative [branch of government] should be always in being; ②it is absolutely necessary that the executive power should be always in being; ③there is not always need of new laws to be made; ④there is always need of execution of the laws that are made. The diagram for this passage is:

which shows that the conclusion of the second argument is stated between the conclusion and premise of the first argument, and that the premise of the first argument is stated between the conclusion and premise of the second argument. The diagram also shows that both conclusions are stated before their premises.

The same diagram exhibits the logical structure of two related arguments of the Roman philosopher Seneca in support of the deterrence theory of punishment:

> ① No one punishes because a sin has been committed, ② but in order that a sin will not be committed. [For] ③ what has passed cannot be recalled, but ④ what lies in the future may be prevented.

That "we do not punish because a sin has been committed" is the conclusion of one argument; its premise is that "what has passed cannot be recalled." That "we do punish in order that a sin will not be committed" is the conclusion of a second argument, whose premise is that "what lies in the future may be prevented."

In sum, diagramming and paraphrasing are useful tools with which we can analyze arguments so as to understand more fully the relations of premises to conclusions.

## Exercises

The following passages—all appearing recently in the *New York Times*—concern important matters of public policy. Analyze the arguments they contain, paraphrasing propositions where that is needed, and diagramming the argument where you find that helpful.

**Example:**

1.  Genes and proteins are discovered, not invented. Inventions are patentable, discoveries are not. Thus, protein patents are intrinsically flawed.

    —Daniel Alroy, "Invention vs. Discovery,"
    *New York Times*, 29 March 2000

**Solution:**

PREMISES:  Proteins are discovered, not invented.
Discoveries are not patentable, although inventions are.
CONCLUSION:  Protein patents are intrinsically flawed.

2.  Why decry the wealth gap? First, inequality is correlated with political instability. Second, inequality is correlated with violent crime. Third, economic inequality is correlated with reduced life expectancy. A fourth reason? Simple justice. There is no moral justification for chief executives being paid hundreds of times more than ordinary employees.

    —Richard Hutchinsons, "When the Rich Get Even Richer,"
    *New York Times*, 26 January 2000

    *⑥ The wealth gap is a form of inequality*

3.  Wall Street, where prices were sinking, saw the recent employment numbers as fresh evidence of a rising inflation rate, if not right away, then by early spring. The concern is that a shortage of workers forces employers to pay higher wages, and then to raise prices to cover the added labor costs.

    —Louis Uchitelle, "387,000 New Jobs"
    *New York Times*, 5 February 2000

4.  Married people are healthier and more economically stable than single people, and children of married people do better on a variety of indicators. Marriage is thus a socially responsible act. There ought to be some way of spreading the principle of support for marriage throughout the tax code.

    —Anya Bernstein, "Marriage, Fairness and Taxes,"
    *New York Times*, 15 February 2000

*5.  If you marry without love, it does not mean you will not later come to love the person you marry. And if you marry the person you love, it does not mean that you will always love that person or have a successful marriage. The divorce rate is very low in many countries that have prearranged marriage. The divorce rate is very high in countries where people base their marriage decisions on love.

    —Alex Hammoud, "I Take This Man, For Richer Only,"
    *New York Times*, 18 February 2000

6. Our entire tax system depends upon the vast majority of taxpayers who attempt to pay the taxes they owe having confidence that they're being treated fairly and that their competitors and neighbors are also paying what is due. If the public concludes that the IRS cannot meet these basic expectations, the risk to the tax system will become very high, and the effects very difficult to reverse.

—David Cay Johnston, "Adding Auditors to Help IRS Catch Tax Cheaters," *New York Times*, 13 February 2000

7. Since 1976, states (in the United States) have executed 612 people, and released 81 from death row who were found to be innocent. Is there any reason to believe that the criminal justice system is more accurate in *non*-capital cases? If the criminal justice system makes half the mistakes in non-capital cases that it makes in capital cases, thousands of innocent people live in our prisons.

—Philip Moustakis, "Missing: A Death Penalty Debate," *New York Times*, 23 February 2000

8. The divergent paths taken by New York and Texas in the 1990s illustrate the futility of over-reliance on prisons as a cure for crime. Texas added more people to prisons in the 1990s (98,081) than New York's entire prison population (73,233). If prisons are a cure for crime, Texas should have mightily outperformed New York from a crime-control standpoint. But from 1990 to 1998 the decline in New York's crime rate exceeded the decline in Texas's crime rate by 26%.

—Vincent Schiraldi, "Prisons and Crime," *New York Times*, 6 October 2000

9. In most presidential elections in the United States, more than half the states are ignored; voters who don't live in so-called swing states are in effect bystanders in these quadrennial events. An Amendment to the U.S. Constitution should replace the archaic electoral vote system with a direct vote. Only in this manner will citizens in all 50 states be able to take part fully in selecting our nation's leaders.

—Lawrence R. Foster, "End the Electoral College," *New York Times*, 27 September 2000

*10. Petitioners' reasoning would allow Congress to regulate any crime so long as the nationwide, aggregated impact of that crime has substantial effects on employment, production, transit, or consumption. If Congress may regulate gender-motivated violence [on these grounds], it would be able to regulate murder or any other type of violence since gender-motivated violence, as a subset of all violent crime, is certain to have lesser economic impacts than the larger class of which it is a part.

—Chief Justice William Rehnquist, U.S. Supreme Court, *U.S. v. Morrison*, Decided 15 May 2000

**\*11.** For discussion:

In a recent murder trial in Virginia, the judge instructed the jury that: "you may fix the punishment of the defendant at death" if the state proved beyond a reasonable doubt at least one of two aggravating circumstances: that the defendant would continue to be a serious threat to society, or that the crime was "outrageously or wantonly vile, horrible or inhuman." The jury, deliberating the sentence after finding the accused guilty, returned to the judge with this question: If we believe that the state has satisfied one of these alternatives, "then is it our duty as a jury to issue the death penalty?" The judge, in response, simply told them to re-read the instructions already given on that point. The jury returned two hours later, some of its members in tears, with a death sentence for the defendant.

This death sentence was appealed, and the case was ultimately reviewed by the U.S. Supreme Court [*Weeks v. Angelone*, No. 99-5746, decided 19 January 2000]. The issue that Court confronted was whether, in the circumstances of this case, the death sentence should be nullified on the ground that the jury had been confused about the instructions they had been given. What arguments would you construct in support of either side of this controversy?

## 1.5 RECOGNIZING ARGUMENTS

### A. Conclusion- and Premiss-Indicators

As we have seen, the order in which propositions appear in an argumentative passage cannot be relied upon to identify the conclusion or the premisses. What then may we use to make this identification? Certain words or phrases, called "conclusion-indicators," are helpful because they typically serve to introduce the conclusion of an argument. Here is a partial list of *conclusion-indicators:*

| | |
|---|---|
| therefore | for these reasons |
| hence | it follows that |
| thus | we may infer |
| so | I conclude that |
| accordingly | which shows that |
| in consequence | which means that |
| consequently | which entails that |
| proves that | which implies that |
| as a result | which allows us to infer that |
| for this reason | which points to the conclusion that |

Other words or phrases typically serve to mark the premisses of an argument and hence are called premiss-indicators. Usually, but not always, what follows any one of these will be the premiss of some argument. Here is a partial list of *premiss-indicators:*

| | |
|---|---|
| since | as indicated by |
| because | the reason is that |
| for | for the reason that |
| as | may be inferred from |
| follows from | may be derived from |
| as shown by | may be deduced from |
| inasmuch as | in view of the fact that |

## B. Arguments in Context

The words and phrases listed above may help us recognize the presence of an argument or identify its premisses or conclusion. But it is not necessary for these terms to appear; the fact that an argument has been presented may be indicated by the setting or by the meaning of the passage. For example, one author extends her sharp criticism of smoking with the following statements:

> Whether or not to smoke is a conscious decision, made in the light of an abundance of information on the lethal effects of tobacco. Surely those who choose unwisely should bear the cost of any resulting ill health.[23]

No premiss or conclusion indicators are used here, yet the argument is unmistakable. Similarly, the following passage contains an argument that is immediately recognizable from the sense of the propositions themselves:

> The deterrence argument has been refuted in recent years. Eighteen of the twenty states with the highest murder rates have and use the death penalty. Of the biggest cities with the highest murder rate, seventeen are in death penalty jurisdictions. Texas has executed more people during the last decade than any other state, but still has three cities with murder rates among the top twenty-five. Over nearly two decades two neighboring states, Michigan, with no death penalty, and Indiana, with a death penalty, have had indistinguishable homicide rates.[24]

The argumentative functions of such passages are exhibited by their contexts and their meanings—just as, if I said that I am taking a lobster home for dinner, you would have little doubt that I intended to eat it, not feed it.

Another argument without conclusion- or premiss-indicators appears in a recent defense of proportional representation:

> The single-member-district system of elections is seen to have a number of serious drawbacks. It routinely denies representation to large numbers of voters, produces legislatures that fail to reflect accurately the views of the public, discriminates against third parties, and discourages voter turnout.[25]

---

[23]Lois Taylor, "Is Smoking About Choice?," *New York Times,* 5 September 2000.

[24]D. C. Leven, "Deterrence Fails," *New York Times,* 3 March 1995.

[25]D. J. Amy, "Elections in Which Every Vote Counts," *The Chronicle of Higher Education,* 12 January 1996.

Although this passage might be regarded as *stating* a widely understood truth and then *illustrating* it with various consequences of the single-member-district system, it can be equally well understood as an argument whose conclusion is stated first and followed by the premises offered in its support.

A somewhat more intricate example of an argument in which neither conclusion-indicators nor premiss-indicators appear is the following passage from a Supreme Court opinion concerning the desegregation of public schools:

> That there was racial imbalance in student attendance was not tantamount to a showing that the school district was in noncompliance with …its duties under the law. Racial balance is not to be achieved for its own sake. It is to be pursued when racial imbalance has been caused by a constitutional violation. Once the racial imbalance due to the *de jure* violation has been remedied, the school district is under no duty to remedy imbalance that is caused by demographic factors.[26]

The first sentence of this passage presents the conclusion of its argument, which may be paraphrased as "the presence of racial imbalance does not show that the school district violated the law." How do we know this? Context is crucial here: the sentences that follow the first one offer reasons for what has gone before. We see that it is the conduct of "the school district," referred to in the first sentence, that is at issue; we discern that the sentences following that one express more general propositions that bear upon the conduct of the school district. The words chosen also give clues; although the phrase "was not tantamount to a showing" is not a conclusion-indicator, it does convey the suggestion that the first sentence is the logical endpoint of the passage.

Passages containing arguments often contain additional material that serves neither as premiss nor conclusion. Sometimes that material supplies background information that enables the reader (or hearer) to understand what the argument is about. In the following passage an argument appears in the concluding sentence, but it would not be intelligible if we had not grasped the sentence before it:

> As the government spends increasingly less on student financial aid, many leading colleges and universities are using a greater percentage of tuition revenues for scholarships. Just as income tax breaks are given for charitable contributions, this portion of tuition should be tax deductible.[27]

Strictly speaking the first sentence in this passage is not part of the argument, but without it we would not understand that "this portion of tuition" is the portion used for scholarships. With that understanding, we can paraphrase the argument as follows:

1. Charitable contributions to the needy are tax-deductible.
2. Substantial portions of tuition revenue are used by colleges as a charitable contribution to scholarships for needy students.

---

[26]*Freeman v. Pitts*, 503 U.S. 467, 1992.

[27]D. Goldin, "Some College Costs Should Be Tax Deductible," *New York Times*, 18 April 1992.

Therefore, that portion of tuition used for scholarships to needy students should be tax-deductible.

Understanding cross-references within the context may thus be essential for understanding the argument itself. An argument by the philosopher Arthur Schopenhauer in defense of suicide illustrates this reliance upon cross-reference:

> If the criminal law forbids suicide, that is not an argument valid in the Church; and besides, the prohibition is ridiculous; for what penalty can frighten a person who is not afraid of death itself?[28]

The material before the first semicolon in this passage is neither premiss nor conclusion—but without it we would not know that in the conclusion of the subsequent argument ("the prohibition is ridiculous"), the "prohibition" referred to is the prohibition of suicide by the criminal law.

## C.   Premisses Not in Declarative Form

In the preceding illustration, the premiss of the argument appears in the form of a question: "What penalty can frighten a person who is not afraid of death itself?" But as we saw in section 1.2, questions assert nothing; they do not express propositions. How then can a question function as a premiss? It can do so when the question is *rhetorical*. That is, a question may suggest or assume a premiss when the question is one whose answer the author believes to be obvious or inescapable. In our illustration, Schopenhauer thought the obvious answer to his question was "none." Thus, though framed in the form of a question, the premiss of Schopenhauer's argument was the implied proposition that "there is no penalty that can frighten a person who is not afraid of death itself."

Arguments in which one of the premisses is a question whose answer is assumed to be evident are very common; they also can be rhetorically effective, as in the following argument of Socrates:

> If there is no one who desires to be miserable, there is no one, Meno, who desires evil; for what is misery but the desire and possession of evil?[29]

Using questions in this way is risky, however. Strictly speaking, the question can be neither true nor false. If the answer that is assumed to be obvious or inescapable is *not* so, the argument is defective, and its defect may be obscured by the question. Was Socrates correct in assuming that misery *is* the desire and possession of evil? The answer to his question is not obvious.

The conclusions of arguments that depend on rhetorical questions are suspect. To avoid responsibility for the forthright assertion of their premisses, authors sometimes ask a question whose answer is supposed to be obvious when that assumed answer actually is dubious or even false.

---

[28]A. Schopenhauer, "On Suicide," 1851.
[29]Plato, *Meno*, 78a.

The use of a genuinely rhetorical question as a premiss can be a very clever technique, however. By suggesting the desired answer and leading readers to provide that answer for themselves, one can augment the persuasiveness of the argument. Consider the use of rhetorical questions in the following two examples. In the New Testament we find this passage:

> If a man say, I love God, and hateth his brother, he is a liar: for he that loves not his brother whom he hath seen, how can he love God whom he hath not seen?[30]

And in a recent critique of the defense of euthanasia, the following argument appears:

> If a right to euthanasia is grounded in self-determination, it cannot reasonably be limited to the terminally ill. If people have a right to die, why must they wait until they are actually dying before they are permitted to exercise that right?[31]

In both examples the supposed answers (that "one who does not love his brother cannot love God," and that "people need not wait until they are actually dying before they are permitted to exercise their right") are assumed to be perfectly evident. These answers serve as premisses that support the conclusions intended: "that one who loves God cannot hate his brother," and that "if there is a right to euthanasia grounded in self-determination it cannot be limited to the terminally ill."

Sometimes the conclusion of an argument takes the form of an imperative, or command. After reasons have been offered to persuade us to perform a given action, we are *directed* to act thus-and-so. In Proverbs, for example, we read:

> Wisdom is the principal thing; therefore get wisdom.

And in *Hamlet*, Polonius gives famous advice to his son, Laertes:

> Neither a borrower nor a lender be;
> For loan oft loses both itself and friend,
> And borrowing dulls the edge of husbandry.[32]

Since a command, like a question, cannot express a proposition, it cannot be (strictly speaking) the conclusion of an argument. But for the sake of simplicity it is useful to regard commands, in these contexts, as no different from propositions in which hearers (or readers) are told that they *should*, or *ought to*, act in the manner specified in the command. The conclusions in the two arguments above may then be rephrased as: "Getting wisdom is what you should do," and "You ought to be neither a lender nor a borrower."

---

[30]1 John 4:20.

[31]Ramsey Colloquium of the Institute on Religion and Public Life, "Always to Care, Never to Kill," *Wall Street Journal*, 17 November 1991.

[32]William Shakespeare, *Hamlet*, act 1, scene 3.

Almost everyone will agree that assertions of this kind can be true or false. Exactly what difference, if any, there is, between a command to do something and a statement that it should be done is a difficult problem that need not be explored here. By ignoring that difference (if there really is one) we are able to deal uniformly with arguments whose conclusions are expressed in this form.

Our aim is to understand arguments more fully. Reformulation can help by clarifying the roles of the argument's constituent propositions while depending as little as possible on context. We want to focus on the propositions themselves; we want to know whether they are true or false, what they imply, whether they are implied by other propositions, and whether they are serving as premiss or as conclusion in some argument. We seek to grasp the substance of the propositions relied on, whatever their grammatical form.

Some reformulations are merely grammatical. Arguments are built of propositions, but the words that express a proposition (and hence a premiss) may take the form of a phrase, rather than a declarative sentence. This is well illustrated in a passage discussing the possibility of extraterrestrial life.

> Is there life beyond the earth? The jury is still out. But with planets aplenty; with creatures that can live without the energy of a nearby star; with abundant cosmic sources of cosmic hydrogen and oxygen to make water; with several natural ways for planets to generate internal heat; with the possibility that life could originate in undersea volcanoes and propagate varieties hardy enough to spread their seeds to other worlds; and with rocky meteorites that could serve as vehicles for interplanetary exchange, the idea that life has evolved elsewhere in the universe seems less daunting than it did just a few years ago.[33]

The conclusion here—that life beyond our earth is a notion at least more acceptable now than it used to be—is supported by six distinct premisses, each calling attention to recently discovered facts or possibilities, and each rendering extraterrestrial life somewhat more plausible. When these premisses are rephrased as declarative sentences, *e.g.,*: (1) There are plenty of other planets; (2) there are creatures that can live without the energy of a nearby star; and so on, the argument expressed in this passage becomes evident.

## D. Unstated Propositions

The analysis of an argument may become yet more complicated when one or more of its constituent propositions is not stated but is assumed to be understood. An example arose at the U.S. Supreme Court in April 2000, involving the famous *Miranda* rules (which prohibit confessions from being admitted at trial unless a suspect in custody has been first advised that he has the right to remain silent, and the right to have an attorney). Defenders of the *Miranda* rules argued thus:

> If the *Miranda* decision is reversed, police will no longer be compelled to give those warnings [of the right to remain silent, etc.]; and if they aren't compelled to give them,

---

[33]Peter G. Brown, "Stardust," *The Sciences*, August 1988.

they won't give them. But because police interrogations take place out of public view, the integrity of such interrogations can be safeguarded only if those *Miranda* warnings are invariably given.[34]

The conclusion of their argument—that those warnings must always be given and that the Supreme Court should *not* reverse the *Miranda* decision—did not need to be stated in that context.

In a very different context, the distinguished novelist Anais Nin described one of her fictional characters by saying that "The dreamer rejects the ordinary. Jay invited the ordinary."[35] We infer what the author sought to convey—"Jay was no dreamer"—even though it is not stated.

One of the premises of an argument may be left unstated because the arguer supposes that it is common knowledge or that it will be readily granted for other reasons. In Shakespeare's *Julius Caesar*, while Marc Antony is delivering his famous speech about Caesar's ambition, one of the listening citizens remarks about Caesar:

> He would not take the crown;
> Therefore 'tis certain he was not ambitious.[36]

This is an argument, but part of it is missing; plainly it relies upon the plausible, but unstated, premiss that "one who would not accept the crown must not have been ambitious." Arguments in everyday discourse often rely on some proposition that is not stated. Such arguments are called **enthymemes.**[37]

Sometimes it may not be obvious just how one would formulate the proposition on which the speaker relies, even though, once formulated, it is readily accepted. In a recent account of the historical controversy over slavery in America and the role of moral argument in that controversy, the author writes:

> If one doesn't believe that moral arguments make any difference, then one doesn't believe in republican government.[38]

In this enthymeme the unstated premise is the claim that "believing in republican government entails that one does believe that moral arguments make a difference"—a claim that most of us would grant.

On the other hand, the unstated proposition on which an enthymeme relies may not be obvious, but disputable—and the absence of an explicit statement of that proposition may serve to shield it from attack. For example, medical

---

[34]The case before the Court was *Dickerson v. United States* (No. 99-5525). The central issue (at oral argument on 19 April 2000) was whether Congress has the authority to overturn *Miranda* by statute.

[35]Anais Nin, *Cities of the Interior* (Denver, CO: Swallow Press, 1959).

[36]William Shakespeare, *Julius Caesar*, act 3, scene 2.

[37]Discussed from another perspective in section 7.5, below.

[38]William L. Miller, *Arguing About Slavery: The Great Battle in the United States Congress* (Knopf, 1995).

research using embryonic stem cells (the undifferentiated cells found in the human embryo that can develop into other types of cells and most types of tissue) is highly controversial. One U.S. senator used the following enthymeme in attacking legislation that would permit government financing of such research:

> This research [involving the use of embryonic stem cells] is illegal, for this reason: The deliberate killing of a human embryo is an essential component of the contemplated research.[39]

The stated premiss is true; if the embryo were not destroyed, research of that kind would be impossible. But the conclusion that such research is illegal depends on the unstated premiss that the killing of a human embryo is illegal—a claim that is very much in dispute.

Enthymemes depend heavily on context, and often on the listener's knowing that some stated proposition is false. When the aim is to emphasize the falsity of some *other* proposition, it is not uncommon for the speaker to construct a hypothetical proposition of which the target component is the antecedent (the "if" component) and a proposition generally known to be false is the consequent (the "then" component). Thus one of the great Bavarian organ-builders of the 18th century, Karl Josef Reipp, was known to express pride in his organs by saying that "If better organs can be found in Europe, then my name is Jack." Since everyone understands intuitively that in a true hypothetical statement the antecedent cannot be true if the consequent is false, the assertion of that hypothetical proposition serves as an enthymematic argument that ridicules the antecedent, the supposition that better organs can be found in Europe. Both the conclusion (No better organs can be found in Europe) and one of the premisses (My name is not Jack) are left unstated.[40]

### Exercises

I.   In each of the following passages, identify the premisses and conclusions of any argument it contains. Paraphrase arguments, or diagram them, as you deem necessary for thorough analysis.

   *1.   The Supreme Court will only uphold federal racial set-asides in light of convincing evidence of past discrimination by the federal government itself; but, for almost 20 years, the federal government has been discriminating in favor of minority contractors rather than against them. Therefore, federal minority preferences in procurement are doomed.

   —Jeffrey Rosen, cited by Ian Ayres, "Remedying Past Discrimination," *Los Angeles Times*, 26 April 1998

---

[39]Senator Sam Brownback, of Kansas, at a Senate hearing in April 2000, on a bill designed to permit such funding, introduced by his Republican colleague Senator Arlen Specter of Pennsylvania.

[40]And Bruno Bettelheim, a distinguished psychiatrist and survivor of the death camps at Dachau and Buchenwald, wrote: "If all men are good, then there never was an Auschwitz."

2. Science studies the natural. That is all we ask of it. If there is any fact or truth beyond nature, science knows nothing about it and has nothing to say on the subject.

—Richard W. Metz, "Don't Throw Crackpottery at Haunted Houses," *New York Times*, 1 August 1996

3. In the *Crito*, Plato presents the position of the Athenian community, personified as "the Laws," speaking to Socrates or to any citizen of the community who may contemplate deliberate disobedience to the state:

> He who disobeys us is, as we maintain, thrice wrong; first, because in disobeying us he is disobeying his parents; secondly, because we are the authors of his education; thirdly, because he has made an agreement with us that he will duly obey our commands.

4. The black-power movement's fundamental problem was that it focused essentially on *power.* We found out that we cannot organize and sustain the organization with just power talk, because we don't have the principles around which to organize. We must now combine the political and the moral.

—Maulana Ron Karenga, "After the Revolution," *The New Yorker*, 29 April 1996

*5. The *New York Times* reported, on 30 May 2000, that some scientists were seeking a way to signal back in time. A critical reader responded thus:

> It seems obvious to me that scientists in the future will never find a way to signal back in time. If they were to do so, wouldn't we have heard from them by now?

—Ken Grunstra, "Reaching Back in Time," *New York Times*, 6 June 2000

6. There could be no such thing as a first event, looked at from a strictly physical perspective. If things had to begin . . . (a big bang?) the question is, "Why only then, why not earlier?" The answer has to be: "Conditions were not yet right." What was it for "conditions to become right"? Something had to happen first (*i.e.,* before the big bang). Thus there is always an event presupposed by any posited "first event." The big bang, even if it is science and not mere "literary conception," is only an interesting event.

—Lawrence Dewan, "Big Bang, If There Was One, Was No Big Deal," *New York Times*, 7 May 1990

7. I reject the argument . . . that the white journalist featured in your series on race should not have written about black drug addicts in Baltimore because it was not "his story to tell." This assumes that only black people can or should write about black people, and

implies that there exists a single, unanimous perspective that all black Americans hold.

—Ian Reifowitz, in a letter to the
*New York Times*, 19 June 2000

8. There can be no resolution of the conflict between the autonomy of the individual and the putative authority of the state. Insofar as a man fulfills his obligation to make himself the author of his decisions, he will . . . deny that he has a duty to obey the laws of the state *simply because they are the laws*. In that sense . . . anarchism is the only political doctrine consistent with the virtue of autonomy.

—Robert Paul Wolff, *In Defense of Anarchism*, 1970

9. Space contains such a huge supply of atoms that all eternity would not be enough time to count them and count the forces which drive the atoms into various places just as they have been driven together in this world. So we must realize that there are other worlds in other parts of the universe with races of different men and different animals.

—Lucretius, *De Rerum Natura*, (1st century B.C.)

*10. The Internal Revenue Code is inordinately complex, imposes an enormous burden on taxpayers, and thus undermines compliance with the law. Repeated efforts to simplify and reform the law have failed. We have reached the point where further patchwork will only compound the problem. It is time to repeal the Internal Revenue Code and start over.

—Shirley D. Peterson, "Death to the Tax Code,"
*New York Times*, 29 July 1995

II. Each of the following passages can be interpreted as containing two arguments, each of which may have more than one premiss. Analyze these arguments, paraphrasing premisses and conclusions where you find that helpful, and exhibit the diagram for each passage.

**Example:**

1. In a recent attack upon the evils of suburban sprawl, the authors argue as follows:

> The dominant characteristic of sprawl is that each component of a community—housing, shopping centers, office parks, and civic institutions—is segregated, physically separated from the others, causing the residents of suburbia to spend an inordinate amount of time and money moving from one place to the next. And since nearly everyone drives alone, even a sparsely populated area can generate the traffic of a much larger traditional town.[41]

---

[41]Paraphrased in part from Andres Duany, Elizabeth Plater-Zyberk, and Jeff Speck, *Suburban Nation: The Rise of Sprawl and the Decline of the American Dream*, (North Point Press, 2000).

**Solution:**

① The dominant characteristic of sprawl is that each component of a community—housing, shopping centers, office parks, and civic institutions—is segregated, physically separated from the others, causing ② the residents of suburbia to spend an inordinate amount of time and money moving from one place to the next. And since ③ nearly everyone drives alone, ④ even a sparsely populated area can generate the traffic of a much larger traditional town.

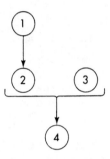

2. The biggest advantage of compulsory voting is that, by enhancing voter turnout, it equalizes participation and removes much of the bias against less-privileged citizens. It also has two other significant advantages. One is that mandatory voting can reduce the role of money in politics, since it does away with the need for candidates and political parties to spend large sums on getting voters to the polls. Second, it reduces the incentives for negative advertising.

   —Arend Lijphart, "Compulsory Voting Is the Best
   Way to Keep Democracy Strong," *The Chronicle
   of Higher Education*, 18 October 1996

3. Life is not simply a "good" that we possess. Our life is our person. To treat our life as a "thing" that we can authorize another to terminate is profoundly dehumanizing. Euthanasia, even when requested by the competent, attacks the distinctiveness and limitations of being human.

   —Ramsey Colloquium of the Institute on Religion
   and Public Life, "Always to Care, Never to Kill,"
   *Wall Street Journal*, 27 November 1991

4. All of the positive contributions that sports make to higher education are threatened by disturbing patterns of abuse, particularly in some big-time programs. These patterns are grounded in institutional indifference, presidential neglect, and the growing commercialization of sport combined with the urge to win at all costs. The sad truth is that on too many campuses big-time revenue sports are out of control.

   —*Keeping Faith with the Student-Athlete: A New Model for
   Intercollegiate Athletics*, Knight Foundation Commission
   on Intercollegiate Athletics, Charlotte, NC, March 1991

**\*5.** The distinguished economist, J. K. Galbraith, long fought to expose and improve a society exhibiting "private opulence and public squalor." In his classic work, *The Affluent Society* (1960), he argued as follows:

> Vacuum cleaners to insure clean houses are praiseworthy and essential in our standard of living. Street cleaners to insure clean streets are an unfortunate expense. Partly as a result, our houses are generally clean and our streets generally filthy."

—cited by John Cassidy in "Height of Eloquence,"
*The New Yorker,* 30 November 1998

**6.** Back in 1884, Democratic nominee Grover Cleveland was confronted by the charge that he had fathered an out-of-wedlock child. While Republicans chanted, "Ma, Ma, where's my Pa," Cleveland conceded that he had been supporting the child. No excuses, no evasions. One of his supporters—one of the first spin doctors—gave this advice to voters:

> Since Grover Cleveland has a terrific public record, but a blemished private life, and since his opponent, James G. Blaine, has a storybook private life but a checkered public record, why not put both where they perform best—return Blaine to private life, keep Cleveland in public life.

**7.** As force is always on the side of the governed, the governors have nothing to support them but opinion. It is therefore on opinion only that government is founded.

—David Hume, cited in Keith Thomas, "Just Say Yes,"
*The New York Review of Books,* 24 November 1988

**8.** Cognitive function depends on neuro-chemical processes in the brain, which are influenced by enzymes. These enzymes are made by genes. It would be dumbfounding if intellectual functioning were without genetic influence.

—Dr. Gerald E. McClearn, "Genes a Lifelong Factor
in Intelligence," *New York Times,* 6 June 1997

**9.** [C]ontemporary standards of decency confirm our judgment that such a young person [15 years old] is not capable of acting with the culpability that can justify the ultimate [death] penalty. Inexperience, less education, and less intelligence make the teenager less able to evaluate the consequences of his or her conduct while at the same time he or she is more apt to be motivated by mere emotion or peer pressure than is an adult.

Juvenile executions could not be expected to deter people under 16 from committing murder, because the likelihood that the teenage offender has made the kind of cost-benefit analysis that attaches any weight to the possibility of execution is so remote as to be virtually nonexistent.

—Justice John Paul Stevens, *Thompson v. Oklahoma*, 487 U.S. 815, 1988

*10. This dichotomy between the "best" and the "best black" is not something manufactured by racists to denigrate the abilities of professionals who are not white. On the contrary, it is reinforced from time to time by those students who demand that universities commit to hiring some pre-set number of minority faculty members . . . saying [in effect] "Go out and hire the best blacks." And it is further reinforced by faculty members who see these demands as nothing more than claims for simple justice.

—Stephen L. Carter, "The Best Black, and Other Tales," *Reconstruction*, vol. 1, Winter 1990

11. Does the past exist? No. Does the future exist? No. Then only the present exists. Yes. But within the present there is no lapse of time? Quite so. Then time does not exist? Oh, I wish you wouldn't be so tiresome.

—Bertrand Russell, *Human Knowledge*, 1948

12. Tipping does not improve service; if it did, taxi drivers would be more courteous than flight attendants. Furthermore, tipping is undignified, since blurring the line between a fee and a gift puts both patron and server in a vulnerable position.

—George Jochnowitz, "Let's Dispense with Tipping Altogether," *New York Times*, 24 January 1997

13. Without dust there would be no twilight, no blue skies, no gorgeous sunsets, none of the ethereal color effects that hold landscape painters in thrall. If light were not scattered by myriad minute dust particles in the air, the sun's heat would be unbearable. Without dust to serve as nucleation sites, rain clouds would not readily form, and so the days would be intensely hot and the nights intensely cold. Dust, in sum, makes life possible on this planet.

—Ivor Smullen, "Homage to a Speck," *The Sciences*, April 1992

14. The lower strata of the middle class—the small tradespeople, shopkeepers, and retired tradesmen generally, the handicraftsmen and peasants—all these sink gradually into the proletariat, partly because their diminutive capital does not suffice for the scale on which modern industry is carried on, and is swamped in the competition with the large capitalists, partly because their specialized

skill is rendered worthless by new methods of production. Thus the proletariat is recruited from all classes of the population.

—Karl Marx and Friedrich Engels,
*The Communist Manifesto*, 1848

*15. Because I had decided, right off, that I liked Nolan Myers, what I heard in his answer was toughness and confidence. Had I decided early on that I didn't like him, I would have heard in that reply arrogance and bluster. The first impression becomes a self-fulfilling prophesy: we hear what we expect to hear. The interview is hopelessly biased in favor of the nice.

—Malcom Gladwell, "The New-Boy Network,"
*The New Yorker*, 29 May 2000

16. No one means all he says, and yet very few say all they mean, for words are slippery and thought is viscous.

—Henry Adams, *The Education of Henry Adams* (1907), chapter 31

17. Natural selection is interested in behavior and isn't so involved in the content of what goes on in the mind. This means that the chance of natural selection supplying people with true beliefs is low, and therefore people have ample reason to doubt the beliefs held in any mind produced by natural selection alone.

—Prof. Alvin Plantinga, quoted in "Science and
Sensibility," *Insight*, 18 August 1997

18. Cuts in tuition can reduce institutional income from government-financed aid programs, which in certain cases are based on total expenses charged, so there is a built-in disincentive to lower prices.

—David Spadafora, "Don't Expect Many Colleges
to Lower Tuition," *New York Times*, 29 January 1996

19. The most powerful tax reform of all is this: cut the capital gains tax rate. Less money and energy would be spent seeking ways to defer capital gains taxes and more effort would be dedicated to entrepreneurial investing. Funds locked into mature investments with a low cost basis would be freed for new risk-taking. Both government tax receipts and new investment would rise, benefiting investors, government, and entrepreneurs all.

—Bruce C. Lueck, "Cut the Capital Gains Tax,"
*New York Times*, 2 December 1996

*20. Native American beliefs about the past and the dead certainly deserve respect, but they should not be allowed to dictate government policy on the investigation and interpretation of early American prehistory. If a choice must be made among competing theories of human origins, primacy should be given to theories based on the scientific method. Only scientific theories are built on empirical evidence; only scientific theories can be adjusted or over-turned.

—R. Bonnichsen and A. L. Schneider,
"Battle of the Bones," *The Sciences*, August 2000

## 1.6 ARGUMENTS AND EXPLANATIONS

Many passages, both written and spoken, that appear to be arguments are in fact not arguments but explanations. The occurrence of certain premiss-or conclusion-indicators such as "because," "for," and "therefore" cannot settle the matter, since those words may be used in both explanations and arguments.[42] What we need to know is the *intention* of the author of the passage.

Compare the following two passages:

1. Lay up for yourselves treasures in heaven, where neither moth nor rust consumes and where thieves do not break in and steal. For where your treasure is, there will your heart be also.

—Matthew 7:19

2. Therefore is the name of it [the tower] called Babel; because the Lord did there confound the language of all the earth.

—Genesis 11:19

The first passage is clearly an argument. Its conclusion, that one ought to lay up treasures in heaven, is supported by the premiss (here marked by the word "for") that one's heart will be where one's treasure is laid up. But the second passage, which uses the word "therefore" quite appropriately, is not an argument. It *explains* why the tower (whose construction is recounted in Genesis) is called Babel. The tower was given this name, we are told, because it was the place where humankind, formerly speaking one language, became confounded by many languages.[43] The passage assumes that the reader knows that the tower had that name; the intention is to explain why that name was given to it. The phrase, "Therefore is the name called Babel" is not a conclusion but a completion of the explanation of the naming. And the clause "because the Lord did there confound the language of all the earth" is not a premiss; it could not serve as a reason for believing that Babel was the name of the tower, since the fact that that *was* the name is known by those to whom the passage is

---

[42]The premiss-indicator "since" often has a *temporal* sense as well. Thus, in the lyric of the famous old song "Stormy Weather," the line "Since my man and I ain't together, keeps rainin' all the time" is deliberately ambiguous, and richly suggestive. (Music by Harold Arlen, words by Ted Koehler, 1933.)

[43]The name "Babel" is derived from the Hebrew word meaning "to confound"; that is, to confuse by mixing up or lumping together in an indiscriminate manner.

addressed. In this context "because" indicates that what follows will *explain* the giving of that name, Babel, to that tower.

The two passages illustrate the fact that passages that are superficially similar may have quite different functions. Whether any given passage is an argument or an explanation depends upon the *purpose* to be served by that passage. If our aim is to establish the truth of some proposition, Q, and to do that we offer some evidence, P, in support of Q, we may appropriately say "Q because P." We are in this way presenting an argument *for* Q, and P is our premiss. But suppose, instead, that Q is known to be true. In that case we don't have to give any reasons to support its truth—but we may wish to give an account of *why* it is true. Here also we may say "Q because P"—but in this case we are giving not an argument *for* Q, but an explanation *of* Q.

In responding to a query about the apparent color of quasars (celestial objects lying far beyond our galaxy) one scientist wrote:

> The most distant quasars look like intense points of infrared radiation. This is because space is scattered with hydrogen atoms (about two per cubic meter) that absorb blue light, and if you filter the blue from visible white light, red is what's left. On its multibillion-light-year journey to earth, quasar light loses so much blue that only infrared remains.[44]

This is not an argument; it does not seek to convince the reader that quasars have the apparent color they do, but rather aims to give the causes for this being so.

Similarly, in discussing the early growth of British influence in Africa, a historian wrote:

> Sierra Leone became a crown colony in 1808 not because it flourished, but because it failed. Burdened by war and stagnant trade, the private Sierra Leone Company could not cover its costs, and a Government that had just abolished the slave trade felt obliged to adopt it.[45]

No argument is given here for the conclusion that Sierra Leone became a crown colony in 1808. It *did* become a crown colony then. But why? Because . . . In this and in the previous example, "because" is plainly the mark of an explanation, not an argument.

How can we tell whether a passage is intended to explain or to convince? Usually we can do so by asking, with reference to the form, "Q because P," what the status of Q is for that author. Is Q a proposition whose truth needs to be established? Then "because P" is probably offering premiss(es) in its support, and hence "Q because P" is an argument. Or is Q a proposition whose truth is known, or at least not in doubt in the context? In that case, "because P" is probably offering some account of why Q has come to be true, and therefore "Q because P" is an explanation.

In an explanation one must distinguish *what* is being explained from what the explanation *is*. In the explanation from Genesis given above, what is being

---

[44]Jeff Greenwald, "Brightness Visible," *New York Times Magazine,* 14 May 2000.

[45]Andrew Porter, in a review of Lawrence James's *The Rise and Fall of the British Empire* (1995), in the *New York Times Book Review,* 14 January 1996.

explained is how the tower came to have the name Babel; the explanation is that it was there that the Lord did confound the language of all the earth. In the historical example just given, what is being explained is Sierra Leone's becoming a British crown colony; the explanation is the failure of the Sierra Leone Company and the British government's response to that failure.

What is called an explanation may in fact be an argument, and vice versa. Not long ago the *New York Times* was criticized by a reader for treating the sexes unequally because it commented on the increased weight of a prominent actress but not on the increased weight of a prominent businessman referred to in the same report. Another reader then responded:

> Ellen R. Fox's complaint—that you noted that Catherine Deneuve was "perhaps not as slender as she once was" but that you did not mention Donald Trump's growing girth—is easily explained. Mr. Trump never appeared nude in a movie that made his shape a matter of interest.[46]

This is not really an explanation but an argument. Its premisses are, first, that nude appearance in a movie makes one's appearance a matter of interest, and second, that Mr. Trump never made such an appearance but that Ms. Deneuve did. It was therefore reasonable (this writer contends) for the newspaper to comment on the shape of the prominent person who did so appear while ignoring the shape of the prominent person who did not. Therefore, the complaint that the sexes had been treated unequally was not justified.

To distinguish explanations from arguments, we must often be sensitive to context, and there will always remain many passages whose purpose cannot be determined. A problematic passage may need to be given alternative, equally plausible "readings"—viewed as an argument when interpreted in one way and as an explanation when interpreted in another.

## Exercises

Some of the following passages contain explanations, some contain arguments, and some may be interpreted as either an argument or an explanation. What is your judgment about the chief function of each passage? What would have to be the case for the passage in question to be an argument? To be an explanation? Where you find an argument, identify its premises and conclusion. Where you find an explanation, indicate what is being explained and what the explanation is.

## Example

1. There is no mystery to why the idea of a flat tax is appealing. The existing tax system can be maddeningly complicated and expensive to comply with. It rewards consumption and penalizes savings, exactly the opposite of economic common sense. And in many cases

---

[46]Andy Rooney, *New York Times*, 29 April 1996.

it is clearly unfair—for example many working couples pay substantially higher taxes on their joint return than do unmarried couples who live together and file separate returns.

—David E. Rosenbaum, "Panel Calls for a Flat Tax,"
*New York Times*, 18 January 1996

**Solution:**

On the surface this passage is an explanation of why the flat tax is appealing: It is appealing because of the deficiencies of the existing tax system, several of which are identified. But the passage may also be viewed as an argument in support of the flat tax. The deficiencies of the present tax system are the premises, and the conclusion (not explicitly stated) is that the present system ought to be replaced by a flat tax.

Which of these interpretations is closer to the intentions of the author depends on the context of the passage. If the context had been an impartial weighing of alternative tax systems, the passage would have served chiefly as an explanation. But since the passage appeared in the report of a panel *calling for* a flat tax, we may conclude that it served in fact mainly as an argument in support of that position.

2. It would be immoral and selfish not to use animals in research today, given the harm that could accrue to future generations if such research were halted.

—*Science, Medicine, and Animals*
(Washington, DC: National Academy of
Sciences, Institute of Medicine, 1991)

3. Animals born without traits that led to reproduction died out, whereas the ones that reproduced the most succeeded in conveying their genes to posterity. Crudely speaking, sex feels good because over evolutionary time the animals that liked having sex created more offspring than the animals that didn't.

—R. Thornhill and C. T. Palmer, "Why Men Rape,"
*The Sciences*, February 2000.

4. Changes are real. Now, changes are only possible in time, and therefore time must be something real.

—Immanuel Kant, *Critique of Pure Reason* (1781),
"Transcendental Aesthetic," section II

*5. A black hole is an object with so much gravity that nothing can escape it—not even light, the fastest thing in the universe. Anything approaching a black hole gets pulled into the object and disappears as if it fell into a hole. Because even light cannot escape, the hole appears black.

—Ken Croswell, "The Best Black Hole in the Galaxy,"
*Astronomy*, March 1992

6. To name causes for a state of affairs is not to excuse it. Things are justified or condemned by their consequences, not by their antecedents.

> —John Dewey, "The Liberal College and Its Enemies,"
> *The Independent*, 1924

7. Because he is my son and because I love him more than anything else in the world, more than I can imagine loving anyone else, more even than I loved his mother, I crawl in beside him, my torso jammed deep into the closet, with my legs stretched over a hooked rug.

> —Michael G. Jaffe, *Dance Real Slow*
> (New York: Farrar, Straus, & Giroux, 1996)

8. I like Wagner's music better than anybody's. It is so loud that one can talk the whole time without people hearing what one says.

> —Oscar Wilde, *The Picture of Dorian Gray*, 1891

9. Every President from Herbert Hoover through Jimmy Carter has donated his Presidential records to the public. Only Nixon sued for payment for such records. For years, Nixon's lawyers argued against any public access to the tapes for privacy reasons. It is absurd for the estate to argue now [1999] that it should be compensated for the tapes, along with the other materials, because Nixon might have cashed in on the evidence that drove him from office.

> —"A Curious Claim by the Nixon Estate,"
> *New York Times*, Editorial, 22 February 1999

*10. Love looks not with the eyes but with the mind;
And therefore is wing'd Cupid painted blind.

> —William Shakespeare, *A Midsummer Night's Dream*,
> act 1, scene 1

11. Members of the primate order have especially long periods of infant dependency compared with other mammals, because, it is believed, juveniles need the time to learn the ropes of their uniquely intricate social world.

> —Meredith F. Small, "Political Animal,"
> *The Sciences*, March 1990

12. That appellate advocacy is largely a written art has two consequences: First, making heads or tails of Supreme Court arguments without having read the briefs is often difficult. Second, the decision in any Court case may bear no relation to the questions asked at oral argument; the decision reflects the arguments made in the briefs. Rather than demystify the process, televising Supreme Court arguments may only contribute to misunderstandings about how the Court operates.

> —Andrew C. Mergen, "Where Words Are Worth
> 1,000 Pictures," *New York Times*, 8 May 1996

13. U.S. Presidents have always been more likely to be killed or disabled by assassins than by diseases, and the Secret Service thus has more to do with the President's health and safety than the President's physicians.

> —George J. Annas, "The Health of the President
> and Presidential Candidates," *New England
> Journal of Medicine*, 5 October 1995

14. People often think of inflammation as merely an annoying symptom. But inflammation doesn't just signal injury; it can—in a vicious cycle—perpetuate injury. That's why disorders like arthritis can be so crippling, chronic, and hard to treat. And that's why patients are willing to risk serious side effects for drugs that offer even a temporary respite.

> —Jerome Groopman, "Superaspirin,"
> *The New Yorker*, 15 June 1998

*15. How do girls become afraid to ask questions in science class? How do they come to think of science as less useful or interesting than boys do? Such attitudes are learned, and parents and teachers teach them.

> —"Why Are There Fewer Women?"
> *Michigan Alumnus*, October 1995

16. Increasing incarceration rates do not result in decreasing crime rates because few crimes result in imprisonment or arrest. This is not because judges are soft on criminals but because 90 percent of crimes are either not reported or go unsolved.

> —Elizabeth Alexander, "Look to More Cost-effective
> Antidotes than Prison," *New York Times*, 25 January 1996

17. One may be subject to laws made by another, but it is impossible to bind oneself in any matter which is the subject of one's own free exercise of will. . . . It follows of necessity that the king cannot be subject to his own laws. For this reason [royal] edicts and ordinances conclude with the formula, "for such is our good pleasure."

> —Jean Bodin, *Six Books of the Commonwealth*, 1576

18. The resistance of the bourgeoisie is increased tenfold by its overthrow (even if only in one country), and its power lies not only in the strength of international capital and the international connections of the bourgeoisie, but also in the force of habit in the strength of small production. For, unfortunately, small production is still very, very widespread in the world, and small production engenders capitalism and the bourgeoisie continuously, daily, hourly, spontaneously, and on a mass scale. For all these reasons the dictatorship of the proletariat is essential, and victory over the bourgeoisie is impossible without a long, stubborn and desperate

war of life and death, a war demanding perseverance, discipline, firmness, indomitableness, and unity of will.

—V. I. Lenin, *"Left Wing" Communism:*
*An Infantile Disorder,* 1920

19. Neither the Federal Communications Commission nor the New York State Public Service Commission receives many complaints about the problem of inaccurate telephone directory assistance. This is because when looking at their bills, people don't realize that they are charged for a mistaken "no listing" answer. And directory assistance providers, paid whether or not they have up-to-date information, have no incentive to improve service.

—Bradley F. Taylor, "No Listing? Dial M for
'Maddening,' " *New York Times,* 29 August 2000

*20. By any standard one wants to set, Americans are not learning science. All too often what is taught as science is better not taught at all. All too often the mind-set against science and the fear of mathematics are solidly installed in grade school. All too often science can be skipped in high school and in most colleges. As for most American college students, the science requirement is a sad joke.

—Leon M. Lederman, "Science Education, Science,
and American Culture," *The Key Reporter,* Winter 1992

21. All animal populations fluctuate in size from year to year, in response to the good conditions (gentle weather, abundant food) and the bad conditions (drought, harsh winters, famine) they encounter; and small populations are more likely to fluctuate to zero when conditions are bad, since zero is never far away. With less margin of security, a small population is also more vulnerable to the various forms of human persecution and natural catastrophe that can deliver a coup de grace. Therefore, small populations face a greater risk of extinction than big populations. And island populations—including those trapped within ecological islands, such as a park surrounded by development—tend to be small.

—David Quammen, "National Parks: Nature's
Dead End," *New York Times,* 28 July 1996

22. Because gravity increases with the mass of an object, heavy objects exert more pull. And gravity grows stronger the closer you get to an object, so objects with small diameters wield greater force. That's why white dwarfs—collapsed stars with a mass about that of the sun packed into a sphere the size of the Earth—exert such strong gravity.

—Marcia Bartusiak, "To the Edge of Space,"
*Astronomy,* July 1998

23. George Mason, one of my ancestors, urged the abolition of slavery at the Constitutional Convention, calling it "disgraceful to

mankind." Failing in this attempt, he urged that his Declaration of Rights be enacted as a bill of rights. It too was turned down. Thus, Mason refused to sign the Constitution.

—Thomas C. Southerland, Jr., "A Virginia Model,"
*New York Times,* 5 July 1997

24. Mother rats give birth to very different ratios of sons and daughters depending on how they are faring. When the rats are doing well and mating with vigorous dominant males, they give birth to an excess of sons. When times are hard, or when they have recently lost a litter, they give birth to more daughters.

Daughters, it seems, are the "cheaper" sex to raise: mothers spend less time licking and nursing them, and they are smaller than sons at weaning. They are also the safer sex, almost assured of having some offspring and thus keeping their mother's genetic legacy alive. Sons, by contrast, are considered the jackpot sex, who in theory could do brilliantly by their mother come their sexual maturity, spawning far more offspring than their sisters ever could manage. Hence there is evolutionary justification for mothers to bear more expensive sons when they have the energy and resources to do so, and opting for fail-safe females when prospects are dim. Somehow the mothers extract relevant information from their habitat and translate it into a changed birth ratio.

—"How Biology Affects Behavior and Vice Versa,"
*New York Times,* 30 May 1995

*25. Black or white, rich or poor, male or female, conservative or liberal: we are willfully blind to the 700,000 black men incarcerated in 1994 (up from 25,000 in 1960) and to the 11,000 killed as a result of homicide in 1993 (both figures from the Bureau of Justice Statistics), to unemployment and life expectancy that lags far behind every other racial and gender classification. This class of Americans doesn't have think tanks, political parties or lobbyists. To paraphrase writer Ralph Wiley, that's why black boys tend to shoot.

—Bill Stephney, "Rap Star's Death Highlights Harsher
Reality," *New York Times,* 18 September 1996

## 1.7 DEDUCTION AND VALIDITY

Every argument makes the claim that its premises provide grounds for the truth of its conclusion. Indeed, that claim is the mark of an argument. But there are two major classes of arguments: *deductive* and *inductive.* These two classes differ fundamentally in the *way* in which their conclusions are supported by their premises. In this section we give a brief account of deduction.

A deductive argument makes the claim that its conclusion is supported by its premises *conclusively.* In contrast, an inductive argument does not make such a claim. If, in interpreting a passage, we judge that such a claim is being made, we treat the argument as deductive; if we judge that such a claim is not being made, we treat it as inductive. Since every argument either makes this claim of conclusiveness or does not, every argument is either deductive or inductive.

When an argument makes the claim that its premisses (if true) provide irrefutable grounds for the truth of its conclusion, that claim will be either correct or not correct. If it is correct, that argument is **valid.** If it is not correct (that is, if the premisses when true fail to establish the conclusion irrefutably), that argument is **invalid.**

For logicians, therefore, the term *validity* is applicable only to deductive arguments. To say that a deductive argument is valid is to say that it is not possible for its conclusion to be false if its premisses are true. Thus we define "validity" as follows: **A deductive argument is valid when, if its premisses are true, its conclusion *must* be true.**

Every deductive argument makes the claim that its premisses guarantee the truth of its conclusion, but not all deductive arguments live up to that claim. Deductive arguments that fail to do so are *invalid.*

Since every deductive argument either succeeds or does not succeed in achieving its objective, every deductive argument is either valid or invalid. This point is important: if a deductive argument is not valid, it must be invalid; if it is not invalid, it must be valid.

The central task of deductive logic (treated at length in Part II of this book) is to discriminate valid arguments from invalid ones. Through the ages logicians have devised powerful techniques to do this. But the traditional techniques for determining validity differ from those employed by most modern logicians. The former, called *classical logic* and rooted in the analytical works of Aristotle, are explained in Chapters 5, 6, and 7 of this book. The techniques of *modern symbolic logic* are presented in detail in Chapters 8, 9, and 10. Although logicians of the two schools differ in their methods and in their interpretations of some arguments, all agree that the fundamental task of deductive logic is to develop the tools that enable us to distinguish arguments that are valid from those that are not.

## **1.8** INDUCTION AND PROBABILITY

Inductive arguments do not claim that their premisses, even if true, support their conclusions with certainty. They make a weaker but nonetheless important claim that their premisses support their conclusions with *probability*, which always falls short of certainty. What was said above about validity and invalidity therefore does not apply to inductive arguments: Inductive arguments are neither valid nor invalid.[47] We can still evaluate them of course. Indeed, the

---

[47] In everyday speech the terms "valid" and "invalid" have taken on much wider and looser meanings. One hears it said, for example, that a fine motion picture "makes a valid statement," or that some emotional response to an act or event is a "valid reaction," and so forth. English is beautifully rich. But as logicians we use the terms *valid* and *invalid* far more narrowly; they indicate nothing more than the success, or lack of success, of a deductive argument in making its claim that if its premisses are true its conclusion must be true.

appraisal of inductive arguments is one of the leading tasks of scientists in every sphere. The premises of an inductive argument provide some support for its conclusion, and the higher the level of probability the premises confer on the conclusion, the greater the merit of the argument. In general, we say that inductive arguments may be "better" or "worse," "weaker" or "stronger," and so on. But even when the premises are all true and provide very strong support for the conclusion, in an inductive argument the conclusion is never certain. The theory of induction, techniques of inductive reasoning, methods for appraising inductive arguments, and methods for quantifying and calculating probabilities are presented at some length in Part III of this book.

The difference between inductive and deductive arguments is deep. Because an inductive argument can yield no more than some degree of probability for its conclusion, it is always possible that additional information will strengthen or weaken it. Newly discovered facts may cause us to change our estimate of the probabilities, and thus may lead us to judge the argument to be better (or worse) than we thought it was. In the world of inductive argument—even when the conclusion is thought to be very highly probable—*all* the evidence is never in. It is this possibility of new data, perhaps conflicting with what was believed earlier, that keeps us from asserting that any inductive conclusion is absolutely certain.

Deductive arguments, on the other hand, cannot gradually become better or worse. They either succeed or do not succeed in exhibiting a compelling relation between premises and conclusion. The fundamental difference between deduction and induction is revealed by this contrast. If a deductive argument is valid, *no* additional premises could possibly add to the strength of that argument. For example, if all humans are mortal, and if Socrates is human, we may conclude without reservation that Socrates is mortal—*and that conclusion will follow from those premises no matter what else may be true in the world, and no matter what other information may be discovered or added.* If we come to learn that Socrates is ugly, or that angels are immortal, or that cows give milk, neither those findings nor any other findings can have any impact on the validity of the original argument.

In the case of every valid deductive argument, the conclusion that follows with certainty from its premises follows from any enlarged set of premises with the same certainty, regardless of the nature of the additional premises. If an argument is valid, nothing in the world can make it more valid; if a conclusion is validly inferred from some set of premises, nothing can be added to that set to make that conclusion follow more strictly, or more logically, or more validly.

But this is not true of inductive arguments, in which the relationship claimed between premises and conclusion is much less strict and different in kind. Consider the following inductive argument:

Most corporation lawyers are conservatives.
Angela Palmieri is a corporation lawyer.
Therefore Angela Palmieri is probably a conservative.

This is a pretty good inductive argument; its first premise is true, and if its second premiss also is true its conclusion is more likely to be true than false. But in this case (in contrast to the argument about Socrates' mortality) new premisses added to the original pair might weaken or (depending on the content of the new premisses) strengthen the original argument. Suppose we also learn that

Angela Palmieri is an officer of the American Civil Liberties Union (ACLU).

and suppose we add the (true) premiss that

Most officers of the ACLU are not conservatives.

Now the conclusion (that Angela Palmieri is a conservative) no longer seems very probable; the original inductive argument has been greatly weakened by the presence of this additional information about Angela Palmieri. Indeed, if the final premiss were to be transformed into the universal proposition

No officers of the ACLU are conservatives.

The opposite of the original conclusion would then follow deductively—that is, validly—from the full set of premisses affirmed.

On the other hand, suppose we enlarge the original set of premisses by adding the following additional premisses:

Angela Palmieri has long been an officer of the National Rifle Association (NRA).

and

Angela Palmieri was appointed a contributing editor of the conservative *National Review.*

The original conclusion would be supported by this enlarged set of premisses with even greater likelihood than it was by the original set.

In sum, the distinction between induction and deduction rests on the nature of the *claims* made by the two types of arguments about the *relations between their premises and their conclusions.* We may characterize the two types of arguments as follows:

**A deductive argument is one whose conclusion is claimed to follow from its premises with absolute necessity, this necessity not being a matter of degree and not depending in any way on whatever else may be the case. In sharp contrast, an inductive argument is one whose conclusion is claimed to follow from its premises only with probability, this probability being a matter of degree and dependent upon what else may be the case.**

Inductive arguments do not always acknowledge explicitly that their conclusions are inferred only with some degree of probability. On the other hand, the mere presence of the word "probability" within an argument is no sure indication that the argument is inductive. This is so because there are some strictly deductive arguments *about* probabilities themselves.* Arguments of this kind, in which the probability of a certain combination of events is deduced from the probabilities of other events, are discussed in Chapter 14.

## 1.9 VALIDITY AND TRUTH

As noted earlier, a successful deductive argument is *valid.* Validity refers to a relation *between* propositions—between the set of propositions that serve as the premises of a deductive argument, and the one proposition that serves as the conclusion of that argument. If the latter follows with logical necessity from the former, we say that the argument is valid. Since logical necessity is never achieved by inductive arguments, validity never applies to them. *Nor can validity ever apply to any single proposition by itself,* since the needed *relation* cannot possibly be found within any one proposition.

Truth and falsity, on the other hand, *are* attributes of individual propositions. A single statement that serves as a premiss in an argument may be true; the statement that serves as its conclusion may be false. That conclusion may have been validly inferred, but it makes no sense to say that any conclusion, or any single premiss, is itself valid or invalid.

Truth is the attribute of a proposition that asserts what really is the case. When I assert that Lake Superior is the largest of the five Great Lakes, I assert what really is the case, what is true. If I said that the largest of the Great Lakes is Lake Michigan, my assertion would not be in accord with the real world; therefore, it would be false. This contrast is important: **truth and falsity are attributes of individual propositions or statements; validity and invalidity are attributes of arguments.**

Just as the concept of validity does not apply to single propositions, the concept of truth does not apply to arguments. Of the several propositions in an argument, some (or all) may be true and some (or all) may be false. But the argument as a whole is neither "true" nor "false." Propositions, which are statements about the world, may be true or false; deductive arguments, which consist of inferences from one set of propositions to other propositions, may be valid or invalid.

The relations *between* true (or false) propositions and valid (or invalid) arguments lie at the heart of deductive logic. Part II of this book is largely devoted to the examination of those complex relations. However, a preliminary discussion of the relation between validity and truth is in order at this point.

We begin by emphasizing that an argument may be valid even if one or more of its premises is not true. Every argument makes a claim about the relation between the premises and the conclusion drawn from them; that relation may hold even if the premises turn out to be false or the truth of the premises is in dispute. This point was made effectively by Abraham Lincoln in

---

*If, for example, we learn that the probability of three successive heads in three tosses of a coin is ⅛, we may infer deductively that the probability of getting at least one tail in three tosses of coin is ⅞.

1858 in one of his debates with Stephen Douglas. Lincoln was attacking the *Dred Scott* decision, which obliged the return of slaves who had escaped into northern states to their owners in the South:

> I think it follows, [from the *Dred Scott* decision] and submit to the consideration of men capable of arguing, whether as I state it in syllogistic form the argument has any fault in it:
>
> Nothing in the Constitution or laws of any State can destroy a right distinctly and expressly affirmed in the Constitution of the United States.
>
> The right of property in a slave is distinctly and expressly affirmed in the Constitution of the United States.
>
> Therefore, nothing in the Constitution or laws of any State can destroy the right of property in a slave.
>
> I believe that no fault can be pointed out in that argument; assuming the truth of the premises, the conclusion, so far as I have capacity at all to understand it, follows inevitably. There *is* a fault in it as I think, but the fault is not in the reasoning; but the falsehood in fact is a fault of the premises. I believe that the right of property in a slave *is not* distinctly and expressly affirmed in the Constitution, and Judge Douglas thinks it *is*. I believe that the Supreme Court and the advocates of that decision [the *Dred Scott* decision] may search in vain for the place in the Constitution where the right of property in a slave is distinctly and expressly affirmed. I say, therefore, that I think one of the premises is not true in fact.[48]

In the argument that he recapitulates and attacks, Lincoln finds the second premiss—that the right of property in a slave is affirmed in the U.S. Constitution—to be plainly false. The reasoning in the argument is not faulty, he points out; nevertheless, its conclusion has not been established. His logical point is correct: *An argument may be valid even when its conclusion and one or more of its premises are false.* For the validity of an argument, we emphasize once again, depends only upon the *relation* of the premises to the conclusion.

There are many possible combinations of true and false premises and conclusions in both valid and invalid arguments. Consider the following illustrative arguments, each of which is prefaced by the statement of the combination it represents. With these illustrations before us, we will be in a position to formulate some important principles concerning the relations between truth and validity.

I.   Some *valid* arguments contain *only true* propositions—true premisses and a true conclusion:

> All mammals have lungs.
> All whales are mammals.
> Therefore all whales have lungs.

II.  Some *valid* arguments contain *only false* propositions:

> All four-legged creatures have wings.
> All spiders have four legs.
> Therefore all spiders have wings.

---

[48]Abraham Lincoln, in Roy R. Basler, ed., *The Collected Works of Abraham Lincoln*, vol. 3. (Rutgers University Press).

This argument is valid because, if its premisses were true, its conclusion would have to be true also—even though we know that in fact both the premisses *and* the conclusion of this argument are false.

III.  Some *invalid* arguments contain *only true* propositions—all their premisses are true, and their conclusions are true as well:

> If I owned all the gold in Fort Knox, then I would be wealthy.
> I do not own all the gold in Fort Knox.
> Therefore I am not wealthy.

IV.  Some *invalid* arguments contain *only true premisses* and have a *false conclusion*. This can be illustrated with an argument exactly like the previous one (III) in form, changed only enough to make the conclusion false:

> If Bill Gates owned all the gold in Fort Knox, then Bill Gates would be wealthy.
> Bill Gates does not own all the gold in Fort Knox.
> Therefore Bill Gates is not wealthy.

The premisses of this argument are true, but its conclusion is false. Such an argument *cannot* be valid because it is impossible for the premisses of a valid argument to be true and its conclusion to be false.

V.  Some *valid* arguments have *false premisses and a true conclusion*:

> All fishes are mammals.
> All whales are fishes.
> Therefore all whales are mammals.

The conclusion of this argument is true, as we know; moreover it may be validly inferred from the two premisses, both of which are wildly false.

VI.  Some *invalid* arguments also have *false premisses and a true conclusion*:

> All mammals have wings.
> All whales have wings.
> Therefore all whales are mammals.

From examples V and VI taken together, it is clear that we cannot tell from the fact that an argument has false premisses and a true conclusion whether it is valid or invalid.

VII.  Some *invalid* arguments, of course, contain *all false propositions*—false premisses and a false conclusion:

> All mammals have wings.
> All whales have wings.
> Therefore all mammals are whales.

These seven examples make it clear that there are valid arguments with false conclusions (Example II), as well as invalid arguments with true conclusions (Examples III and VI). Hence it is clear that *the truth or falsity of an argument's conclusion does not by itself determine the validity or invalidity of that argument.* Moreover, *the fact that an argument is valid does not guarantee the truth of its conclusion* (Example II).

Two tables (referring to the seven examples on the preceding pages) will make very clear the variety of possible combinations. The first table shows that invalid arguments can have every possible combination of true and false premisses and conclusions:

| INVALID ARGUMENTS | | |
| --- | --- | --- |
| | TRUE CONCLUSION | FALSE CONCLUSION |
| TRUE PREMISSES | Example III | Example IV |
| FALSE PREMISSES | Example VI | Example VII |

The second table shows that valid arguments can have only three of those combinations of true and false premisses and conclusions:

| VALID ARGUMENTS | | |
| --- | --- | --- |
| | TRUE CONCLUSION | FALSE CONCLUSION |
| TRUE PREMISSES | Example I | |
| FALSE PREMISSES | Example V | Example II |

The one blank position in the second table exhibits a fundamental point: *If an argument is valid and its premisses are true, we may be certain that its conclusion is true also.* To put it another way: *If an argument is valid and its conclusion is false, not all of its premisses can be true.* Some perfectly valid arguments do have false conclusions—but any such argument must have at least one false premiss.

When an argument is valid, *and* all of its premisses are true, we call it "sound." The conclusion of a sound argument obviously must be true—and only a sound argument can establish the truth of its conclusion. If a deductive argument is not sound—that is, if the argument is not valid, *or* if not all of its premisses are true—it fails to establish the truth of its conclusion *even if in fact the conclusion is true.*

To test the truth or falsehood of premisses is the task of science in general, since premisses may deal with any subject matter at all. The logician is not interested in the truth or falsehood of propositions so much as in the logical relations between them. By "logical" relations between propositions we mean those relations that determine the correctness or incorrectness of the arguments in which they occur. The task of determining the correctness or incorrectness of arguments falls squarely within the province of logic. The logician is interested in the correctness even of arguments whose premises may be false.

Why not confine ourselves to arguments with true premises, ignoring all others? Because the correctness of arguments whose premises are not known to be true may be of great importance. In science, for example, we verify theories by deducing testable consequences—but we cannot know beforehand which theories are true. In everyday life as well, we must often choose between alternative courses of action, deducing the consequences of each. To avoid deceiving ourselves we must reason correctly about the consequences of the alternatives, taking each as a premise. If we were interested only in arguments with true premises, we would not know which set of consequences to trace out until we knew which of the alternative premises was true. But if we knew which of the alternative premises was true, we would not need to reason about it at all, since our purpose in reasoning was to help us decide which alternative premiss to *make* true. To confine our attention to arguments with premisses known to be true would therefore be self-defeating.

Effective methods for establishing the validity or invalidity of deductive arguments are presented and explained in Part II of this book.

## 1.10  COMPLEX ARGUMENTATIVE PASSAGES

**■Advanced Material**  Arguments can be very complicated. Passages in which several arguments are interwoven, with many propositions appearing, some of which serve only as premises and some of which serve as both premises and sub-conclusions, can be difficult to analyze. The diagramming technique is very helpful, but there is no mechanical way to assure that the diagram we construct represents the passage accurately. Moreover, because the passage may be subject to varying plausible interpretations, there may be more than one diagram that can reasonably be considered to exhibit the logical structure of the passage.

To analyze complex passages fairly we must strive to understand the flow of the author's reasoning and identify the role of each element of the passage. The examples that follow (in which component propositions have been numbered for purposes of analysis) exhibit the ways in which we can set forth the connections between premises and conclusions. Once we have identified the arguments within a passage and their relations, we can go about deciding whether the conclusions do indeed follow from the premises affirmed.

In the following set of arguments the final conclusion of the passage appears in the very first statement, which is not unusual. There are four premises directly supporting this conclusion; two of these are sub-conclusions, which in turn are supported in different ways, by other premises affirmed in the passage:

①  It is very unlikely that research using animals will be unnecessary or poorly done.
②  Before an experiment using a vertebrate animal is carried out, the protocol for that experiment must be reviewed by an institutional committee that includes a veterinarian and a member of the public, and ③ during the research the animal's health and

care are monitored regularly. ④ Researchers need healthy animals for study in science and medicine, because ⑤ unhealthy animals could lead to erroneous results. This is a powerful incentive for ⑥ scientists to make certain that any animals they use are healthy and well nourished. Furthermore, ⑦ research involving animals is expensive, and because ⑧ funding is limited in science, ⑨ only high quality research is able to compete effectively for support.[49]

The following diagram exhibits the logical structure of this passage. In examining such diagrams, it is helpful to "read" them by replacing the numbers with the indicated propositions, beginning with those highest on the page and therefore earliest in the logical cascade. In this way one can follow each of the several paths of reasoning to the final conclusion.

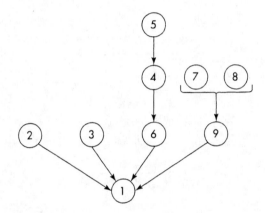

Within an argument, individual propositions are sometimes repeated in differently worded sentences, sometimes for emphasis and other times by oversight. This repetition complicates the task of analysis. Diagramming helps because we can assign the same number to different formulations of the same proposition. The following passage comprising three distinct arguments, exhibits this confusing duplication of propositions:

① The Big Bang theory is crumbling.... ② According to orthodox wisdom, the cosmos began with the Big Bang—an immense, perfectly symmetrical explosion 20 billion years ago. The problem is that ③ astronomers have confirmed by observation the existence of huge conglomerations of galaxies that are simply too big to have been formed in a mere 20 billion years.... Studies based on new data collected by satellite, and backed up by earlier ground surveys, show that ④ galaxies are clustered into vast ribbons that stretch billions of light years, and ⑤ are separated by voids hundreds of millions of light years across. Because ⑥ galaxies are observed to travel at only a small fraction of the speed of light, mathematics shows that ⑦ such large clumps of matter must have taken at least one hundred billion years to come together—five times as long as the time since the hypothetical Big Bang.... ③ Structures as big as those now seen can't be made in 20 billion years.... ② The Big Bang theorizes that matter was

[49] *Science, Medicine, and Animals,* National Academy of Sciences, Washington, DC, 1991.

54

spread evenly through the universe. From this perfection, ③ there is no way for such vast clumps to have formed so quickly.[50]

In this passage the premisses that report observational evidence, ④, ⑤, and ⑥, give reasons for ⑦, the great length of time that would have had to elapse since the Big Bang. This passage of time is used to support the subconclusion (formulated in three slightly different ways) that ③ structures as big as those now seen are too big to have been formed in that period of time. From that subconclusion, combined with ②, a short statement (formulated in two slightly different ways) of the original symmetry and spread that the Big Bang theory supposes, we infer the final conclusion of the passage ①: that the Big Bang theory is crumbling—the proposition with which the passage begins. The following diagram exhibits this set of logical relations:

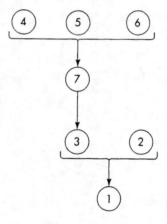

The analysis of an argument must take into account the fact that premisses may appear in compressed form, sometimes as a short noun phrase. In the following argument the phrase, "the scattering in the atmosphere" serves as a premiss, ④, that may be reformulated as "the sun's energy is scattered in the atmosphere." This compression, along with repetition, makes it more difficult to analyze this argument:

① Solar-powered cars can never be anything but experimental devices. ② Solar power is too weak to power even a mini-car for daily use. ③ The solar power entering the atmosphere is about 1 kilowatt per square yard. Because of ④ the scattering in the atmosphere, and because ⑤ the sun shines half a day on the average at any place on earth, ⑥ average solar power received is 1/6 kilowatt, or 4 kilowatt hours a day....Tests on full-size cars indicate that ⑦ 300,000 watt hours are required in a battery for an electric car to perform marginally satisfactorily. So, ⑧ 40 square yards of cells would be needed to charge the car batteries, about the size of the roof of a tractor-trailer. ① It is not undeveloped technologies that put solar power out of the running to be anything but a magnificently designed experimental car. It is cosmology.[51]

[50]Eric J. Lerner, "For Whom the Bang Tolls," *New York Times*, 3 June 1991.
[51]Victor Wouk, "You Can't Drive Solar Cars to Work," *New York Times*, 15 July 1991.

The first proposition in this passage, asserting that "solar powered cars can never be more than experimental" is the final conclusion. It is repeated in more elaborate form at the end of the passage, as a diagram of the passage shows:

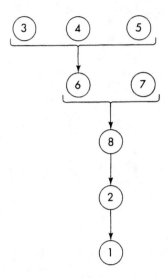

When we analyze complex argumentative passages, even ones that contain many premises and subconclusions, we often find them to be coherent and clear. Consider the following passage, by an editor defending her highly controversial editorial policy:

> The *Journal* [*New England Journal of Medicine*] has taken the position that ① it will not publish reports of unethical research, regardless of their scientific merit....
>     There are three reasons for our position. First, ② the policy of publishing only ethical research, if generally applied, would deter unethical work. ③ Publication is an important part of the reward system in medical research, and ④ investigators would not undertake unethical studies if they knew the results would not be published. Furthermore, ⑤ any other policy would tend to lead to more unethical work, because, as I have indicated, ⑥ such studies may be easier to carry out and thus ⑦ may give their practitioners a competitive edge. Second, ⑧ denying publication even when the ethical violations are minor protects the principle of the primacy of the research subject. ⑨ If small lapses were permitted we would become inured to them, and ⑩ this would lead to larger violations. And finally, ⑪ refusal to publish unethical work serves notice to society at large that even scientists do not consider science the primary measure of a civilization. ⑫ Knowledge, although important, may be less important to a decent society than the way it is obtained.[52]

Again the final conclusion appears at the beginning of the passage, and the three major premises that support it directly, ②, ⑧ and ⑪, are themselves supported by various other premises arranged differently. But each of the

---

[52]Dr. Marcia Angell, "The Nazi Hypothermia Experiments and Unethical Research Today," *New England Journal of Medicine,* 17 May 1990.

many propositions in the passage has a clear logical role in leading to the conclusion that the passage aims to justify: reports of research done in unethical ways will not be published in the *New England Journal of Medicine,* regardless of their scientific merit. The following diagram exhibits the logical structure of this complicated but carefully reasoned passage:

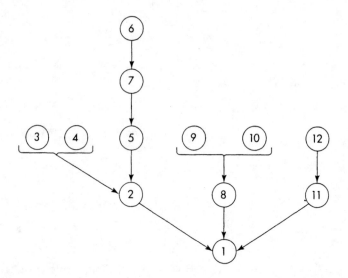

Arguments in everyday life often fall short of this standard. They may include statements whose role is unclear; connections among the statements in the argument may be tangled or misstated; even in the mind of its author the flow of the argument may be confused. Logical analysis, supported by diagrams, can expose such deficiencies. By exposing the *structure* of a reasoning process we can see how it was intended to work and what its strengths and weaknesses may be. The special province of logic is the evaluation of arguments; successful evaluation requires a clear grasp of the argument we are analyzing.

### Exercises

Each of the following passages can best be interpreted as containing several arguments, whose premises and conclusions are arranged in a variety of ways. Analyze these passages, paraphrasing premises and conclusions where necessary, and construct a diagram for each passage.

*1. Democractic laws generally tend to promote the welfare of the greatest possible number; for they emanate from the majority of the citizens, who are subject to error, but who cannot have an interest opposed to their own advantage. The laws of an aristocracy tend, on the contrary, to concentrate wealth and power in the hands of the minority; because an aristocracy, by its very nature, constitutes a minority. It may therefore be asserted, as a general proposition, that the purpose of a democracy in its legislation is more useful to humanity than that of an aristocracy.

—Alexis de Tocqueville, *Democracy in America*, 1835

2. Paternal and maternal genes can be antagonistic to one another. Consider pregnancy. In most mammals, the mother's body regards the growing embryo as an intruder, and tries to limit the demands it places on her resources. The father, of course, does not bear the young and so is unaffected by such considerations. His genetic interest is unambiguous: to stimulate the embryo's growth and to shield it from the mother's defenses. Thus only males contribute the genes that foster the growth of the protective organ known as the placenta; females do not. Uniparental mouse eggs, created from the genes of the mother alone, develop into normal embryos, but the embryos lack a placenta and so do not flourish.

—Laurence Marschall, in a review of *Genome*,
by Matt Ridley (HarperCollins, 2000),
appearing in *The Sciences*, August 2000

3. A question arises: whether it be better [for a prince] to be loved than feared or feared than loved? One should wish to be both, but, because it is difficult to unite them in one person, it is much safer to be feared than loved, when, of the two, one must be dispensed with. Because this is to be asserted in general of men, that they are ungrateful, fickle, false, cowards, covetous . . . and that prince who, relying entirely on their promises, has neglected other precautions, is ruined, because friendships that are obtained by payments may indeed be earned but they are not secured, and in time of need cannot be relied upon. Men have less scruple in offending one who is beloved than one who is feared, for love is preserved by the link of obligation which, owing to the baseness of men, is broken at every opportunity for their advantage; but fear preserves you by a dread of punishment which never fails.

—N. Machiavelli, *The Prince*, 1515

4. Consider why the federal government is involved in student lending: it is in the national interest to have an educated populace. On average, college graduates earn almost twice the annual salary of high-school graduates. The cost of the nation's investment in the education of student borrowers is recouped many times over through increased productivity and greater earnings. By making a college education possible for millions of Americans, federally sponsored student loans produce a tremendous return for the U.S. Treasury and students, whose incomes—and tax payments—are greatly increased with their college degrees.

But most college students are not creditworthy borrowers. The typical student is cash poor, owner of few if any assets that could be used as collateral, and often earns too little to be considered a good credit risk. If such a borrower could get a loan, in all likelihood it would carry a high interest rate—high enough to lead many students to decide not to go on to higher education. That is why student loans are backed by federal money and the interest charged on those loans is capped.

—Richard W. Riley, "Should Washington
Have a Bigger Share of the Student-loan
Industry? Yes!" *Insight*, 29 April 1996

*5. ". . . You appeared to be surprised when I told you, on our first meeting, that you had come from Afghanistan."

"You were told, no doubt."

"Nothing of the sort. I *knew* you came from Afghanistan. From long habit the train of thoughts ran so swiftly through my mind that I arrived at the conclusion without being conscious of intermediate steps. There were such steps, however. The train of reasoning ran, 'Here is a gentleman of medical type, but with the air of a military man. Clearly an army doctor, then. He has just come from the tropics, for his face is dark, and that is not the natural tint of his skin, for his wrists are fair. He has undergone hardship and sickness, as his haggard face says clearly. His left arm has been injured. He holds it in a stiff and unnatural manner. Where in the tropics could an English army doctor have seen much hardship and got his arm wounded? Clearly in Afghanistan.' The whole train of thought did not occupy a second. I then remarked that you came from Afghanistan, and you were astonished."

"It is simple enough as you explain it," I said, smiling.

—A. Conan Doyle, *A Study in Scarlet*, 1887

6. One of the most difficult problems associated with quantum research is how to observe subatomic particles in their natural states without affecting them—observing them non-destructively, so to speak. It's difficult for two reasons. First, atoms and subatomic particle are the smallest constituents of matter. Since any medium used to observe them emits energy of its own, that energy must affect the energy of the observed particles. Second, in isolation, atomic components exist in two quantum states simultaneously— particles and waves. It's as if they were packets of statistical probability. Only when they interact with other components do they display one manifestation or the other.

—"Skinning Schrodinger's Cat," *Insight*, 15 July 1996

7. Is there any room left at all in science for divine things? Michael J. Behe [in *Darwin's Black Box* (The Free Press, 1996)] contends that there is. He argues that the origin of intracellular processes underlying the foundation of life cannot be explained by natural selec-

tion or by any other mechanism based purely on chance. When examined with the powerful tools of modern biology, life on a biochemical level can be the product (this practicing biochemist believes) only of intelligent design.

The crux of his argument is that fundamental systems within the cell are "irreducibly complex"; they are composed of several specific, interacting components, each of which plays a vital role in the functioning of the system as a whole. Take out any step in the complex cascade of reactions that leads to the coagulation of blood, for example, and a wounded organism's lifeblood would leak out like water from a broken cup; but remove a single enzyme that limits the clotting process to the area of the wound, and the entire blood supply hardens up instead. Since either of these conditions would be fatal, the molecular components of clotting could not have come together gradually through natural selection and then assembled themselves into a functioning system.

8. In the U.S. Postal Service there is no straightforward mechanism to correct problems or force the agency to change. No citizens can own tradable shares. The income and security of managers and workers are guaranteed by the monopoly on first-class mail, public funding and the employees' political clout with Congress. The public cannot shift its business to more efficient competitors, because competition is prohibited. Consequently, the gross postal inefficiencies are not the result of the character or personality of the individuals who happen to occupy positions and jobs; they stem from the structure of the Postal Service itself.

> —Douglas K. Adie, "Privatizing Will Improve Mail Service Posthaste," *Insight*, 30 January 1995

9. Eliminating a tax on marriage sounds like a great idea. But it is also a sound idea to set higher rates on wealthier people and to tax families with the same total income the same no matter how their income is split between spouses. No tax code can satisfy these three goals simultaneously. Two people whose individual incomes are low enough to be taxed at 15 percent can, under a progressive code, hit the 28 percent bracket when their incomes are combined. Congress can eliminate the marriage tax, but only by sacrificing progressivity.

> —"Temptations of a Balanced Budget," Editorial in *New York Times*, 31 December 1997

*10. Nothing is demonstrable unless the contrary implies a contradiction. Nothing that is distinctly conceivable implies a contradiction. Whatever we conceive as existent, we can also conceive as nonexistent. There is no being, therefore, whose non-existence implies a contradiction. Consequently there is no being whose existence is demonstrable.

—David Hume, *Dialogues Concerning Natural Religion,*
Part IX, 1779 ∎

## 1.11  REASONING

**For Enrichment**     Logic, we have said, is the study of the methods and principles used to distinguish correct from incorrect reasoning. Reasoning is the process with which one advances, with arguments, from premises known (or affirmed for the purpose) to conclusions. Thus far we have been analyzing and evaluating the arguments of others. Arguments of our own we construct every day, of course, in deciding how we shall act, in judging the acts of others, in defending our moral or political convictions, and so on. Skill in building and applying good arguments is of enormous value.

This skill in reasoning can be improved with practice. To encourage such practice the various games of reasoning (chess, go, and Mastermind, for examples) are splendid instruments. But also quite useful are puzzles with which we may strengthen and test our logical skills. Reasoning is not only an essential activity, it is also an enjoyable activity—and the enjoyment it can yield is apparent when we solve logical problems designed both to stimulate and to entertain.

Contrived problems will be *neater* than those arising in real life, and usually simpler too. But solving them can be challenging, and often requires extended reasoning in patterns not very different from those employed by a detective, or a journalist, or a juror. Chains of inferences are likely to be needed, in which the sub-conclusions reached are used as premises in subsequent arguments. Insight may be called for too; finding the path to solution may require the creative recombination of information earlier given or discovered. Solving contrived problems can prove difficult, sometimes frustrating—but success, achieved through the successful application of reason, is very satisfying. Logical games and puzzles—in addition to being models for the employment of reason—are good fun. "The enjoyment of the doubtful," wrote the American philosopher, John Dewey, " is a mark of the educated mind."

One common type of reasoning problem is the brainteaser in which, using only the clues provided, we are asked to untangle and identify the names, or roles, or other facts about several specified characters. Here is a relatively simple example:

> In a certain flight crew, the positions of pilot, copilot, and flight engineer are held by three persons, Allen, Brown, and Carr, though not necessarily in that order.
> The copilot, who is an only child, earns the least.
> Carr, who married Brown's sister, earns more than the pilot.
> What position does each of the three persons hold?

To solve such problems we look first for a sphere in which we have enough information to reach some conclusions going beyond what is given in the premisses. In this case we know most about Carr: he is not the pilot, because he earns more than the pilot; and he is not the copilot because the copilot earns the least. By elimination we may infer that Carr must be the flight engineer.

Using that sub-conclusion we can determine Brown's position. Brown is not the copilot because he has a sister and the copilot is an only child; he is not the flight engineer because Carr is. Brown must therefore be the pilot. Allen, the only one left, must therefore be the copilot.

In addressing problems of this type (which can become very intricate) it is useful to construct a graphic display of the alternatives, called a *matrix*, which we fill in as we accumulate new information. To appreciate the helpfulness of such a matrix, consider the following puzzle:

> Alonzo, Kurt, Rudolf, and Willard are four creative artists of great talent. One is a dancer, one is a painter, one is a singer, and one is a writer, though not necessarily in that order.
>
> (1) Alonzo and Rudolf were in the audience the night the singer made his debut on the concert stage.
>
> (2) Both Kurt and the writer have had their portraits painted from life by the painter.
>
> (3) The writer, whose biography of Willard was a best-seller, is planning to write a biography of Alonzo.
>
> (4) Alonzo has never heard of Rudolf.
>
> What is each man's artistic field?

To keep the many facts asserted in these premisses in mind, and also to remember the several subconclusions that may have been inferred from them, would be a demanding task. Writing our inferences down in the form of notes might prove helpful but could also result in a confusing clutter. We need a method for storing the information given and the intermediate conclusions drawn, a method that will keep what is known and what is inferred in order and available for use as the number of inferences increases and the chain of arguments lengthens. In the matrix we construct there will be room to represent all the relevant possibilities and to record each inference drawn.

The matrix for this problem must display an array of the four persons (in four rows) and the four artistic professions (in four columns) that they hold. It would look like this:

|  | DANCER | PAINTER | SINGER | WRITER |
|---|---|---|---|---|
| ALONZO | ✓ | ✗ | ✗ | ✗ |
| KURT | ✗ | ✗ | ✓ | ✗ |
| RUDOLF | ✗ | ✗ | ✗ | ✓ |
| WILLARD | ✗ | ✓ | ✗ | ✗ |

When we conclude that the individual whose name is at the left of one of the rows cannot be the artist whose profession is at the top of one of the columns, we write an N (for "no," or a "−") in the box to the right of that person's name and in the column headed by that profession. We can immediately infer (from premiss 1) that neither Alonzo nor Rudolph is the singer, so we place an N to the right of their names, in the third (singer) column. Similarly, we can infer from premiss 2 that Kurt is neither the painter nor the writer, so we enter an N to the right of his name in the second (painter) and fourth (writer) columns. From premiss 3 we see that the writer is neither Alonzo nor Willard, so we enter N to the right of their names in the fourth column. The entries we have made thus far are all justified by the information originally given, and our matrix now looks like this:

|  | DANCER | PAINTER | SINGER | WRITER |
|---|---|---|---|---|
| ALONZO |  |  | N | N |
| KURT |  | N |  | N |
| RUDOLF |  |  | N |  |
| WILLARD |  |  |  | N |

From the information now available we can conclude by elimination that Rudolf must be the writer, so we enter a Y (for "yes," or a "+") in the box to the right of Rudolf's name in the fourth (writer) column, and we place an N in the other boxes to the right of his name. The array now makes it evident that the painter must be either Alonzo or Willard, and we can eliminate Alonzo in this way: Rudolf had his portrait painted by the painter (from premiss 2), and Alonzo has never heard of Rudolf (from premiss 4)—therefore Alonzo cannot be the painter. Thus we enter an N to the right of Alonzo's name under column two (painter).

We next conclude that Alonzo must be the dancer, so we enter a Y to the right of Alonzo's name in the first (dancer) column. Now we can enter an N in the dancer column for both Kurt and Willard. The only possible category remaining for Kurt is singer, and therefore we enter a Y in that box and an N in the singer column to the right of Willard's name. Again by elimination we conclude that Willard must be the painter and put a Y in the last empty box in the matrix. Our completed graphic display looks like this:

|  | DANCER | PAINTER | SINGER | WRITER |
|---|---|---|---|---|
| ALONZO | Y | N | N | N |
| KURT | N | N | Y | N |
| RUDOLF | N | N | N | Y |
| WILLARD | N | Y | N | N |

From the filled-in matrix we can read off the solution: Alonzo is the dancer; Kurt is the singer; Rudolf is the writer; Willard is the painter.

Brainteasers of this general kind become more complicated when solutions on several dimensions are called for. Some such problems are very challenging and almost impossible to solve without using a matrix.[53]

Other reasoning problems present a different kind of challenge. Here is one that is elegant and amusing, but not very difficult. Try solving it before turning to the solution that follows.

You are confronted by six balls: two red, two green, and two blue. In each color pair you know that one ball is heavier than the other. You also know that all three of the heavier balls weigh the same, as do all three of the lighter balls. The six balls (call them R1, R2, G1, G2, B1, and B2) are otherwise indistinguishable. You have only a balance scale.

## The Problem:

With no more than two weighings on the scale, how can one identify the heavier and the lighter balls in all three pairs?

## Solution:  First weighing: R1 + G1 // R2 + B1

If they balance: Of the pair R1 and R2, one is heavy and the other light. With the two red balls on opposite sides of the scale, we know that if the two sides balance there must be a heavy and a light ball on each side—because two heavies on one side would have to go down, and two lights on one side would have to go up. Therefore we know that either: G1 is heavy and B1 is light, or G1 is light and B1 is heavy.

**If the two sides balance on the first weighing, the second weighing is: G1 // B1.** Whatever the outcome of this weighing all balls will be identifiable:

If (on this weighing) G1 goes down:

— G1 is heavy (and G2 is light), and
— B1 is light (and B2 is heavy), and
— R1 is light (and R2 is heavy).

If (on this weighing) G1 goes up: the reverse is true.

But what if on the first weighing (R1 + G1 // R2 + B1) the two sides do not balance? Suppose R1 + G1 goes down. (If R1 + G1 goes up, the solution that follows is simply reversed.)

We know that in this case R1 (the red ball on the side that goes down) must be heavy; because if R1 were light, R2 would be heavy; and if R2 were heavy, R1 + G1 could not have gone down.

---

[53]Readers who find logical problems of this kind enjoyable will encounter a feast of such delights in a series entitled *Original Logic Problems,* and published by The Penny Press, Norwalk, CT.

Since R1 is heavy, one of the following three combinations must be the case:

**(a)** G1 is light    and B1 is light;    or
**(b)** G1 is heavy    and B1 is heavy;    or
**(c)** G1 is heavy    and B1 is light

**If R1 + G1 go down on the first weighing, the second weighing is: R1 + R2 // G1 + B1.**

We already know that R1 is heavy. On this second weighing, R1 + R2 (heavy + light) must either go down or go up, or the two sides will balance. Whichever the outcome, we can identify all the balls as follows:

(x) If R1 + R2 go down, G1 and B1 must both be light (since a heavy and a light can outweigh only two lights). In this case the combination must be pattern (a) above: G1 is light and B1 is light—and all are solved.

(y) If R1 + R2 go up, G1 and B1 must both be heavy (since heavy + light can be outweighed only by two heavies). In this case the combination must be pattern (b) above: G1 is heavy and B1 is heavy—and all are solved.

(z) If the two sides balance, G1 and B1 must also be heavy + light. In this case the combination must be pattern (c) above: G1 is heavy and B1 is light—and all are solved.

Before giving this problem to your friends, practice explaining the solution!

In the real world we are often called upon to reason from some present state of affairs to its causes, from what *is* to what *was*. Scientists—especially archeologists, geologists, astronomers, and physicians—commonly confront events or conditions whose origins are problematic. Reasoning that seeks to explain how things must have developed from what went before is called *retrograde analysis*. For example, to the amazement of astronomers, comet Hyakutake, streaking by the earth in 1996, was found to be emitting variable X-rays 100 times stronger than anyone had ever predicted a comet might emit. A comet expert at the Max Planck Institute in Germany remarked: "We have our work cut out for us in explaining these data—but that's the kind of problem you love to have."

We do love to have them, and because we do, problems in retrograde analysis are often devised for amusement. Such problems present a special difficulty, however: the logical framework that in the real world is supplied by scientific or historical knowledge must somehow be provided by the problem itself. Some rules or laws must be set forth within which logical analysis can proceed.

The chessboard is the setting for the most famous of all problems in retrograde analysis; the rules of chess provide the needed theoretical

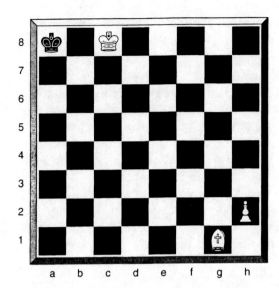

**FIGURE 1-1**

context. No skill in playing chess is required, but readers who are not familiar with the rules of chess may skip the illustration that follows.

Retrograde problems in chess commonly take this form: An arrangement of pieces on the chessboard is given; it was reached in a game of chess in which all the rules of the game were obeyed. What move, or series of moves has just been completed? An example of such a problem follows. The diagram presents a position reached in an actual game of chess, all moves in that game having been made in accordance with the rules of chess.

For the purpose of analysis the rows are numbered from bottom to top, 1 to 8, and the columns are lettered from left to right, a to h. Each square on the board then can be identified by a unique letter–number combination: the black king is on a8, the white pawn on h2, and so on. The problem is this: The last move was made by black. What was that move? And what was white's move just before that? Can you reason out the solution before reading the next paragraph?

Solution: The black king has just moved. Since the two kings may never rest on adjacent squares, it could not have moved to its present position from b7 or from b8; therefore, we may be certain that the black king has moved from a7, where it was in check.

That much is easily deduced. But what preceding white move could have put the black king in check? No move by the white bishop (on g1) could have done, it, because there would have been no way for that bishop to move to that square, g1, without the black king having been in check with white to move! Therefore it must be that the check was *discovered* by the movement of a white piece that had been blocking the bishop's attack and was captured by the black king on its move to a8. What white piece could have been on that black diagonal and moved from there to the white square in the corner? Only a knight that had been on b6. We may therefore be certain that before black's last move (the black king from a7 to a8) white's last move was that of a white knight from b6 to a8.[54]

The problems of reasoning that confront us in the real world are rarely as tidy as the puzzles discussed in this section, of course. Many real problems are not accurately described, and their misdescription may prove so misleading that no solution can be reached. In cases of that kind, some part or parts of the description of the problem need to be rejected or replaced. But we cannot do this when we are seeking to solve logical puzzles of the sort presented in this chapter.

Some problems in the real world, moreover, even when they are described accurately, may be incomplete in that something not originally available may be essential for the solution. The solution may depend on some additional scientific discovery, or some previously unimagined invention or equipment, or the search of some as-yet-unexplored territory. But in the statement of a logical puzzle, as in the writing of a good murder mystery, all the information that is sufficient for the solution must be given; otherwise we feel that the mystery writer, or the problem-maker, has been unfair to us.

Finally, the logical puzzle presents an explicit question (*e.g.,* Which member of the artistic foursome is the singer? What were black's and white's last moves?) whose answer, if given and proved, solves the problem definitively. But that is not the form in which many real-world problems arise. Real problems are often identified, initially at least, only by the recognition of some inconsistency or the occurrence of an unusual event, or perhaps just by the feeling that something is amiss—rather than by a well-formed question with a clearly defined answer.

In spite of these differences, problems designed to be solved through systematic reasoning are similar enough to problems in the real world to justify their use in the study of logic.

### Exercises

The following problems require reasoning for their solution. To prove that an answer is correct requires an argument (often containing subsidiary arguments) whose premises are contained in the statement of the problem—and whose final conclusion is the answer to it. If the answer is correct, it is possible to construct a valid argument proving it. In working these problems, readers are urged to concern themselves not merely with discovering the answers but also with formulating arguments to prove that those answers are correct.

---

[54]Readers who find retrograde analysis enjoyable will take delight in a collection of such problems, compiled by the logician Raymond Smullyan and entitled *The Chess Mysteries of Sherlock Holmes* (New York: Alfred A. Knopf, 1979).

**\*1.** In a certain mythical community, politicians never tell the truth, and nonpoliticians always tell the truth. A stranger meets three natives and asks the first of them, "Are you a politician?" The first native answers the question. The second native then reports that the first native denied being a politician. The third native says that the first native *is* a politician.

    How many of these three natives are politicians?

**2.** Of three prisoners in a certain jail, one had normal vision, the second had only one eye, and the third was totally blind. The jailor told the prisoners that, from three white hats and two red hats, he would select three and put them on the prisoners' heads. None could see what color hat he wore. The jailor offered freedom to the prisoner with normal vision if he could tell what color hat he wore. To prevent a lucky guess, the jailor threatened execution for any incorrect answer. The first prisoner could not tell what hat he wore. Next the jailor made the same offer to the one-eyed prisoner. The second prisoner could not tell what hat he wore either. The jailor did not bother making the offer to the blind prisoner, but he agreed to extend the same terms to that prisoner when he made the request. The blind prisoner said:

> I do not need to have my sight;
> From what my friends with eyes have said,
> I clearly see my hat is _____ !

How did he know?

**3.** On a certain train, the crew consists of the brakeman, the fireman, and the engineer. Their names listed alphabetically are Jones, Robinson, and Smith. On the train are also three passengers with corresponding names, Mr. Jones, Mr. Robinson, and Mr. Smith. The following facts are known:
  **a.** Mr. Robinson lives in Detroit.
  **b.** The brakeman lives halfway between Detroit and Chicago.
  **c.** Mr. Jones earns exactly $20,000 a year.
  **d.** Smith once beat the fireman at billiards.
  **e.** The brakeman's next-door neighbor, one of the three passengers mentioned, earns exactly three times as much as the brakeman.
  **f.** The passenger living in Chicago has the same name as the brakeman.
What is the engineer's name?

**4.** The employees of a small loan company are Mr. Black, Mr. White, Mrs. Coffee, Miss Ambrose, Mr. Kelly, and Miss Earnshaw. The positions they occupy are manager, assistant manager, cashier, stenographer, teller, and clerk, though not necessarily in that order. The assistant manager is the manager's grandson, the cashier is the stenographer's son-in-law, Mr. Black is a bachelor, Mr. White is twenty-two years old, Miss Ambrose is the teller's step-sister, and Mr. Kelly is the manager's neighbor.

Who holds each position?

*5. Benno Torelli, genial host at Miami's most exclusive nightclub, was shot and killed by a racketeer gang because he fell behind in his protection payments. After considerable effort on the part of the police, five suspects were brought before the district attorney, who asked them what they had to say for themselves. Each of them made three statements, two true and one false. Their statements were

LEFTY:   I did not kill Torelli. I never owned a revolver in all my life. Spike did it.

RED:   I did not kill Torelli. I never owned a revolver. The others are all passing the buck.

DOPEY:   I am innocent. I never saw Butch before. Spike is guilty.

SPIKE:   I am innocent. Butch is the guilty one. Lefty did not tell the truth when he said I did it.

BUTCH:  I did not kill Torelli. Red is the guilty one. Dopey and I are old pals.

Whodunnit?

6. Mr. Short, his sister, his son, and his daughter are fond of golf and often play together. The following statements are true of their foursome:
(1)   The best player's twin and the worst player are of the opposite sex.
(2)   The best player and the worst player are the same age.
Which one of the foursome is the best player?

7. Daniel Kilraine was killed on a lonely road, two miles from Pontiac, Michigan, at 3:30 A.M. on March 17 of last year. Otto, Curly, Slim, Mickey, and the Kid were arrested a week later in Detroit and questioned. Each of the five made four statements, three of which were true and one of which was false. One of these persons killed Kilraine.

Their statements were

OTTO:   I was in Chicago when Kilraine was murdered. I never killed anyone. The Kid is the guilty one. Mickey and I are pals.

CURLY:   I did not kill Kilraine. I never owned a revolver in my life. The Kid knows me. I was in Detroit the night of March 17.

SLIM:   Curly lied when he said he never owned a revolver. The murder was committed on St. Patrick's Day. Otto was in Chicago at this time. One of us is guilty.

MICKEY:   I did not kill Kilraine. The Kid has never been in Pontiac. I never saw Otto before. Curly was in Detroit with me on the night of March 17.

THE KID:   I did not kill Kilraine. I have never been in Pontiac. I never saw Curly before. Otto erred when he said I am guilty.

Whodunnit?

8.   Picture a checkerboard (or chessboard like that on p. 63) having eight rows and eight columns of squares, alternately colored red and black. We are given a package of oblong dominoes, each one covering two of the squares of the chessboard, and asked to cover the chessboard completely. Obviously 32 dominoes are needed to cover the entire board.

But suppose we are given only 31 dominoes, so that, seeking to cover the chessboard, we must leave two squares empty. Suppose also that the upper-left-hand corner of the chessboard is left empty, so that one other square will also have to be left uncovered. Can the 31 dominoes be placed in such a way as to leave, as the other empty square, the square in the lower-right-hand corner? If so, how? And if not, why not?

9.   In the same mythical community described in Exercise 1, a stranger meets three other natives and asks them, "How many of you are politicians?" The first native replies, "We are all politicians." The second native says, "No, just two of us are politicians." The third native then says, "That isn't true either."

Is the third native a politician?

*10.   Imagine a room with four walls, a nail placed in the center of each wall, as well as in the ceiling and floor, six nails in all. The nails are connected to each other by strings, each nail connected to every other nail by a separate string. These strings are of two colors, red and blue, and of no other color. All these strings obviously make many triangles, since any three nails may be considered the apexes of a triangle.

Can the colors of the strings be distributed so that no one triangle has all three sides (strings) of the same color? If so, how? And if not, why not?

## Challenge to the Reader

Here is a final reasoning problem whose solution requires the construction of a set of sustained arguments. It isn't easy—but solving it is well within your power and will give you great pleasure.

**\*11.** You are presented with a set of twelve metal balls, apparently identical in every respect: size, color, and so on. In fact, eleven of them are identical, but one of them is "odd": It differs from all the rest in weight only; it is either heavier, or lighter, than all the others. You are given a balance scale, on which the balls can be weighed against one another. If the same number of balls are put on each side of the balance, and the "odd" ball is on one side, that side will go down if the odd ball is heavier, or up if the odd ball is lighter; the two sides will balance if the odd ball is not among those weighed and the same number of balls are placed on each side. You are allowed three weighings only; any removal or addition of a ball constitutes a separate weighing.

Your challenge is this: Devise a set of three weighings that will enable you to identify the odd ball wherever it may lie in a random mixing of the twelve balls, *and* that will enable you to determine whether the odd ball is heavier or lighter than the rest. ∎

## Summary of Chapter 1

In this chapter we introduced and illustrated the most fundamental concepts of logic.

In section 1.1 we defined logic as **the study of the methods and principles used to distinguish correct from incorrect reasoning,** and explained this definition.

In section 1.2 we explained **propositions**—which may be asserted or denied, and which are either true or false—and distinguished them from the sentences in which they may be expressed.

In section 1.3 we introduced and explained the concept of **an argument**—a cluster of propositions in which one is the **conclusion** and the other(s) are **premisses** offered in its support.

In section 1.4 we explained and illustrated **how arguments may be analyzed**—either by **paraphrasing,** in which the propositions are reformulated and arranged in logical order; or by **diagramming,** in which the propositions are numbered and the numbers are laid out on a page and connected in ways that exhibit the logical relations among the propositions.

In section 1.5 we discussed several aspects of the task of **recognizing arguments,** including conclusion- and premiss-indicators; the role of context in identifying premisses and conclusions; the nondeclarative forms in which premisses may appear; and arguments containing propositions that are not explicitly stated.

In section 1.6 we discussed the differences between **arguments** and **explanations.** We explained why it is often difficult to make this distinction, which depends on context and the purpose of the author of the passage.

In section 1.7 we discussed **deduction** and **validity.** We defined a deductive argument as one in which the conclusion is claimed to follow from the premisses with necessity, and a valid deductive argument as one in which the conclusion is necessarily true if the premisses are true.

In section 1.8 we discussed **induction** and **probability.** We defined an inductive argument as one whose conclusion has some degree of probability but in which the claim of necessity is not made. Inductive arguments, we explained, may be judged as better or worse but cannot be characterized as valid or invalid.

In section 1.9 we discussed some of the complicated relations between the **validity (or invalidity) of deductive arguments** and the **truth (or falsity) of propositions.**

In section 1.10 we discussed **complex argumentative passages,** showing how the diagramming technique is useful analyzing them.

In section 1.11 we discussed **problems of reasoning,** exhibiting the ways in which such problems can exercise and strengthen reasoning skills, while affording genuine intellectual pleasure.

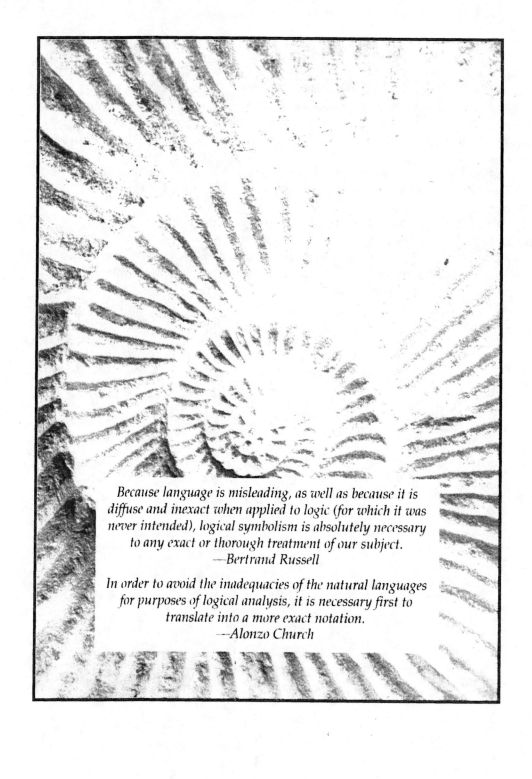

*Because language is misleading, as well as because it is diffuse and inexact when applied to logic (for which it was never intended), logical symbolism is absolutely necessary to any exact or thorough treatment of our subject.*
—Bertrand Russell

*In order to avoid the inadequacies of the natural languages for purposes of logical analysis, it is necessary first to translate into a more exact notation.*
—Alonzo Church

# CHAPTER 8

# SYMBOLIC LOGIC

## 8.1 THE SYMBOLIC LANGUAGE OF MODERN LOGIC

We seek techniques for the analysis and appraisal of deductive arguments. The theory of deduction aims to provide these techniques, and two different branches of this theory have been developed to do this: the *classical* or *Aristotelian logic*, examined in the three preceding chapters, and *modern symbolic logic*, which we will be our subject in this and the following two chapters.

The analyzing and appraising of arguments is often made difficult, however, by the peculiarities of the language—English, or any natural language—in which the arguments are presented. The words used may be vague or equivocal, the construction of the arguments may be ambiguous, metaphors and idioms may confuse or mislead, emotional appeals may distract—problems that were discussed in Part One. To avoid these difficulties, and thus move directly to the logical heart of an argument, logicians construct an artificial symbolic language, free of linguistic defects. With a symbolic language we can formulate an argument with precision.

Symbols also facilitate our thinking about an argument. "By the aid of symbolism," wrote one of the greatest of modern logicians, "we can make transitions in reasoning almost mechanically by the eye, which otherwise would call into play the higher faculties of the of the brain."[1] It may seem paradoxical, but a symbolic language helps us to accomplish some intellectual tasks without having to think too much.

The ancient and classical logicians also recognized the value of a special logical notation. Aristotle used variables in his own analyses, and the refined Aristotelian logic uses symbols in very sophisticated ways, as the preceding

---

[1] Alfred North Whitehead, *An Introduction to Mathematics*, 1911.

chapters have shown.[2] During the twentieth century very great steps have been taken to advance this process.

In modern logic, it is not syllogisms (as in the Aristotelian tradition) that are central, but logical *connectives*, the relations between elements that every deductive argument, syllogism or not, must employ. The *internal structure* of propositions and arguments is the focus of modern logic. To understand this structure we must first master the special symbols that are used in modern logical analysis.

Modern symbolic logic is not encumbered (as Aristotelian logic was) by the need to transform deductive arguments into syllogistic form. That task can be laborious, as we have seen in Chapter 7. Freed from the need to make such transformations, we can pursue the aims of deductive analysis more directly. The symbolic notation of modern logic set forth here is an exceedingly powerful tool for the analysis of arguments. With it we can more fully achieve the central aim of deductive logic: to discriminate valid arguments from invalid arguments.

## 8.2 THE SYMBOLS FOR CONJUNCTION, NEGATION, AND DISJUNCTION

In this chapter we shall be concerned with relatively simple arguments such as

The blind prisoner has a red hat or the blind prisoner has a white hat.
The blind prisoner does not have a red hat.
Therefore the blind prisoner has a white hat.

and

If Mr. Robinson is the brakeman's next-door neighbor, then Mr. Robinson lives halfway between Detroit and Chicago.
Mr. Robinson does not live halfway between Detroit and Chicago.
Therefore Mr. Robinson is not the brakeman's next-door neighbor.

Every argument of this general type contains at least one compound statement. In studying such arguments we divide all statements into two general categories, simple and compound. **A simple statement is one that does not contain any other statement as a component.** For example, "Charlie's neat" is a simple statement. **A compound statement is one that**

---

[2] The Arabic numerals we use today also illustrate very nicely how symbols can facilitate our reasoning. These numerals (1, 2, 3, . . .) replaced the old Roman numerals (i, ii, iii, . . .), which were much more cumbersome to manipulate. To multiply 113 by 9 is easy, but to multiply CXIII by IX is not so easy. Think of the difficulties of multiplying MCCCXLVIII by DCCLXIV! So awkward is calculation using the old numerals that even the ancient Romans were driven to devise a more efficient symbolism for arithmetic; some scholars contend that they actually relied on a Western version of the Oriental abacus, which they called a "counting board." We too must manipulate concepts. The more efficient our logical notation, the easier will be the tasks of deductive analysis, and the more likely that the resulting analyses will be accurate.

does contain another statement as a component. For example, "Charlie's neat and Charlie's sweet" is a compound statement, for it contains two simple statements as components. Of course, the components of a compound statement may themselves be compound.[3]

## A. Conjunction

There are several types of compound statements, each requiring its own logical notation. The first type of compound statement to be considered is the *conjunction*. **We can form the *conjunction* of two statements by placing the word "and" between them; the two statements so combined are called *conjuncts*.** Thus the compound statement "Charlie's neat and Charlie's sweet" is a conjunction whose first conjunct is "Charlie's neat" and whose second conjunct is "Charlie's sweet."

The word "and" is a short and convenient word, but it has other uses besides that of connecting statements. For example, the statement "Lincoln and Grant were contemporaries" is *not* a conjunction but a simple statement expressing a relationship. To have a unique symbol whose only function is to connect statements conjunctively, we introduce the dot "•" as our symbol for conjunction. Thus the previous conjunction can be written as "Charlie's neat • Charlie's sweet." More generally, where $p$ and $q$ are any two statements whatever, their conjunction is written $p • q$.

We know that every statement is either true or false. Therefore we say that **every statement has a *truth value*, where the truth value of a true statement is *true*, and the truth value of a false statement is *false*.** Using this concept of "truth value" we can divide compound statements into two distinct categories, according to whether or not the truth value of the compound statement is determined wholly by the truth values of its components, or determined by anything other than the truth values of its components.

---

[3] In formulating definitions and principles in logic one must be very precise. What appears simple often proves more complicated than had been supposed. The notion of a "component of a statement" is a good illustration of this need for caution.

One might have supposed that a *component* of a statement is simply a part of a statement that is itself a statement. But this account does not define the term with enough precision, because one statement may be a *part* of a larger statement and yet not a *component* of it in the strict sense. For example, consider the statement: "The man who shot Lincoln was an actor." Plainly the last four words of this statement are a part of it, and could indeed be regarded as a statement; it is either true or it is false that Lincoln was an actor. But the statement that "Lincoln was an actor," although undoubtedly a part of the larger statement, is not a *component* of that larger statement.

We can explain this by noting that, for part of a statement to be a component of that statement, two conditions must be satisfied: (1) The part must be a statement in its own right; *and* (2) If the part is replaced in the larger statement by any other statement, the result of that replacement must be meaningful, must make sense.

The first of these conditions is satisfied in the Lincoln example just above, but the second is not. Suppose the part "Lincoln was an actor" were replaced by "there are lions in Africa." The result of this replacement would be nonsense: "The man who shot there are lions in Africa." The term *component* is not a difficult one to understand but—like all logical terms—it must be defined accurately and applied carefully.

We apply this distinction to conjunctions. The truth value of the conjunction of two statements is determined wholly and entirely by the truth values of its two conjuncts. If both its conjuncts are true, the conjunction is true; otherwise it is false. For this reason a conjunction is said to be a *truth-functional* compound statement, and its conjuncts are said to be *truth-functional* components of it.

Not every compound statement is truth-functional, however. For example, the truth value of the compound statement "Othello believes that Desdemona loves Cassio" is not in any way determined by the truth value of its component simple statement "Desdemona loves Cassio," for it could be true that Othello believes that Desdemona loves Cassio regardless of whether she does so or not. So the component "Desdemona loves Cassio" is not a truth-functional component of the statement "Othello believes that Desdemona loves Cassio," and the statement itself is not a truth-functional compound statement.

For our present purposes we define a *component* of a compound statement as being a **truth-functional component of it provided that, if the component is replaced in the compound by any different statements having the same truth value as each other, the different compound statements produced by those replacements will also have the same truth values as each other.** And now we define a *compound statement* as being a **truth-functional compound statement if all of its components are truth-functional components of it.**[4]

We shall be concerned only with those compound statements that are truth-functionally compound. In the remainder of this book, therefore, we shall use the term *simple statement* to refer to **any statement that is not truth-functionally compound.**

A conjunction is a truth-functional compound statement, so our dot symbol is a **truth-functional connective.** Given any two statements, $p$ and $q$, there are only four possible sets of truth values they can have. These four possible cases, and the truth value of the conjunction in each, can be displayed as follows:

> Where $p$ is true and $q$ is true, $p \bullet q$ is true.
> Where $p$ is true and $q$ is false, $p \bullet q$ is false.
> Where $p$ is false and $q$ is true, $p \bullet q$ is false.
> Where $p$ is false and $q$ is false, $p \bullet q$ is false.

If we represent the truth values "true" and "false" by the capital letters **T** and **F**, the determination of the truth value of a conjunction by the truth values of its conjuncts can be represented more briefly and more clearly by means of a "truth table":

| $p$ | $q$ | $p \bullet q$ |
|-----|-----|-----|
| T | T | T |
| T | F | F |
| F | T | F |
| F | F | F |

---

[4] Somewhat more complicated definitions have been proposed by David H. Sanford in his "What Is a Truth Functional Component?" *Logique et Analyse* 14 (1970), 483–486.

This truth table can be taken as defining the dot symbol, since it explains what truth values are assumed by $p \cdot q$ in every possible case.

We shall find it convenient to abbreviate simple statements by capital letters, generally using for this purpose a letter that will help us remember which statement it abbreviates. Thus we should abbreviate "Charlie's neat and Charlie's sweet" as $N \cdot S$. Some conjunctions both of whose conjuncts have the same subject term—for example, "Byron was a great poet and Byron was a great adventurer"—are more briefly and perhaps more naturally stated in English by placing the "and" between the predicate terms and not repeating the subject term, as in "Byron was a great poet and a great adventurer." For our purposes, we regard the latter as formulating the same statement as the former and symbolize either one indifferently as $P \cdot A$. If both conjuncts of a conjunction have the same predicate term, as in "Lewis was a famous explorer and Clark was a famous explorer," again the conjunction usually would be stated in English by placing the "and" between the subject terms and not repeating the predicate, as in "Lewis and Clark were famous explorers." Either formulation is symbolized as $L \cdot C$.

As shown by the truth table defining the dot symbol, a conjunction is true if and only if both of its conjuncts are true. But the word "and" has another use in which it signifies not *mere* (truth-functional) conjunction but has the sense of "and subsequently," meaning temporal succession. Thus the statement "Jones entered the country at New York and went straight to Chicago" is significant and might be true, whereas "Jones went straight to Chicago and entered the country at New York" is hardly intelligible. And there is quite a difference between "He took off his shoes and got into bed" and "He got into bed and took off his shoes."[5] Consideration of such examples emphasizes the desirability of having a special symbol with an exclusively truth-functional conjunctive use.

Note that the English words "but," "yet," "also," "still," "although," "however," "moreover," "nevertheless," and so on, and even the comma and the semicolon, can also be used to conjoin two statements into a single compound statement, and in their conjunctive sense they can all be represented by the dot symbol.

## B.  Negation

The *negation* (or contradictory or denial) of a statement in English is often formed by the insertion of a "not" in the original statement. Alternatively, one can express the negation of a statement in English by prefixing to it the phrase "it is false that" or "it is not the case that." It is customary to use the symbol "~" (called a "curl" or a "tilde") to form the negation of a statement. Thus, where $M$ symbolizes the statement "All humans are mortal," the various statements "Not all humans are mortal," "Some humans are not mortal," "It is false that all humans are mortal," and "It is not the case that all humans are mortal"

---

[5]And in *The Victoria Advocate*, Victoria, Texas, 27 October 1990, appeared the following report: "Ramiro Ramirez Garza, of the 2700 block of Leary Lane, was arrested by police as he was threatening to commit suicide and flee to Mexico."

are all indifferently symbolized as $\sim M$. More generally, where $p$ is any statement whatever, its negation is written $\sim p$. It is obvious that the curl is a truthfunctional operator. The negation of any true statement is false, and the negation of any false statement is true. This fact can be presented very simply and clearly by means of a truth table:

| $p$ | $\sim p$ |
|---|---|
| T | F |
| F | T |

This truth table may be regarded as the definition of the negation symbol "$\sim$".

## C.   Disjunction

**The *disjunction* (or alternation) of two statements is formed in English by inserting the word "or" between them. The two component statements so combined are called "disjuncts" (or "alternatives").**

The English word "or" is ambiguous, having two related but distinguishable meanings. One of them is exemplified in the statement "Premiums will be waived in the event of sickness or unemployment." The intention here is obviously that premiums are waived not only for sick persons and for unemployed persons, but also for persons who are *both* sick *and* unemployed. This sense of the word "or" is called *weak* or *inclusive*. An inclusive disjunction is true in case one or the other or both disjuncts are true; only if both disjuncts are false is their inclusive disjunction false. The inclusive "or" has the sense of "either, possibly both." Where precision is at a premium, as in contracts and other legal documents, this sense is made explicit by the use of the phrase "and/or."

The word "or" is also used in a *strong* or *exclusive* sense, in which the meaning is not "at least one" but "at least one and at most one." Where a restaurant lists "salad or dessert" on its dinner menu, it is clearly meant that, for the stated price of the meal, the diner may have one or the other *but not both*. Where precision is at a premium and the exclusive sense of "or" is intended, the phrase "but not both" is usually added.

We interpret the inclusive disjunction of two statements as an assertion that at least one of the statements is true, and we interpret their exclusive disjunction as an assertion that at least one of the statements is true but not both are true. Note that the two kinds of disjunction have a part of their meanings in common. This partial common meaning, that at least one of the disjuncts is true, is the *whole* meaning of the inclusive "or" and a *part* of the meaning of the exclusive "or."

Although disjunctions are stated ambiguously in English, they are unambiguous in Latin. Latin has two different words corresponding to the two different senses of the English word "*or*." The Latin word *vel* signifies weak or inclusive disjunction, and the Latin word *aut* corresponds to the word "or" in its strong or exclusive sense. It is customary to use the initial letter of the word *vel* to stand for "or" in its weak, inclusive sense. Where $p$ and $q$ are any two statements whatever, their weak or inclusive disjunction is written $p \vee q$. Our symbol for inclusive disjunction (called a "wedge" or, less frequently, a "vee") is also a truth-functional connective. A weak disjunction is false only in case both of its disjuncts are false. We may regard the wedge as being defined by the following truth table:

| $p$ | $q$ | $p \vee q$ |
|-----|-----|------------|
| T | T | T |
| T | F | T |
| F | T | T |
| F | F | F |

The first specimen argument presented in this section was a Disjunctive Syllogism.[6]

> The blind prisoner has a red hat or the blind prisoner has a white hat.
> The blind prisoner does not have a red hat.
> Therefore the blind prisoner has a white hat.

Its form is characterized by saying that its first premiss is a disjunction; its second premiss is the negation of the first disjunct of the first premiss; and its conclusion is the same as the second disjunct of the first premiss. It is evident that the disjunctive syllogism, so defined, is valid on either interpretation of the word "or"; that is, regardless of whether an inclusive or exclusive disjunction is intended.[7] Since the typical valid argument that has a disjunction for a premiss is, like the disjunctive syllogism, valid on either interpretation of the word "or," a simplification may be effected by translating the English word "or" into our logical symbol "$\vee$"—*regardless of which meaning of the English word "or" is intended.* In general, only a close examination of the context, or an explicit questioning of the speaker or writer, can reveal which sense of "or" is intended. This problem, often impossible to resolve, can be avoided if we agree to treat *any* occurrence of the word "or" as inclusive. On the other hand, if it is explicitly stated that the disjunction is intended to be exclusive, by means of the added phrase "but not both" for example, we have the symbolic machinery to formulate that additional sense, as will be shown directly.

Where both disjuncts have either the same subject term or the same predicate term, it is often natural to compress the formulation of their disjunction in English by so placing the "or" that there is no need to repeat the common part of the two disjuncts. Thus "Either Smith is the owner or Smith is the manager" might equally well be stated as "Smith is either the owner or the manager," and either one is properly symbolized as $O \vee M$. And "Either Red is guilty or Butch is guilty" would often be stated as "Either Red or Butch is guilty," either one being symbolized as $R \vee B$.

---

[6] A *syllogism* is a deductive argument consisting of two premises and a conclusion.

[7] Note that the term "disjunctive syllogism" is being used in a narrower sense here than it was in the preceding chapter.

The word "unless" is often used to form the disjunction of two statements. Thus, "You will do poorly on the exam unless you study" is correctly symbolized as $P \lor S$. The reason is that we use "unless" to mean that if the one proposition is not true, the other is or will be true. The sentence above can be understood to mean "If you don't study, you will do poorly on the exam"—and that is the thrust of the disjunction, since it asserts that one of the disjuncts is true, and hence that if one of them is false, the other must be true. Of course you may study *and* do poorly on the exam.

But the word "unless" is sometimes used to convey more information than that; it may mean that one or the other proposition is true but that not both are true. That is, "unless" may be intended as an *exclusive* disjunction. Thus Jeremy Bentham wrote, "What is politically good cannot be morally bad, unless the rules of arithmetic, which are good for a large number, are bad for a small one."[8] Here the author did mean that at least one of the two disjuncts is true, but he plainly also suggested that they cannot both be true. Other uses of "unless" are somewhat ambiguous. When we say, "The picnic will be held unless it rains" (or, "Unless it rains, the picnic will be held"), we surely do mean that the picnic will be held if it does not rain. But do we mean that it will not be held if it does rain? That may be uncertain. Here, as elsewhere, it is wise policy to treat every disjunction as weak or inclusive; "unless" is best symbolized simply with the wedge ($\lor$).

## D. Punctuation

In English, punctuation is absolutely required if complicated statements are to be clear. A great many different punctuation marks are used, without which many sentences would be highly ambiguous. For example, quite different meanings attach to "The teacher says John is a fool" when it is given different punctuations. Other sentences require punctuation for their very intelligibility, as, for example, "Jill where Jack had had had had had had had had had had had the teacher's approval." Punctuation is equally necessary in mathematics. In the absence of a special convention, no number is uniquely denoted by $2 \times 3 + 5$, although when it is made clear how its constituents are to be grouped, it denotes either 11 or 16: the first when punctuated $(2 \times 3) + 5$, the second when punctuated $2 \times (3 + 5)$. To avoid ambiguity, and to make meaning clear, punctuation marks in mathematics appear in the form of parentheses, ( ), which are used to group individual symbols; brackets, [ ], which are used to group expressions that include parentheses; and braces, { }, which are used to group expressions that include brackets.

In the language of symbolic logic those same punctuation marks—parentheses, brackets, and braces—are equally essential, because in logic compound statements are themselves often compounded together into more complicated ones. Thus $p \bullet q \lor r$ is ambiguous: It might mean the conjunction of $p$ with the disjunction of $q$ with $r$, or it might mean the disjunction whose first disjunct is

---

[8] Jeremy Bentham, *Principles of Legislation* (1802).

the conjunction of $p$ and $q$ and whose second disjunct is $r$. We distinguish between these two different senses by punctuating the given formula as $p \cdot (q \vee r)$ or else as $(p \cdot q) \vee r$. That the different ways of punctuating the original formula do make a difference can be seen by considering the case in which $p$ is false and $q$ and $r$ are both true. In this case the second punctuated formula is true (since its second disjunct is true), whereas the first one is false (since its first conjunct is false). Here the difference in punctuation makes all the difference between truth and falsehood, for different punctuations can assign different truth values to the ambiguous $p \cdot q \vee r$.

The word "either" has a variety of different meanings and uses in English. It has conjunctive force in the sentence "There is danger on either side." More often it is used to introduce the first disjunct in a disjunction, as in "Either the blind prisoner has a red hat or the blind prisoner has a white hat." There it contributes to the rhetorical balance of the sentence, but it does not affect its meaning. Perhaps the most important use of the word "either" is to punctuate a compound statement. Thus the sentence

> The organization will meet on Thursday and Anand
> will be elected or the election will be postponed.

can have its ambiguity resolved in one direction by placing the word "either" at its beginning, or in the other direction by inserting the word "either" before the name "Anand." Such punctuation is effected in our symbolic language by parentheses. The ambiguous formula $p \cdot q \vee r$ discussed in the preceding paragraph corresponds to the ambiguous sentence just examined. The two different punctuations of the formula correspond to the two different punctuations of the sentence effected by the two different insertions of the word "either."

The negation of a disjunction is often formed by use of the phrase "neither–nor." Thus the statement "Either Fillmore or Harding was the greatest American president" can be contradicted by the statement "Neither Fillmore nor Harding was the greatest American president." The disjunction would be symbolized as $F \vee H$, and its negation as either $\sim(F \vee H)$ or as $(\sim F) \cdot (\sim H)$. (The logical equivalence of these two symbolic formulas will be discussed in section 8.5.) It should be clear that to deny a disjunction stating that one or another statement is true requires that both be stated to be false.

The word "both" in English has a very important role in logical punctuation, and it deserves the most careful attention. When we say "Both Jamal and Derek are not . . ." we are saying, as noted just above, that "Neither Jamal nor Derek is . . ."; we are applying the negation to each of them. But when we say "Jamal and Derek are not both . . ." we are saying something very different; we are applying the negation to the pair of them taken together, saying that it is not the case that they are both . . ." This difference is very substantial. Entirely different meanings arise when the word both is placed differently in the English sentence. Consider the great difference between the meanings of

> Jamal and Derek will not both be elected.

and

> Jamal and Derek will both not be elected.

The first denies the conjunction $J \bullet D$ and may be symbolized as $\sim(J \bullet D)$. The second says that each one of the two will not be elected, and is symbolized as $\sim(J) \bullet \sim(D)$. Merely changing the *position* of the two words "both" and "not" alters the logical force of what is asserted.

Of course the word "both" does not always have this role; sometimes we use it only to add emphasis. When we say that "Both Lewis and Clark were great explorers," we use the word only to state more emphatically what is said by "Lewis and Clark were great explorers." But when the task is that of logical analysis, the punctuational role of "both" must be very carefully determined.

In the interest of brevity—that is, to decrease the number of parentheses required—it is convenient to establish the convention that **in any formula the negation symbol will be understood to apply to the smallest statement that the punctuation permits.** Without this convention, the formula $\sim p \vee q$ is ambiguous, meaning either $(\sim p) \vee q$, or $\sim(p \vee q)$. But by our convention we take it to mean the first of these alternatives, for the curl *can* (and therefore by our convention *does*) apply to the first component, $p$, rather than to the larger formula $p \vee q$.

Given a set of punctuation marks for our symbolic language, it is possible to write not merely conjunctions, negations, and weak disjunctions in it, but exclusive disjunctions as well. The exclusive disjunction of $p$ and $q$ asserts that at least one of them is true but not both are true, which is written quite simply as $(p \vee q) \bullet \sim(p \bullet q)$.

Any compound statement constructed from simple statements using only the truth-functional connectives—dot, curl, and wedge—has its truth value completely determined by the truth or falsehood of its component simple statements. If we know the truth values of simple statements, the truth value of any truth-functional compound of them is easily calculated. In working with such compound statements we always begin with their inmost components and work outward. For example, if $A$ and $B$ are true and $X$ and $Y$ are false statements, we calculate the truth value of the compound statement $\sim[\sim(A \bullet X) \bullet (Y \vee \sim B)]$ as follows. Since $X$ is false, the conjunction $A \bullet X$ is false, and so its negation $\sim(A \bullet X)$ is true. $B$ is true; so its negation $\sim B$ is false, and since $Y$ is false also, the disjunction of $Y$ with $\sim B$, $Y \vee \sim B$, is false. The bracketed formula $[\sim(A \bullet X) \bullet (Y \vee \sim B)]$ is the conjunction of a true with a false statement and is therefore false. Hence its negation, which is the entire statement, is true. Such a stepwise procedure always enables us to determine the truth value of a compound statement from the truth values of its components.

In some circumstances we may be able to determine the truth value of a truth-functional compound statement even if we cannot determine the truth or falsehood of one or more of its component simple statements. We do this by first calculating the truth value of the compound statement on the assumption that a given simple component is true, and then by calculating the truth value of the compound statement on the assumption that that same simple component is false, doing the same for each component whose truth value is unknown. If both these calculations yield the *same* truth value for the compound statement in question, we will have determined the truth value of the compound statement without having had to determine the truth value of its components, because we know that the truth value cannot be other than true or false.

## Exercises

I.  Using the truth table definitions of the dot, the wedge, and the curl, determine which of the following statements are true.

*1.  Rome is the capital of Italy ∨ Rome is the capital of Spain.

2.  ~(London is the capital of England • Stockholm is the capital of Norway).

3.  ~London is the capital of England • ~Stockholm is the capital of Norway.

4.  ~(Rome is the capital of Spain ∨ Paris is the capital of France).

*5.  ~Rome is the capital of Spain ∨ ~Paris is the capital of France.

6.  London is the capital of England ∨ ~London is the capital of England.

7.  Stockholm is the capital of Norway • ~Stockholm is the capital of Norway.

8.  (Paris is the capital of France • Rome is the capital of Spain) ∨ (Paris is the capital of France • ~Rome is the capital of Spain).

9.  (London is the capital of England ∨ Stockholm is the capital of Norway) • (~Rome is the capital of Italy • ~Stockholm is the capital of Norway).

*10.  Rome is the capital of Spain ∨ ~(Paris is the capital of France • Rome is the capital of Spain).

11.  Rome is the capital of Italy • ~(Paris is the capital of France ∨ Rome is the capital of Spain).

12.  ~(~Paris is the capital of France • ~Stockholm is the capital of Norway).

13.  ~[~(~Rome is the capital of Spain ∨ ~Paris is the capital of France) ∨ ~(~Paris is the capital of France ∨ Stockholm is the capital of Norway)].

14.  ~[~(~London is the capital of England • Rome is the capital of Spain) • ~(Rome is the capital of Spain • ~Rome is the capital of Spain)].

*15.  ~[~(Stockholm is the capital of Norway ∨ Paris is the capital of France) ∨ ~(~London is the capital of England • ~Rome is the capital of Spain)].

16.  Rome is the capital of Spain ∨ (~London is the capital of England ∨ London is the capital of England).

17. Paris is the capital of France • ~(Paris is the capital of France • Rome is the capital of Spain).

18. London is the capital of England • ~(Rome is the capital of Italy • Rome is the capital of Italy).

19. (Stockholm is the capital of Norway ∨ ~Paris is the capital of France) ∨ ~(~Stockholm is the capital of Norway • ~London is the capital of England).

*20. (Paris is the capital of France ∨ ~Rome is the capital of Spain) ∨ ~(~Paris is the capital of France • ~Rome is the capital of Spain).

21. ~[~(Rome is the capital of Spain • Stockholm is the capital of Norway) ∨ ~(~Paris is the capital of France ∨ ~Rome is the capital of Spain)].

22. ~[~(London is the capital of England • Paris is the capital of France) ∨ ~(~Stockholm is the capital of Norway ∨ ~Paris is the capital of France)].

23. ~[(~Paris is the capital of France ∨ Rome is the capital of Italy) • ~(~Rome is the capital of Italy ∨ Stockholm is the capital of Norway)].

24. ~[(~Rome is the capital of Spain ∨ Stockholm is the capital of Norway) • ~(~Stockholm is the capital of Norway ∨ Paris is the capital of France)].

*25. ~[(~London is the capital of England • Paris is the capital of France) ∨ ~(~Paris is the capital of France • Rome is the capital of Spain)].

II. If *A*, *B*, and *C* are true statements and *X*, *Y*, and *Z* are false statements, which of the following are true?

*1. ~A ∨ B

2. ~B ∨ X

3. ~Y ∨ C

4. ~Z ∨ X

*5. (A • X) ∨ (B • Y)

6. (B • C) ∨ (Y • Z)

7. ~(C • Y) ∨ (A • Z)

8. ~(A • B) ∨ (X • Y)

9. ~(X • Z) ∨ (B • C)

*10. ~(X • ~Y) ∨ (B • ~C)

11. (A ∨ X) • (Y ∨ B)

12. (B ∨ C) • (Y ∨ Z)

13. (X ∨ Y) • (X ∨ Z)

14. ~(A ∨ Y) • (B ∨ X)

*15. ~(X ∨ Z) • (~X ∨ Z)

16. ~(A ∨ C) ∨ ~(X • ~Y)

17. ~(B ∨ Z) • ~(X ∨ ~Y)

18. ~[(A ∨ ~C) ∨ (C ∨ ~A)]

19. ~[(B • C) • ~(C • B)]

*20. ~[(A • B) ∨ ~(B • A)]

21. [A ∨ (B ∨ C)] • ~[(A ∨ B) ∨ C]

22. [X ∨ (Y • Z)] ∨ ~[(X ∨ Y) • (X ∨ Z)]

23. [A • (B ∨ C)] • ~[(A • B) ∨ (A • C)]

24. ~{[(~A • B) • (~X • Z)] • ~[(A • ~B) ∨ ~(~Y • ~Z)]}

*25. ~{~[(B • ~C) ∨ (Y • ~Z)] • [(~B ∨ X) ∨ (B ∨ ~Y)]}

**III.** If *A* and *B* are known to be true and *X* and *Y* are known to be false, but the truth values of *P* and *Q* are not known, of which of the following statements can you determine the truth values?

 **\*1.** $A \lor P$      **2.** $Q \cdot X$

 **3.** $Q \lor {\sim}X$     **4.** ${\sim}B \cdot P$

 **\*5.** $P \lor {\sim}P$     **6.** ${\sim}P \lor (Q \lor P)$

 **7.** $Q \cdot {\sim}Q$     **8.** $P \cdot ({\sim}P \lor X)$

 **9.** ${\sim}(P \cdot Q) \lor P$   **\*10.** ${\sim}Q \cdot [(P \lor Q) \cdot {\sim}P]$

 **11.** $(P \lor Q) \cdot {\sim}(Q \lor P)$   **12.** $(P \cdot Q) \cdot ({\sim}P \lor {\sim}Q)$

 **13.** ${\sim}P \lor [{\sim}Q \lor (P \cdot Q)]$  **14.** $P \lor {\sim}({\sim}A \lor X)$

 **\*15.** $P \cdot [{\sim}(P \lor Q) \lor {\sim}P]$  **16.** ${\sim}(P \cdot Q) \lor (Q \cdot P)$

 **17.** ${\sim}[{\sim}({\sim}P \lor Q) \lor P] \lor P$  **18.** $({\sim}P \lor Q) \cdot {\sim}[{\sim}P \lor (P \cdot Q)]$

 **19.** $({\sim}A \lor P) \cdot ({\sim}P \lor Y)$

 **\*20.** ${\sim}[P \lor (B \cdot Y)] \lor [(P \lor B) \cdot (P \lor Y)]$

 **21.** $[P \lor (Q \cdot A)] \cdot {\sim}[(P \lor Q) \cdot (P \lor A)]$

 **22.** $[P \lor (Q \cdot X)] \cdot {\sim}[(P \lor Q) \cdot (P \lor X)]$

 **23.** ${\sim}[{\sim}P \lor ({\sim}Q \lor X)] \lor [{\sim}({\sim}P \lor Q) \lor ({\sim}P \lor X)]$

 **24.** ${\sim}[{\sim}P \lor ({\sim}Q \lor A)] \lor [{\sim}({\sim}P \lor Q) \lor ({\sim}P \lor A)]$

 **\*25.** ${\sim}[(P \cdot Q) \lor (Q \cdot {\sim}P)] \cdot {\sim}[(P \cdot {\sim}Q) \lor ({\sim}Q \cdot {\sim}P)]$

**IV.** Using the letters *E, I, J, L,* and *S* to abbreviate the simple statements "Egypt's food shortage worsens," "Iran raises the price of oil," "Jordan requests more American aid," "Libya raises the price of oil," and "Saudi Arabia buys 500 more warplanes," symbolize these statements.

 **\*1.** Iran raises the price of oil but Libya does not raise the price of oil.

 **2.** Either Iran or Libya raises the price of oil.

 **3.** Iran and Libya both raise the price of oil.

 **4.** Iran and Libya do not both raise the price of oil.

 **\*5.** Iran and Libya both do not raise the price of oil.

 **6.** Iran or Libya raises the price of oil but they do not both do so.

 **7.** Saudi Arabia buys 500 more warplanes and either Iran raises the price of oil or Jordan requests more American aid.

 **8.** Either Saudi Arabia buys 500 more warplanes and Iran raises the price of oil or Jordan requests more American aid.

 **9.** It is not the case that Egypt's food shortage worsens, and Jordan requests more American aid.

 **\*10.** It is not the case that either Egypt's food shortage worsens or Jordan requests more American aid.

 **11.** Either it is not the case that Egypt's food shortage worsens or Jordan requests more American aid.

12. It is not the case that both Egypt's food shortage worsens and Jordan requests more American aid.

13. Jordan requests more American aid unless Saudi Arabia buys 500 more warplanes.

14. Unless Egypt's food shortage worsens, Libya raises the price of oil.

*15. Iran won't raise the price of oil unless Libya does so.

16. Unless both Iran and Libya raise the price of oil neither of them does.

17. Libya raises the price of oil and Egypt's food shortage worsens.

18. It is not the case that neither Iran nor Libya raises the price of oil.

19. Egypt's food shortage worsens and Jordan requests more American aid, unless both Iran and Libya do not raise the price of oil.

*20. Either Iran raises the price of oil and Egypt's food shortage worsens, or it is not the case both that Jordan requests more American aid and that Saudi Arabia buys 500 more warplanes.

21. Either Egypt's food shortage worsens and Saudi Arabia buys 500 more warplanes, or either Jordan requests more American aid or Libya raises the price of oil.

22. Saudi Arabia buys 500 more warplanes, and either Jordan requests more American aid or both Libya and Iran raise the price of oil.

23. Either Egypt's food shortage worsens or Jordan requests more American aid, but neither Libya nor Iran raises the price of oil.

24. Egypt's food shortage worsens, but Saudi Arabia buys 500 more warplanes and Libya raises the price of oil.

*25. Libya raises the price of oil and Egypt's food shortage worsens; however, Saudi Arabia buys 500 more warplanes and Jordan requests more American aid.

## **8.3** CONDITIONAL STATEMENTS AND MATERIAL IMPLICATION

**Where two statements are combined by placing the word "if" before the first and inserting the word "then" between them, the resulting compound statement is a *conditional* (also called a "hypothetical," an "implication," or an "implicative statement").** In a conditional, the component statement that follows the "if" is called the **antecedent** (or the "implicans" or—rarely—the "protasis"), and the component statement that follows the "then" is the **consequent** (or the "implicate" or—rarely—the "apodosis"). For example, "If Mr. Jones is the brakeman's next-door neighbor, then Mr. Jones earns exactly three times as much as the brakeman" is a conditional statement in which "Mr. Jones is the brakeman's next-door neighbor" is the antecedent and "Mr. Jones earns exactly three times as much as the brakeman" is the consequent.

A conditional statement asserts that in any case in which its antecedent is true, its consequent is true also. It does not assert that its antecedent is true, but only that *if* its antecedent is true, its consequent is true also. It does not assert that its consequent is true, but only that its consequent is true *if* its antecedent is true. The essential meaning of a conditional statement is the *relationship* asserted to hold between its antecedent and consequent, in that order. To understand the meaning of a conditional statement, then, we must understand what the relationship of implication is.

"Implication" plausibly appears to have more than one meaning. We found it useful to distinguish different senses of the word "or" before introducing a special logical symbol to correspond exactly to a single one of the meanings of the English word. Had we not done so, the ambiguity of the English would have infected our logical symbolism and prevented it from achieving the clarity and precision aimed at. It will be equally useful to distinguish the different senses of "implies" or "if–then" before we introduce a special logical symbol in this connection.

Consider the following four conditional statements, each of which seems to assert a different type of implication, and to each of which corresponds a different sense of "if–then":

**A.** If all humans are mortal and Socrates is a human, then Socrates is mortal.
**B.** If Leslie is a bachelor, then Leslie is unmarried.
**C.** If this piece of blue litmus paper is placed in acid, then this piece of blue litmus paper will turn red.
**D.** If State loses the homecoming game, then I'll eat my hat.

Even a casual inspection of these four conditional statements reveals that they are of quite different types. The consequent of **A** follows *logically* from its antecedent, whereas the consequent of **B** follows from its antecedent by the very *definition* of the term "bachelor," which means unmarried man. The consequent of **C** does not follow from its antecedent either by logic alone or by the definition of its terms; the connection must be discovered empirically, for the implication stated here is *causal.* Finally, the consequent of **D** does not follow from its antecedent either by logic or by definition, nor is there any causal law involved—in the usual sense of the term. Most causal laws, those discovered in physics and chemistry, for example, describe what happens in the world regardless of people's hopes or desires. There is no such law connected with statement **D,** of course. That statement reports a *decision* of the speaker to behave in the specified way under the specified circumstances.

The four conditional statements examined in the preceding paragraph are different in that each asserts a different type of implication between its antecedent and consequent. But they are not completely different; all assert types of implication. Is there any identifiable common meaning, any partial meaning that is common to these admittedly different types of implication, although perhaps not the whole or complete meaning of any one of them?

The search for a common partial meaning takes on added significance when we recall our procedure in working out a symbolic representation for the

English word "or." In that case, we proceeded as follows. First, we emphasized the difference between the two senses of that word, contrasting inclusive with exclusive disjunction. The inclusive disjunction of two statements was observed to mean that at least one of the statements is true, and the exclusive disjunction of two statements was observed to mean that at least one of the statements is true but not both are true. Second, we noted that these two types of disjunction had a common *partial* meaning. This partial common meaning, that at least one of the disjuncts is true, was seen to be the *whole* meaning of the weak, inclusive "or," and a *part* of the meaning of the strong, exclusive "or." We then introduced the special symbol "∨" to represent this common partial meaning (which was the entire meaning of "or" in its inclusive sense). Third, we noted that the symbol representing the common partial meaning was an adequate translation of either sense of the word "or" for the purpose of retaining the Disjunctive Syllogism as a valid form of argument. It was admitted that translating an exclusive "or" into the symbol "∨" ignored and lost part of the word's meaning. But the part of its meaning that is preserved by this translation is all that is needed for the Disjunctive Syllogism to remain a valid form of argument. Since the Disjunctive Syllogism is typical of arguments involving disjunction, with which we are here concerned, this partial translation of the word "or," which may abstract from its "full" or "complete" meaning in some cases, is wholly adequate for our present purposes.

Now we wish to proceed in the same way, this time in connection with the English phrase "if–then." The first part is already accomplished: We have already emphasized the differences among some four senses of the "if–then" phrase, corresponding to four different types of implication. We are now ready for the second step, which is to discover a sense that is at least a part of the meaning of all four different types of implication.

One way of approaching this problem is to ask what circumstances would suffice to establish the falsehood of a given conditional statement. Under what circumstances should we agree that the conditional statement

> If this piece of blue litmus paper is placed in that solution, then this piece of blue litmus paper will turn red.

is *false?* It is important to realize that this conditional does not assert that any blue litmus paper is actually placed in the solution, or that any litmus paper actually turns red. It asserts merely that *if* this piece of blue litmus paper is placed in the solution, *then* this piece of blue litmus paper will turn red. It is proved false if this piece of blue litmus paper is actually placed in the solution and does not turn red. The acid test, so to speak, of the falsehood of a conditional statement is available when its antecedent is true, for if its consequent is false while its antecedent is true, the conditional itself is thereby proved false.

Any conditional statement "If $p$ then $q$" is known to be false in case the conjunction $p \bullet \sim q$ is known to be true; that is, in case its antecedent is true and its consequent is false. For a conditional to be true, then, the indicated conjunction must be false; that is, its negation $\sim(p \bullet \sim q)$ must be true. In other words, for any conditional "If $p$ then $q$" to be true, $\sim(p \bullet \sim q)$, the negation of the conjunction of its antecedent with the negation of its consequent, must also be true. We may, then, regard $\sim(p \bullet \sim q)$ as a part of the meaning of "If $p$ then $q$."

Every conditional statement means to deny that its antecedent is true and its consequent false, but this need not be the whole of its meaning. A conditional such as **A** on page 313 also asserts a logical connection between its antecedent and consequent, as **B** asserts a definitional connection, **C** a causal connection, and **D** a decisional connection. But no matter what type of implication is asserted by a conditional statement, part of its meaning is the negation of the conjunction of its antecedent with the negation of its consequent.

We now introduce a special symbol to represent this common partial meaning of the "if–then" phrase. **We define the new symbol "⊃" (called a "horseshoe") by taking $p \supset q$ as an abbreviation of** $\sim(p \bullet \sim q)$. The exact significance of the "⊃" symbol can be indicated by means of a truth table:

| $p$ | $q$ | $\sim q$ | $p \bullet \sim q$ | $\sim(p \bullet \sim q)$ | $p \supset q$ |
|-----|-----|----------|--------------------|--------------------------|---------------|
| T | T | F | F | T | T |
| T | F | T | T | F | F |
| F | T | F | F | T | T |
| F | F | T | F | T | T |

Here the first two columns are the guide columns; they simply lay out all possible combinations of truth and falsehood for $p$ and $q$. The third column is filled in by reference to the second, the fourth by reference to the first and third, the fifth by reference to the fourth, and the sixth is identical to the fifth by definition.

The symbol "⊃" is not to be regarded as denoting *the* meaning of "if–then," or standing for *the* relation of implication. That would be impossible, for there is no single meaning of "if–then"; there are several meanings. There is no unique relation of implication to be thus represented; there are several different implication relations. Nor is the symbol "⊃" to be regarded as somehow standing for *all* the meanings of "if–then." These are all different, and any attempt to abbreviate all of them by a single logical symbol would render that symbol ambiguous—as ambiguous as the English phrase "if–then" or the English word "implication." The symbol "⊃" is completely unambiguous. What $p \supset q$ abbreviates is $\sim(p \bullet \sim q)$, whose meaning is included in the meanings of each of the various kinds of implications considered but which does not constitute the entire meaning of any of them.

We can regard the symbol "⊃" as representing another kind of implication, and it will be expedient to do so, since a convenient way to read $p \supset q$ is "If $p$ then $q$." But it is not the same kind of implication as any of those mentioned earlier. It is called *material implication* by logicians, who in giving it a special name admit that it is a special notion, not to be confused with other, more usual, types of implication.

Not all conditional statements in English need assert one of the four types of implication previously considered. Material implication constitutes a fifth type that may be asserted in ordinary discourse. Consider the remark "If Hitler was a military genius, then I'm a monkey's uncle." It is quite clear that it does not assert logical, definitional, or causal implication. It cannot represent a decisional implication, since it scarcely lies in the speaker's power to make the consequent true. No "real connection," whether logical, definitional, or causal, obtains between antecedent and consequent here. A conditional of this sort is often used as an emphatic or humorous method of denying its antecedent. The consequent of such a conditional is usually a statement that is obviously or ludicrously false. And since no true conditional can have both its antecedent true and its consequent false, to affirm such a conditional amounts to denying that its antecedent is true. The full meaning of the present conditional seems to be the denial that "Hitler was a military genius" is true when "I'm a monkey's uncle" is false. And since the latter is so obviously false, the conditional must be understood to deny the former.

The point here is that no "real connection" between antecedent and consequent is suggested by a material implication. All it asserts is that, as a matter of fact, it is not the case that the antecedent is true when the consequent is false. Note that the material implication symbol is a truth-functional connective, like the symbols for conjunction and disjunction. As such, it is defined by the truth table

| $p$ | $q$ | $p \supset q$ |
|-----|-----|---------------|
| T | T | T |
| T | F | F |
| F | T | T |
| F | F | T |

As thus defined by the truth table, the horseshoe symbol "$\supset$" has some features that may at first appear odd: The assertion that a false antecedent materially implies a true consequent is true; and the assertion that a false antecedent materially implies a false consequent is also true. This apparent strangeness can be dissipated in part by the following considerations. Because the number 2 is smaller than the number 4 (a fact notated symbolically as $2 < 4$), it follows that *any* number smaller than 2 is smaller than 4. The conditional formula

$$\text{If } x < 2 \text{ then } x < 4$$

is true for any number $x$ whatsoever. If we focus on the numbers 1, 3, and 4, and replace the number variable $x$ in the preceding conditional formula by each of them in turn, we can make the following observations. In

$$\text{If } 1 < 2 \text{ then } 1 < 4$$

both antecedent and consequent are true, and of course the conditional is true. In

If 3 < 2 then 3 < 4

the antecedent is false and the consequent is true, and of course the conditional is again true. In

If 4 < 2 then 4 < 4

both antecedent and consequent are false, but the conditional remains true. These three cases correspond to the first, third, and fourth rows of the table defining the horseshoe symbol "⊃". So it is not particularly remarkable or surprising that a conditional should be true where both antecedent and consequent are true, where the antecedent is false and the consequent is true, or where antecedent and consequent are both false. Of course, there is no number that is smaller than 2 but not smaller than 4; that is, there is no true conditional statement with true antecedent and false consequent. This is exactly what the defining truth table for "⊃" lays down.

Now we propose to translate any occurrence of the "if–then" phrase into our logical symbol "⊃". This proposal means that in translating conditional statements into our symbolism, we treat them all as merely material implications. Of course most conditional statements assert that more than a merely material implication holds between their antecedents and consequents. So our proposal amounts to suggesting that we ignore, or put aside, or "abstract from," part of the meaning of a conditional statement when we translate it into our symbolic language. How can this proposal be justified?

The previous proposal to translate both inclusive and exclusive disjunctions by means of the "∨" symbol was justified on the grounds that the validity of the Disjunctive Syllogism was preserved even if the additional meaning that attaches to the exclusive "or" was ignored. Our present proposal to translate all conditional statements into the merely material implication symbolized by "⊃" may be justified in exactly the same way. Many arguments contain conditional statements of various different kinds, but the validity of all valid arguments of the general type with which we will be concerned is preserved even if the additional meanings of their conditional statements are ignored. This remains to be proved, of course, and will occupy our attention in the next section.

Conditional statements can be formulated in a variety of ways. The statement

If he has a good lawyer then he will be acquitted.

can equally well be stated without the use of the word "then" as

If he has a good lawyer he will be acquitted.

Antecedent and consequent can have their order reversed, provided that the "if" still directly precedes the antecedent, as

He will be acquitted if he has a good lawyer.

It should be clear that, in any of the examples just given, the word "if" can be replaced by such phrases as "in case," "provided that," "given that," or "on condition that," without any change in meaning. Minor adjustments in the phrasings of antecedent and consequent permit such alternative phrasings of the same conditional as

> That he has a good lawyer implies that he will be acquitted.

or

> His having a good lawyer entails his acquittal.

A shift from active to passive voice accompanies a reversal of order of antecedent and consequent, to yield the logically equivalent

> His being acquitted is implied (or entailed) by his having a good lawyer.

Any of these is symbolized as $L \supset A$.

The notions of necessary and sufficient conditions provide other formulations of conditional statements. For any specified event, there are many circumstances necessary for its occurrence. Thus, for a normal car to run, it is necessary that there be fuel in its tank, its spark plugs properly adjusted, its oil pump working, and so on. So if the event occurs, every one of the conditions necessary for its occurrence must have been fulfilled. Hence to say

> That there is fuel in its tank is a necessary condition for the car to run.

can equally well be stated as

> The car runs only if there is fuel in its tank.

which is another way of saying that

> If the car runs then there is fuel in its tank.

Any of these is symbolized as $R \supset F$. In general, "$q$ **is a necessary condition for** $p$" **and** "$p$ **only if** $q$" **are symbolized as** $p \supset q$.

For a specified situation there are many alternative circumstances, any one of which is sufficient to produce that situation. Thus, for a purse to contain over a dollar, it would be sufficient for it to contain one hundred and one pennies, twenty-one nickels, eleven dimes, five quarters, and so on. If any one of these circumstances obtains, the specified situation will be realized. Hence, to say "That the purse contains five quarters is a sufficient condition for it to contain over a dollar" is to say the same as "If the purse contains five quarters then it contains over a dollar." In general, "$p$ **is a sufficient condition for** $q$" **is symbolized as** $p \supset q$.

If $p$ is a sufficient condition for $q$, we have $p \supset q$, and $q$ must be a necessary condition for $p$. If $p$ is a necessary condition for $q$, we have $q \supset p$, and $q$ must be a sufficient condition for $p$. Hence, if $p$ is necessary *and* sufficient for $q$, then $q$ is sufficient *and* necessary for $p$.

Not every statement containing the word "if" is a conditional. None of the following statements is a conditional: "There is food in the refrigerator if you want some," "Your table is ready, if you please," "There is a message for you if you're interested," "The meeting will be held even if no permit is obtained." The presence or absence of particular words is never decisive. In every case, one must understand what a given sentence means, and then restate that meaning in a symbolic formula.

There is no necessary or logical relation between the words "if" and "iffy," though there is often a suggestion that what is preceded by the word "if" is somewhat doubtful. This is illustrated by the following anecdote:

> George Bernard Shaw once sent Winston Churchill two tickets for the opening night of one of his new plays, noting, "Bring a friend—if you have one"; to which Churchill wrote back to say that he was otherwise engaged opening night, but would appreciate tickets for the second performance, "if there is one."[9]

## Exercises

I.  If $A$, $B$, and $C$ are true statements and $X$, $Y$, and $Z$ are false statements, determine which of the following are true, using the truth tables for the horseshoe, the dot, the wedge, and the curl.

*1.  $A \supset B$       2.  $A \supset X$

3.  $B \supset Y$       4.  $Y \supset Z$

*5.  $(A \supset B) \supset Z$       6.  $(X \supset Y) \supset Z$

7.  $(A \supset B) \supset C$       8.  $(X \supset Y) \supset C$

9.  $A \supset (B \supset Z)$       *10.  $X \supset (Y \supset Z)$

11.  $[(A \supset B) \supset C] \supset Z$       12.  $[(A \supset X) \supset Y] \supset Z$

13.  $[A \supset (X \supset Y)] \supset C$       14.  $[A \supset (B \supset Y)] \supset X$

*15.  $[(X \supset Z) \supset C] \supset Y$       16.  $[(Y \supset B) \supset Y] \supset Y$

17.  $[(A \supset Y) \supset B] \supset Z$

18.  $[(A \bullet X) \supset C] \supset [(A \supset C) \supset X]$

19.  $[(A \bullet X) \supset C] \supset [(A \supset X) \supset C]$

*20.  $[(A \bullet X) \supset Y] \supset [(X \supset A) \supset (A \supset Y)]$

21.  $[(A \bullet X) \vee (\sim A \bullet \supset X)] \supset [(A \supset X) \bullet (X \supset A)]$

22.  $\{[A \supset (B \supset C)] \supset [(A \bullet B) \supset C]\} \supset [(Y \supset B) \supset (C \supset Z)]$

23.  $\{[(X \supset Y) \supset Z] \supset [Z \supset (X \supset Y)]\} \supset [(X \supset Z) \supset Y]$

24.  $[(A \bullet X) \supset Y] \supset [(A \supset X) \bullet (A \supset Y)]$

*25.  $[A \supset (X \bullet Y)] \supset [(A \supset X) \vee (A \supset Y)]$

---

[9] Andreas I. Aristides, "The Gentle Art of the Resounding Put-Down," *The American Scholar* (Summer 1987).

94

II. If $A$ and $B$ are known to be true, and $X$ and $Y$ are known to be false, but the truth values of $P$ and $Q$ are not known, of which of the following statements can you determine the truth values?

*1. $P \supset A$      2. $X \supset Q$

3. $(Q \supset A) \supset X$      4. $(P \bullet A) \supset B$

*5. $(P \supset P) \supset X$      6. $(X \supset Q) \supset X$

7. $X \supset (Q \supset X)$      8. $(P \bullet X) \supset Y$

9. $[P \supset (Q \supset P)] \supset Y$      *10. $(Q \supset Q) \supset (A \supset X)$

11. $(P \supset X) \supset (X \supset P)$      12. $(P \supset A) \supset (B \supset X)$

13. $(X \supset P) \supset (B \supset Y)$      14. $[(P \supset B) \supset B] \supset B$

*15. $[(X \supset Q) \supset Q] \supset Q$      16. $(P \supset X) \supset (\sim X \supset \sim P)$

17. $(X \supset P) \supset (\sim X > Y)$      18. $(P \supset A) \supset (A \supset \sim B)$

19. $(P \supset Q) \supset (P \supset Q)$      *20. $(P \supset \sim\sim P) \supset (A \supset \sim B)$

21. $\sim(A \bullet P) \supset (\sim A \vee \sim P)$      22. $\sim(P \bullet X) \supset \sim(P \vee \sim X)$

23. $\sim(X \vee Q) \supset (\sim X \bullet \sim Q)$

24. $[P \supset (A \vee X)] \supset [(P \supset A) \supset X]$

*25. $[Q \vee (B \bullet Y)] \supset [(Q \vee B) \bullet (Q \vee Y)]$

III. Symbolize the following, using capital letters to abbreviate the simple statements involved.

*1. If Argentina mobilizes then if Brazil protests to the UN then Chile will call for a meeting of all the Latin American states.

2. If Argentina mobilizes then either Brazil will protest to the UN or Chile will call for a meeting of all the Latin American states.

3. If Argentina mobilizes then Brazil will protest to the UN and Chile will call for a meeting of all the Latin American states.

4. If Argentina mobilizes then Brazil will protest to the UN, and Chile will call for a meeting of all the Latin American states.

*5. If Argentina mobilizes and Brazil protests to the UN then Chile will call for a meeting of all the Latin American states.

6. If either Argentina mobilizes or Brazil protests to the UN then Chile will call for a meeting of all the Latin American states.

7. Either Argentina will mobilize or if Brazil protests to the UN then Chile will call for a meeting of all the Latin American states.

8. If Argentina does not mobilize then either Brazil will not protest to the UN or Chile will not call for a meeting of all the Latin American states.

9. If Argentina does not mobilize then neither will Brazil protest to the UN nor will Chile call for a meeting of all the Latin American states.

*10. It is not the case that if Argentina mobilizes then both Brazil will protest to the UN and Chile will call for a meeting of all the Latin American states.

11. If it is not the case that Argentina mobilizes then Brazil will not protest to the UN, and Chile will call for a meeting of all the Latin American states.

12. Brazil will protest to the UN if Argentina mobilizes.

13. Brazil will protest to the UN only if Argentina mobilizes.

14. Chile will call for a meeting of all the Latin American states only if both Argentina mobilizes and Brazil protests to the UN.

*15. Brazil will protest to the UN only if either Argentina mobilizes or Chile calls for a meeting of all the Latin American states.

16. Argentina will mobilize if either Brazil protests to the UN or Chile calls for a meeting of all the Latin American States.

17. Brazil will protest to the UN unless Chile calls for a meeting of all the Latin American States.

18. If Argentina mobilizes, then Brazil will protest to the UN unless Chile calls for a meeting of all the Latin American States.

19. Brazil will not protest to the UN unless Argentina mobilizes.

*20. Unless Chile calls for a meeting of all the Latin American States, Brazil will protest to the UN.

21. Argentina's mobilizing is a sufficient condition for Brazil to protest to the UN.

22. Argentina's mobilizing is a necessary condition for Chile to call for a meeting of all the Latin American states.

23. If Argentina mobilizes and Brazil protests to the UN, then both Chile and the Dominican Republic will call for a meeting of all the Latin American states.

24. If Argentina mobilizes and Brazil protests to the UN, then either Chile or the Dominican Republic will call for a meeting of all the Latin American states.

*25. If neither Chile nor the Dominican Republic calls for a meeting of all the Latin American states, then Brazil will not protest to the UN unless Argentina mobilizes.

## 8.4 ARGUMENT FORMS AND ARGUMENTS

### A. Refutation by Logical Analogy

In this section, we specify more precisely what is meant by the term "valid." We relate our formal definition to more familiar and intuitive notions by considering the method of refutation by logical analogy.[10] Presented with the argument

---

[10] Just as in analyzing the categorical syllogism, we discuss refutation by logical analogy in section 6.2.

> If Bacon wrote the plays attributed to Shakespeare, then Bacon was a great writer.
> Bacon was a great writer.
> Therefore Bacon wrote the plays attributed to Shakespeare.

we may agree with the premises but disagree with the conclusion, judging the argument to be invalid. One way of proving invalidity is by the method of logical analogy. "You might as well argue," we could retort, "that

> If Washington was assassinated, then Washington is dead.
> Washington is dead.
> Therefore Washington was assassinated.

And you cannot seriously defend this argument," we should continue, "because here the premises are known to be true and the conclusion known to be false. This argument is obviously invalid; your argument is of the *same form:* so yours is invalid also." This type of refutation is very effective.

This method of refutation by logical analogy, points the way to an excellent general technique for testing arguments. To prove the invalidity of an argument, it suffices to formulate another argument that (1) has exactly the same form as the first and (2) has true premises and a false conclusion. This method is based upon the fact that validity and invalidity are purely *formal* characteristics of arguments, which is to say that any two arguments having exactly the same form are either both valid or both invalid, regardless of any differences in the subject matter with which they are concerned.[11]

A given argument exhibits its form very clearly when the simple statements that appear in it are abbreviated by capital letters. Thus we may abbreviate the statements "Bacon wrote the plays attributed to Shakespeare," "Bacon was a great writer," "Washington was assassinated," and "Washington is dead" by the letters $B$, $G$, $A$, and $D$, respectively, and using the familiar three dot symbol "∴" for "therefore," symbolize the two preceding arguments as

$$
\begin{array}{ccc}
B \supset G & & A \supset D \\
G & \text{and} & D \\
\therefore B & & \therefore A
\end{array}
$$

So written, their common form is easily seen.

To discuss forms of arguments rather than particular arguments having those forms, we need some method of symbolizing argument forms themselves. To achieve such a method, we introduce the notion of a *variable.* In the preceding sections we used capital letters to symbolize particular simple statements. To avoid confusion, we use small, or lowercase, letters from the middle part of the alphabet $p, q, r, s, \ldots$ as *statement variables.* A **statement variable,** as

---

[11] Here we assume that the simple statements involved are neither logically true (*e.g.,* "All chairs are chairs") nor logically false (*e.g.,* "Some chairs are nonchairs"). We also assume that the only logical relations among the simple statements involved are those asserted or entailed by the premises. The point of these restrictions is to limit our considerations, in this chapter and the next, to truth-functional arguments alone, and to exclude other kinds of arguments whose validity turns on more complex logical considerations not appropriately introduced at this place.

we shall use the term, **is simply a letter for which, or in place of which, a statement may be substituted.** Compound statements as well as simple statements may be substituted for statement variables.

We define an *argument form* as any array of symbols containing statement variables but no statements, such that when statements are substituted for the statement variables—the same statement being substituted for the same statement variable throughout—the result is an argument. For definiteness, we establish the convention that in any argument form $p$ shall be the first statement variable that occurs in it, $q$ shall be the second, $r$ the third, and so on. Thus the expression

$$p \supset q$$
$$q$$
$$\therefore p$$

is an argument form, for when the statements $B$ and $G$ are substituted for the statement variables $p$ and $q$, respectively, the result is the first argument in this section. If the statements $A$ and $D$ are substituted for the variables $p$ and $q$, the result is the second argument. **Any argument that results from the substitution of statements for statement variables in an argument form is called a** *substitution instance* **of that argument form.** It is clear that any substitution instance of an argument form may be said to have that form, and that any argument that has a certain form is a substitution instance of that form.

For any argument there are usually several argument forms that have the given argument as a substitution instance. For example, the first argument of this section

$$B \supset G$$
$$G$$
$$\therefore B$$

is a substitution instance of each of the four argument forms

| $p \supset q$ | $p \supset q$ | $p \supset q$ | $p$ |
| $q$ | $r$ | $r$ | $q$ |
| $\therefore p$ | $\therefore p$ | $\therefore s$ | $\therefore r$ |

Thus we obtain the given argument by substituting $B$ for $p$ and $G$ for $q$ in the first argument form; by substituting $B$ for $p$ and $G$ for both $q$ and $r$ in the second; $B$ for both $p$ and $s$ and $G$ for both $q$ and $r$ in the third; and $B \supset G$ for $p$, $G$ for $q$, and $B$ for $r$ in the fourth. Of these four argument forms, the first corresponds more closely to the structure of the given argument than do the others. It does so because the given argument results from the first argument form by substituting a different simple statement for each different statement variable in it. We call the first argument form the *specific form* of the given argument. Our definition of the specific form of a given argument is the following: **In case an argument is produced by substituting consistently a different simple statement for each different statement variable in an argument form, that argument form is the** *specific form* **of that argument.** For any given argument, there is a unique argument form that is the specific form of that argument.

The technique of refutation by logical analogy can now be described more precisely. If the specific form of a given argument has any substitution instance whose premisses are true and whose conclusion is false, then the given argument is invalid. We may define the term "invalid" as applied to argument forms as follows: **An argument form is invalid if and only if it has at least one substitution instance with true premisses and a false conclusion.** Refutation by logical analogy is based on the fact that any argument whose specific form is an *invalid argument form* is an *invalid argument*. Any argument form that is not invalid must be valid. Hence **an argument form is valid if and only if it has no substitution instances with true premisses and a false conclusion.** And since validity is a formal notion, **an argument is valid if and only if the specific form of that argument is a valid argument form.**

A given argument is proved invalid if a refuting analogy for it can be found, but "thinking up" such refuting analogies may not always be easy. Happily, it is not necessary, because for arguments of this type there is a simpler, purely mechanical test based upon the same principle. Given any argument, we test the specific form of that argument, because its validity or invalidity determines the validity or invalidity of the argument.

## B.   Testing Arguments on Truth Tables

To test an argument form, we examine all possible substitution instances of it to see if any one of them has true premisses and a false conclusion. Of course any argument form has an infinite number of substitution instances, but we need not worry about having to examine them one at a time. Because we are interested only in the truth or falsehood of their premisses and conclusions, we need consider only the truth values involved. The arguments that concern us here contain only simple statements and compound statements that are built up out of simple statements by means of the truth-functional connectives symbolized by the dot, curl, wedge, and horseshoe. Hence we obtain all possible substitution instances whose premisses and conclusions have different truth values by examining all possible different arrangements of truth values for the statements that can be substituted for the different statement variables in the argument form to be tested.

Where an argument form contains just two different statement variables, $p$ and $q$, all of its substitution instances are the result of either substituting true statements for both $p$ and $q$, or a true statement for $p$ and a false one for $q$, or a false one for $p$ and a true one for $q$, or false statements for both $p$ and $q$. These different cases are assembled most conveniently in the form of a truth table. To decide the validity of the argument form

$$p \supset q$$
$$q$$
$$\therefore p$$

we construct the following truth table:

| *p* | *q* | *p* ⊃ *q* |
|-----|-----|-----------|
| T | T | T |
| T | F | F |
| F | T | T |
| F | F | T |

Each row of this table represents a whole class of substitution instances. The **T**'s and **F**'s in the two initial or guide columns represent the truth values of the statements substituted for the variables *p* and *q* in the argument form. We fill in the third column by referring back to the initial or guide columns and the definition of the horseshoe symbol. The third column heading is the first "premiss" of the argument form, the second column is the second "premiss," and the first column is the "conclusion." In examining this truth table, we find that in the third row there are **T**'s under both premises and an **F** under the conclusion, which indicates that there is at least one substitution instance of this argument form that has true premises and a false conclusion. This row suffices to show that the argument form is invalid. Any argument of this specific form (that is, any argument the specific argument form of which is the given argument form) is said to commit the fallacy of affirming the consequent, since its second premiss affirms the consequent of its conditional first premiss.

Truth tables, although simple in concept, are powerful tools. In using them to establish the validity or the invalidity of an argument form, it is critically important that the table first be constructed correctly. To construct the truth table correctly there must be a guide column for each statement variable in the argument form, *p, q, r,* etc. The array must exhibit all the possible combinations of the truth and falsity of all these variables, so there must be a number of horizontal rows sufficient to do this: four rows if there are two variables, eight rows if there are three variables, and so on. And there must be an additional vertical column for each of the premises and for the conclusion, and also a column for each of the symbolic expressions out of which the premises and conclusion are built. The construction of a truth table in this fashion is essentially a mechanical task; it requires only careful counting and the careful placement of **T**'s and **F**'s in the appropriate columns, all governed by our understanding of the several truth-functional connectives—the dot, the wedge, the horseshoe—and the circumstances under which each truth-functional compound is true and the circumstances under which it is false.

Once the table has been constructed and the completed array is before us, it is essential to *read* it correctly, that is, to use it correctly to make the appraisal of the argument form in question. We must note carefully which columns are those representing the premises of the argument being tested, and which column represents the conclusion of that argument. In testing the argument just above, which we found invalid, we noted that it was the second and third columns of the truth table that represent the premises, while the conclusion was represented by the first (leftmost) column. But, depending upon which argument form we are testing, and the order in which we have placed the columns as the table was built, it is possible for the premisses and the conclusion to appear in any order at the top of the table. Their position to the right or to the left is not significant; we, who use the table, must understand which column represents what, and we must understand what we are in search of. *Is there any one case,* we ask ourselves, *any single row in which all the premisses are true and the conclusion false?* If there is such a row the argument form is invalid; if there is no such row the argument form must be valid. After the full array has been neatly and accurately set forth, great care in reading the truth table accurately is of the utmost importance.

## C. Some Common Valid Argument Forms

### Disjunctive Syllogism

One of the simplest valid argument forms relies on the fact that, in every true disjunction, at least one of the disjuncts must be true. Therefore, if one of them is false, the other must be true. We symbolize the Disjunctive Syllogism as follows:

$$p \vee q$$
$$\sim p$$
$$\therefore q$$

And to show its validity we construct the following truth table:

| $p$ | $q$ | $p \vee q$ | $\sim p$ |
|-----|-----|------------|----------|
| T | T | T | F |
| T | F | T | F |
| F | T | T | T |
| F | F | F | T |

Here, too, the initial or guide columns exhibit all possible different truth values of statements that may be substituted for the variables $p$ and $q$. We fill in the third column by referring back to the first two, and the fourth by reference to the first alone. Now the third row is the only one in which **T**'s appear under both premisses (the third and fourth columns), and there a **T** appears under the conclusion also (the second column). The truth table thus shows that the argument form has no substitution instance having true premisses and a false conclusion, and thereby proves the validity of the argument form being tested.[12]

---

[12]As used in this chapter, the term "Disjunctive Syllogism" is the name of an elementary argument form, here proved valid. This form is always valid, of course, and therefore, in modern logic "Disjunctive Syllogism" always refers to an elementary argument form that is valid. But in traditional logic the expression "disjunctive syllogism" is used more broadly, to refer to any syllogism that contains a disjunctive premiss; some such syllogisms may of course be invalid. One must be clear whether the expression is being used in the broader or the narrower sense. Here we use it in the narrower sense.

Here as always it is essential that the truth table be *read* accurately; the column representing the conclusion (second from the left) and the columns representing the premises (third and fourth from the left) being carefully identified. Only by using those three columns correctly can we reliably determine the validity (or invalidity) of the argument form in question. Note that the very same truth table could be used to test the validity of a very different argument form, one whose premises are represented by the second and third columns and whose conclusion is represented by the fourth column. That argument form, as we can see from the top row of the table, is invalid.

The truth-table technique provides a completely mechanical method for testing the validity of any argument of the general type here considered. We are now in a position to justify our proposal to translate any occurrence of the "if–then" phrase into our material implication symbol "⊃". In the preceding section, the claim was made that all valid arguments of the general type with which we are here concerned that involve "if–then" statements remain valid when those statements are interpreted as affirming merely material implications. Truth tables can be used to substantiate this claim, and will justify our translation of "if–then" into the horseshoe symbol.

### Modus Ponens

The simplest type of intuitively valid argument involving a conditional statement is illustrated by the argument:

> If the second native told the truth, then only one native is a politician.
> The second native told the truth.
> Therefore only one native is a politician.

The specific form of this argument, known as *modus ponens* ("the method of putting, or affirming") is

$$p \supset q$$
$$p$$
$$\therefore q$$

and is proved valid by the following truth table:

| $p$ | $q$ | $p \supset q$ |
|-----|-----|---------------|
| T | T | T |
| T | F | F |
| F | T | T |
| F | F | T |

Here the two premises are represented by the third and first columns, and the conclusion is represented by the second. Only the first row represents substitution instances in which both premises are true, and the **T** in the second column shows that in these arguments the conclusion is true also. This truth table establishes the validity of any argument of the form *modus ponens*.

## Modus Tollens

We have seen that if a conditional statement is true, then if the consequent is false the antecedent must be false. This form of argument is very commonly used to establish the falsehood of some proposition in doubt. To illustrate: In a recent match for the world Scrabble championship, the team of Matt Graham and Joel Sherman met the computer program called Maven. At one point in the match the men's tiles permitted the word "triduum," which they found; but for a bingo—using of all eight tiles in one word—their remaining "s" would also have to be used. "Triduum" is definitely a word, said Joel to his partner, but is "triduums" the right plural? Matt's answer was in the form of a very common valid argument: "It has to be. If the plural were "tridua," we'd know that word, and we don't."[13]

The argument would be symbolized as:

$$p \supset q$$
$$\sim q$$
$$\therefore \sim p$$

The validity of this argument form, called **modus tollens** ("the method of taking away or denying"), may be shown by the following truth table:

| $p$ | $q$ | $p \supset q$ | $\sim q$ | $\sim p$ |
|---|---|---|---|---|
| T | T | T | F | F |
| T | F | F | T | F |
| F | T | T | F | T |
| F | F | T | T | T |

Here again there is no substitution instance, no line, on which the premisses, $p \supset q$ and $\sim q$, are both true and the conclusion, $\sim p$, is false.

## Hypothetical Syllogism

Another common type of intuitively valid argument contains only conditional statements. Here is an example:

> If the first native is a politician, then the first native lies.
> If the first native lies, then the first native denies being a politician.
> Therefore if the first native is a politician, then the first native denies being a politician.

The specific form of this argument is

---

[13] "Humankind Battles for Scrabble Supremacy," *New York Times Magazine*, 24 May 1998. A "triduum" is a period of three days, especially a three-day period of prayers. "Triduums" was indeed a bingo—but the match was won by the computer, 6–3.

$$p \supset q$$
$$q \supset r$$
$$\therefore p \supset r$$

Since this argument, called *Hypothetical Syllogism*,[14] contains three distinct statement variables, the truth table here must have three initial or guide columns and will require eight rows for the listing of all possible substitution instances. Besides the initial columns, three additional columns are required: two for the premises, the third for the conclusion. The table appears as

| p | q | r | p⊃q | q⊃r | p⊃r |
|---|---|---|-----|-----|-----|
| T | T | T | T | T | T |
| T | T | F | T | F | F |
| T | F | T | F | T | T |
| T | F | F | F | T | F |
| F | T | T | T | T | T |
| F | T | F | T | F | T |
| F | F | T | T | T | T |
| F | F | F | T | T | T |

In constructing it, we fill in the fourth column by referring back to the first and second, the fifth by reference to the second and third, and the sixth by reference to the first and third. Examining the completed table, we observe that the premises are true only in the first, fifth, seventh, and eighth rows, and that in all of these the conclusion is true also. This truth table establishes the validity of the argument form and proves that the Hypothetical Syllogism also remains valid when its conditional statements are translated by means of the horseshoe symbol.

Enough examples have been provided to illustrate the proper use of the truth-table technique for testing arguments. And perhaps enough have been given to show that the validity of any valid argument involving conditional statements is preserved when its conditionals are translated into merely material implications. Any doubts that remain can be allayed by the reader's providing, translating, and testing any similar examples.

As more complicated argument forms are considered, larger truth tables are required to test them, because a separate initial or guide column is required for each different statement variable in the argument form. Only two are required for a form with just two variables, and that table will have four rows. But three initial columns are required for a form with three variables, such as the Hypothetical Syllogism, and such truth tables will have eight rows. To test the validity of an argument form such as that of the Constructive Dilemma,

$$(p \supset q) \bullet (r \supset s)$$
$$p \vee r$$
$$\therefore q \vee s$$

---

[14] Called a "pure hypothetical syllogism" in Chapter 7.

which contains four distinct statement variables, a truth table with four initial columns and 16 rows is required. In general, in order to test an argument form containing $n$ distinct statement variables we require a truth table with $n$ initial columns and $2^n$ rows.

## D. Some Common Invalid Argument Forms

Two invalid argument forms deserve special notice, because they bear superficial resemblances to valid forms and therefore often tempt careless writers or readers. The **fallacy of affirming the consequent,** discussed also in section 7.7, is symbolized as

$$p \supset q$$
$$q$$
$$\therefore p$$

Although the shape of this form is something like that of *modus ponens,* the two argument forms are, in fact, very different, and this form certainly is not valid. When it is argued, for example, that since membership in the American Civil Liberties Union is indicative of strong support for freedom of speech, one who defends that freedom must be a supporter of the ACLU, the fallacy of affirming the consequent has been committed.

Another invalid form, called the **fallacy of denying the antecedent,** has a shape somewhat like that of *modus tollens* and may be symbolized as

$$p \supset q$$
$$\sim p$$
$$\therefore \sim q$$

An example of this fallacy is the campaign slogan used by a candidate for mayor of New York city some years ago: "If you don't know the buck, you don't know the job—and Abe knows the buck." The unstated conclusion to which the voter was deliberately tempted was that "Abe knows the job"—a proposition that does not follow from the stated premises.

Both of these common fallacies may readily be shown to be invalid by means of truth tables. In each case there is one line of the truth table on which the premises of these fallacious arguments are all true, but the conclusion false.

## E. Substitution Instances and Specific Forms

A given argument can be a substitution instance of several different argument forms, as we noted earlier when defining "argument form." Hence the valid disjunctive syllogism examined on page 305, which may be symbolized as

$$R \vee W$$
$$\sim R$$
$$\therefore W$$

is a substitution instance of the valid argument form

$$p \vee q$$
$$\sim p$$
$$\therefore q$$

and is *also* a substitution instance of the *in*valid argument form

$$p$$
$$q$$
$$\therefore r$$

It is obvious, in this last form, that from two premisses, $p$ and $q$, we could not validly infer $r$. So it is clear that an invalid argument form *can* have a valid argument, *or* an invalid argument, as a substitution instance. Therefore, in determining whether any given argument is valid, *we must look to the specific form of the argument* in question. Only the specific form of the argument accurately reveals the full logical structure of that argument, and because it does, we can know that if the specific form of an argument is valid, the argument itself must be valid.

In the illustration just given, we see an argument (R $\vee$ W, $\sim$R, therefore W), and two argument forms of which that argument could be a substitution instance. The first of these argument forms ($p \vee q$, $\sim p$, therefore $q$) is valid, and because that form is the *specific* form of the given argument, its validity establishes that the given argument is valid. The second of those argument forms is invalid, but because it is *not* the specific form of the given argument it cannot be used to show that the given argument is invalid.

This point should be emphasized: An argument form that is valid can have only valid arguments as substitution instances. That is, all of the substitution instances of a valid form *must* be valid. This is proved by the truth-table proof of validity for the valid argument form, which shows that there is no possible substitution instance of a valid form that has true premises and a false conclusion.

## Exercises

I. Following will be found a group of arguments (Group A, lettered a–o) and a group of argument forms (Group B, numbered 1–24). For each of the arguments (in Group A), indicate which of the argument forms (in Group B), if any, have the given argument as a *substitution instance*. In addition, for each given argument (in Group A), indicate which of the argument forms (in Group B), if any, is the *specific form* of that argument.

## Examples:

Argument **a** in Group A: Examining all the argument forms in Group B, we find that the only one of which Argument **a** is a **substitution instance** is Number 3. Number 3 *is* also the **specific form** of Argument **a**.

Argument **j** in Group A: Examining all the argument forms in Group B, we find that Argument **j** is a **substitution instance** *both* of Number 6 and of Number 23. But *only* number 23 is the **specific form** of Argument **j**.

Argument **m** in Group A: Examining all the argument forms in Group B, we find that Argument **m** is a **substitution instance** *both* of Number 3 and of Number 24. But there is *no* argument form in Group B that is the **specific form** of Argument **m**.

## Group A—Arguments

a.  $A \bullet B$
    $\therefore A$

b.  $C \supset D$
    $\therefore C \supset (C \bullet D)$

c.  $E$
    $\therefore E \vee F$

d.  $G \supset H$
    $\sim H$
    $\therefore \sim G$

\*e. $I$
    $J$
    $\therefore I \bullet J$

f.  $(K \supset L) \bullet (M \supset N)$
    $K \vee M$
    $\therefore L \vee N$

g.  $O \supset P$
    $\sim O$
    $\therefore \sim P$

h.  $Q \supset R$
    $Q \supset S$
    $\therefore R \vee S$

i.  $T \supset U$
    $U \supset V$
    $\therefore V \supset T$

j.  $(W \bullet X) \supset (Y \bullet Z)$
    $\therefore (W \bullet X) \supset [(W \bullet X) \bullet (Y \bullet Z)]$

k.  $A \supset B$
    $\therefore (A \supset B) \vee C$

l.  $(D \vee E) \bullet \sim F$
    $\therefore D \vee E$

m.  $[G \supset (G \bullet H)] \bullet [H \supset (H \bullet G)]$
    $\therefore G \supset (G \bullet H)$

n.  $(I \vee J) \supset (I \bullet J)$
    $\sim (I \vee J)$
    $\therefore \sim (I \bullet J)$

\*o. $(K \supset L) \bullet (M \supset N)$
    $\therefore K \supset L$

## Group B—Argument Forms

\*1. $p \supset q$
    $\therefore \sim q \supset \sim p$

2.  $p \supset q$
    $\therefore \sim p \supset \sim q$

3.  $p \bullet q$
    $\therefore p$

4.  $p$
    $\therefore p \vee q$

\*5. $p$
    $\therefore p \supset q$

6.  $p \supset q$
    $\therefore p \supset (p \bullet q)$

7.  $(p \vee q) \supset (p \bullet q)$
    $\therefore (p \supset q) \bullet (q \supset p)$

8.  $p \supset q$
    $\sim p$
    $\therefore \sim q$

9.  $p \supset q$
    $\sim q$
    $\therefore \sim p$

\*10. $p$
    $q$
    $\therefore p \bullet q$

11. $p \supset q$
    $p \supset r$
    $\therefore q \vee r$

12. $p \supset q$
    $q \supset r$
    $\therefore r \supset p$

13. $p \supset (q \supset r)$
    $p \supset q$
    $\therefore p \supset r$

14. $p \supset (q \bullet r)$
    $(q \vee r) \supset \sim p$
    $\therefore \sim p$

*15. $p \supset (q \supset r)$
    $q \supset (p \supset r)$
    $\therefore (p \vee q) \supset r$

16. $(p \supset q) \bullet (r \supset s)$
    $p \vee r$
    $\therefore q \vee s$

17. $(p \supset q) \bullet (r \supset s)$
    $\sim q \vee \sim s$
    $\therefore \sim p \vee \sim s$

18. $p \supset (q \supset r)$
    $q \supset (r \supset s)$
    $\therefore p \supset s$

19. $p \supset (q \supset r)$
    $(q \supset r) \supset s$
    $\therefore p \supset s$

*20. $(p \supset q) \bullet [(p \bullet q) \supset r]$
    $p \supset (r \supset s)$
    $\therefore p \supset s$

21. $(p \vee q) \supset (p \bullet q)$
    $\sim (p \vee q)$
    $\therefore \sim (p \bullet q)$

22. $(p \vee q) \supset (p \bullet q)$
    $(p \bullet q)$
    $\therefore p \vee q$

23. $(p \bullet q) \supset (r \bullet s)$
    $\therefore (p \bullet q) \supset [(p \bullet q) \bullet (r \bullet s)]$

24. $(p \supset q) \bullet (r \supset s)$
    $\therefore p \supset q$

II. Use truth tables to prove the validity or invalidity of each of the argument forms in Group B, in Exercise 1.

III. Use truth tables to determine the validity or invalidity of each of the following arguments.

*1. $(A \vee B) \supset (A \bullet B)$
    $A \vee B$
    $\therefore A \bullet B$

2. $(C \vee D) \supset (C \bullet D)$
    $C \bullet D$
    $\therefore C \vee D$

3. $E \supset F$
    $F \supset E$
    $\therefore E \vee F$

4. $(G \vee H) \supset (G \bullet H)$
    $\sim (G \bullet H)$
    $\therefore \sim (G \vee H)$

*5. $(I \vee J) \supset (I \bullet J)$
    $\sim (I \vee J)$
    $\therefore \sim (I \bullet J)$

6. $K \vee L$
    $K$
    $\therefore \sim L$

7. $M \vee (N \bullet \sim N)$
    $M$
    $\therefore \sim (N \bullet \sim N)$

8. $(O \vee P) \supset Q$
    $Q \supset (O \bullet P)$
    $\therefore (O \vee P) \supset (O \bullet P)$

9. $(R \vee S) \supset T$
    $T \supset (R \bullet S)$
    $\therefore (R \bullet S) \supset (R \vee S)$

*10. $U \supset (V \vee W)$
    $(V \bullet W) \supset \sim U$
    $\therefore \sim U$

IV. Use truth tables to determine the validity or invalidity of the following arguments.

*1. If Angola achieves stability, then both Botswana and Chad will adopt more liberal policies. But Botswana will not adopt a more liberal policy. Therefore Angola will not achieve stability.

2. If Denmark refuses to join the European Community, then, if Estonia remains in the Russian sphere of influence, then Finland will reject a free trade policy. Estonia will remain in the Russian sphere of influence. So if Denmark refuses to join the European community, then Finland will reject a free trade policy.

3. If Greece strengthens its democratic institutions, then Hungary will pursue a more independent policy. If Greece strengthens its democratic institutions, then the Italian government will feel less threatened. Hence, if Hungary pursues a more independent policy, then the Italian government will feel less threatened.

4. If Japan continues to increase the export of automobiles, then either Korea or Laos will suffer economic decline. Korea will not suffer economic decline. It follows that if Japan continues to increase the export of automobiles, then Laos will suffer economic decline.

*5. If Montana suffers a severe drought, then, if Nevada has its normal light rainfall, Oregon's water supply will be greatly reduced. Nevada does have its normal light rainfall. So if Oregon's water supply is greatly reduced, then Montana suffers a severe drought.

6. If equality of opportunity is to be achieved, then those people previously disadvantaged should now be given special opportunities. If those people previously disadvantaged should now be given special opportunities, then some people receive preferential treatment. If some people receive preferential treatment, then equality of opportunity is not to be achieved. Therefore equality of opportunity is not to be achieved.

7. If terrorists' demands are met, then lawlessness will be rewarded. If terrorists' demands are not met, then innocent hostages will be murdered. So either lawlessness will be rewarded or innocent hostages will be murdered.

8. If people are entirely rational, then either all of a person's actions can be predicted in advance or the universe is essentially deterministic. Not all of a person's actions can be predicted in advance. Thus, if the universe is not essentially deterministic, then people are not entirely rational.

9. If oil consumption continues to grow, then either oil imports will increase or domestic oil reserves will be depleted. If oil imports increase and domestic oil reserves are depleted, then the nation eventually will go bankrupt. Therefore, if oil consumption continues to grow, then the nation eventually will go bankrupt.

**\*10.** If oil consumption continues to grow, then oil imports will increase and domestic oil reserves will be depleted. If either oil imports increase or domestic oil reserves are depleted, then the nation will soon be bankrupt. Therefore, if oil consumption continues to grow, then the nation will soon be bankrupt.

## 8.5  STATEMENT FORMS AND MATERIAL EQUIVALENCE

### A.  Statement Forms and Statements

We now make explicit a notion tacitly assumed in the preceding section, the notion of a "statement form." There is an exact parallel between the relation of argument to argument form, on the one hand, and the relation of statement to statement form, on the other. The definition of "statement form" makes this evident: **A *statement form* is any sequence of symbols containing statement variables but no statements, such that when statements are substituted for the statement variables—the same statement being substituted for the same statement variable throughout—the result is a statement.** Thus $p \lor q$ is a statement form, for when statements are substituted for the variables $p$ and $q$, a statement results. Since the resulting statement is a disjunction, $p \lor q$ is called a "disjunctive statement form." Analogously, $p \bullet q$ and $p \supset q$ are called "conjunctive" and "conditional statement forms," and $\sim p$ is called a "negation form" or "denial form." Just as any argument of a certain form is said to be a substitution instance of that argument form, so **any statement of a certain form is said to be a substitution instance of that statement form.** And just as we distinguished the *specific form* of a given argument, so we distinguish the **specific form of a given statement as that statement form from which the statement results by substituting consistently a different simple statement for each different statement variable.** Thus $p \lor q$ is the *specific form* of the statement "The blind prisoner has a red hat or the blind prisoner has a white hat."

### B.  Tautologous, Contradictory, and Contingent Statement Forms

It is perfectly natural to feel that, although the statements "Lincoln was assassinated" (symbolized as $L$) and "Either Lincoln was assassinated or else he wasn't" (symbolized as $L \lor \sim L$) are both *true*, they are true "in different ways" or have "different kinds" of truth. Similarly, it is perfectly natural to feel that, although the statements "Washington was assassinated" (symbolized as $W$) and "Washington was both assassinated and not assassinated" (symbolized as $W \bullet \sim W$) are both *false*, they are false "in different ways" or have "different kinds" of falsehood. While not pretending to give any psychological explanation of these "feelings," we can nevertheless point out certain logical differences to which they are appropriate.

The statement $L$ is true and the statement $W$ is false; these are historical facts. There is no logical necessity about them. Events might have occurred differently, and the truth values of such statements as $L$ and $W$ must be discovered by an empirical study of history. But the statement $L \vee \sim L$, although true, is not a truth of history. There is logical necessity here: Events could not have been such as to make it false, and its truth can be known independently of any particular empirical investigation. The statement $L \vee \sim L$ is a logical truth, a formal truth, true in virtue of its form alone. It is a substitution instance of a statement form all of whose substitution instances are true statements.

**A statement form that has only true substitution instances is called a *tautologous statement form*,** or a ***tautology***. To show that the statement form $p \vee \sim p$ is a tautology, we construct the following truth table:

| $p$ | $\sim p$ | $p \vee \sim p$ |
|-----|----------|-----------------|
| T   | F        | T               |
| F   | T        | T               |

There is only one initial or guide column to this truth table, since the form under consideration contains only one statement variable. Consequently, there are only two rows, which represent all possible substitution instances. There are only **T**'s in the column under the statement form in question, and this fact shows that all of its substitution instances are true. Any statement that is a substitution instance of a tautologous statement form is true in virtue of its form, and is itself said to be tautologous, or a tautology.

**A statement form that has only false substitution instances is said to be *self-contradictory*,** or a ***contradiction***, and is logically false. The statement form $p \bullet \sim p$ is self-contradictory, for in its truth table only **F**'s occur under it, signifying that all of its substitution instances are false. Any statement, such as $W \bullet \sim W$, which is a substitution instance of a self-contradictory statement form, is false in virtue of its form and is itself said to be self-contradictory, or a contradiction.

**Statement forms that have both true and false statements among their substitution instances are called *contingent statement forms*.** Any statement whose specific form is contingent is called a "contingent statement."[15] Thus $p$, $\sim p, p \bullet q, p \vee q$, and $p \supset q$ are all contingent statement forms. And such statements as $L, \sim L, L \bullet W, L \vee W$, and $L \supset W$ are contingent statements, since their truth values are dependent or contingent on their contents rather than on their forms alone.

Not all statement forms are so obviously tautological or self-contradictory or contingent as the simple examples cited. For example, the statement form $[(p \supset q) \supset p] \supset p$ is not at all obvious, though its truth table will show it to be a tautology. It even has a special name, "Peirce's law."

---

[15] It will be recalled that we are assuming here that no simple statements are either logically true or logically false. Only contingent simple statements are admitted here. See footnote 11 in this chapter, on page 322.

## C.  Material Equivalence

Material equivalence is a truth functional connective, just as disjunction and material implication are truth functional connectives. The truth value of any truth functional connective, as earlier explained, depends upon (is a function of) the truth or falsity of the statements it connects. Thus, we say that the disjunction of A and B is true if either A is true or B is true or if they are both true. Material equivalence is the truth functional connective that asserts that the statements it connects have the *same* truth value. Two statements that are equivalent in truth value, therefore, are materially equivalent. One straightforward definition is this: **Two statements are "materially equivalent" when they are both true, or both false.**

Just as the symbol for disjunction is the wedge, and the symbol for material implication is the horseshoe, there is also a special symbol for material equivalence, the three-bar sign "≡". And just as we gave truth-table definitions for the wedge and the horseshoe, we can do so for the three-bar sign as well. Here is the truth table for material equivalence, "≡":

| $p$ | $q$ | $p \equiv q$ |
|-----|-----|--------------|
| T | T | T |
| T | F | F |
| F | T | F |
| F | F | T |

Any two true statements materially imply one another; that is a consequence of the meaning of material implication. And any two false statements also materially imply one another. Therefore any two statements that are materially equivalent must imply one another, since they are either both true, or both false.

Since any two statements, A and B, that are materially equivalent imply one another, we may infer from their material equivalence that B is true *if* A is true, and also that B is true *only if* A is true. Since both of these relations are entailed by material equivalence, we can read the three-bar sign, ≡, to say "*if and only if.*"

In everyday discourse we use this logical relation only occasionally. I will go to the championship game, one may say, if and only if I can acquire a ticket. I will go *if* I do acquire a ticket, but I can go *only if* I acquire a ticket. So my going to the game, and my acquiring a ticket to the game, are materially equivalent.

Every implication is a *conditional* statement, as we earlier noted. Two statements, A and B, that are materially equivalent entail the truth of the conditional A ⊃ B, and also entail the truth of the conditional B ⊃ A. Since the implication goes both ways when material equivalence holds, a statement of the form A ≡ B is often called a *biconditional.*

There are four truth-functional connectives upon which deductive argument commonly depends: *conjunction, disjunction, material implication,* and *material equivalence.* Our discussion of the set of four is now complete.

---

### TRUTH-FUNCTIONAL CONNECTIVES

A truth-functional connective is a logical connective within a truth-functionally compound proposition. A truth-functionally compound proposition is one whose truth (or falsity) depends *wholly* upon the truth or falsity of the components of that compound. Four truth-functional connectives are of central importance:

• **The Dot.** Symbolizes **conjunction.** Read as: "P and Q."
    P • Q is true if and only if P is true *and* Q is true.

∨ **The Wedge.** Symbolizes **disjunction.** Read as: "P or Q."
    P ∨ Q is true if and only if P is true, *or* Q is true,
    *or* P and Q are both true.

⊃ **The Horseshoe.** Symbolizes **material implication.** Read as: "P implies Q."
    P ⊃ Q is true if and only if it is not the case that P is true and Q is false;
    that is, if and only if P is false or Q is true.

≡ **Three bars.** Symbolizes **material equivalence.** Read as: "P if and only if Q."
    P ≡ Q is true if and only if P and Q have the same truth value, that is, if
    and only if P is true and Q is true *or* P is false and Q is false.

---

## D.   Arguments, Conditional Statements, and Tautologies

To every argument there corresponds a conditional statement whose antecedent is the conjunction of the argument's premisses and whose consequent is the argument's conclusion. Thus, an argument having the form of *modus ponens*

$$p \supset q$$
$$p$$
$$\therefore q$$

may be expressed as a conditional statement of the form $[(p \supset q) • p] \supset q$. If the argument expressed as a conditional has a valid argument form, then its conclusion must in every case follow from its premisses, and therefore the conditional statement of it may be shown on a truth table to be a tautology. That is, the statement that the conjunction of the premisses implies the conclusion will (if the argument is valid) have all and only true instances.

Truth tables are powerful devices for the evaluation of arguments. **An argument form is valid if and only if its truth table has a T under the conclusion in every row in which there are T's under all of its premisses.** This follows from the precise meaning of "validity." Now, if the conditional statement expressing that argument form is made the heading of one column of the truth table, an **F** can occur in that column only in a row in which there are **T**'s under all the premisses and an **F** under the conclusion. But there will be no such row if the argument is valid. Hence only **T**'s will occur under a conditional statement that corresponds to a valid argument, and that conditional statement *must* be a tautology. We may therefore say that **an argument form is valid if, and only if, its expression in the form of a conditional statement** (of which the antecedent is the conjunction of the premisses of the given argument form and the consequent is the conclusion of the given argument form) **is a tautology.**

For every *invalid* argument of the truth-functional variety, however, the corresponding conditional statement will not be a tautology. The statement that the conjunction of its premisses implies its conclusion is (for an invalid argument) either contingent or contradictory.

## Exercises

I.  For each statement in the left-hand column, indicate which, if any, of the statement forms in the right-hand column have the given statement as a substitution instance, and indicate which, if any, is the specific form of the given statement.

| | | | |
|---|---|---|---|
| *1. | $A \lor B$ | a. | $p \bullet q$ |
| 2. | $C \bullet \sim D$ | b. | $p \supset q$ |
| 3. | $\sim E \supset (F \bullet G)$ | c. | $p \lor q$ |
| 4. | $H \supset (I \bullet J)$ | d. | $p \bullet \sim q$ |
| *5. | $(K \bullet L) \lor (M \bullet N)$ | e. | $p \equiv q$ |
| 6. | $(O \lor P) \supset (P \bullet Q)$ | f. | $(p \supset q) \lor (r \bullet s)$ |
| 7. | $(R \supset S) \lor (T \bullet \sim U)$ | g. | $[(p \supset q) \supset r] \supset s$ |
| 8. | $V \supset (W \lor \sim W)$ | h. | $[(p \supset q) \supset p] \supset p$ |
| 9. | $[(X \supset Y) \supset X] \supset X$ | i. | $(p \bullet q) \lor (r \bullet s)$ |
| *10. | $Z \equiv \sim\sim Z$ | j. | $p \supset (q \lor \sim r)$ |

II.  Use truth tables to characterize the following statement forms as tautologous, self-contradictory, or contingent.

*1.  $[p \supset (p \supset q)] \supset q$        2.  $p \supset [(p \supset q) \supset q]$

3.  $(p \bullet q) \bullet (p \supset \sim q)$        4.  $p \supset [\sim p \supset (q \lor \sim q)]$

*5.  $p \supset [p \supset (q \bullet \sim q)]$        6.  $(p \supset p) \supset (q \bullet \sim q)$

7.  $[p \supset (q \supset r)] \supset [(p \supset q) \supset (p \supset r)]$

8.  $[p \supset (q \supset p)] \supset [(q \supset q) \supset \sim(r \supset r)]$

9.  $\{[(p \supset q) \bullet (r \supset s)] \bullet (p \lor r)\} \supset (q \lor s)$

*10.  $\{[(p \supset q) \bullet (r \supset s)] \bullet (q \lor s)\} \supset (p \lor r)$

III.  Use truth tables to decide which of the following biconditionals are tautologies.

*1.  $(p \supset q) \equiv (\sim q \supset \sim p)$        2.  $(p \supset q) \equiv (\sim p \supset \sim q)$

3.  $[(p \supset q) \supset r] \equiv [(q \supset p) \supset r]$        4.  $[p \supset (q \supset r)] \equiv [q \supset (p \supset r)]$

*5.  $p \equiv [p \bullet (p \lor q)]$        6.  $p \equiv [p \lor (p \bullet q)]$

7.  $p \equiv [p \bullet (p \supset q)]$        8.  $p \equiv [p \bullet (q \supset p)]$

9. $p \equiv [p \vee (p \supset q)]$    *10. $(p \supset q) \equiv [(p \vee q) \equiv q]$

11. $p \equiv [p \vee (q \bullet \sim q)]$    12. $p \equiv [p \bullet (q \bullet \sim q)]$

13. $p \equiv [p \bullet (q \vee \sim q)]$    14. $p \equiv [p \vee (q \vee \sim q)]$

*15. $[p \bullet (q \vee r)] \equiv [(p \bullet q) \vee (p \bullet r)]$

16. $[p \bullet (q \vee r)] \equiv [(p \vee q) \bullet (p \vee r)]$

17. $[p \vee (q \bullet r)] \equiv [(p \bullet q) \vee (p \bullet r)]$

18. $[p \vee (q \bullet r)] \equiv [(p \vee q) \bullet (p \vee r)]$

19. $[(p \bullet q) \supset r] \equiv [p \supset (q \supset r)]$

*20. $[(p \supset q) \bullet (q \supset p)] \equiv [(p \bullet q) \vee (\sim p \bullet \sim q)]$

## 8.6  LOGICAL EQUIVALENCE

At this point we introduce a new relation, important and very useful, but not a connective, and somewhat more complicated than any of the truth-functional connectives just discussed.

Statements are materially equivalent when they have the same truth value. Because two materially equivalent statements are either both true, or both false, we can readily see that they must (materially) imply one another, since a false antecedent (materially) implies any statement, and a true consequent is (materially) implied by any statement. We may therefore read the three-bar sign, $\equiv$, as "if and only if."

But statements that are materially equivalent most certainly cannot be substituted for one another. Knowing that they are materially equivalent, we know only that their truth values are the same. The statements "Jupiter is larger than the Earth" and "Tokyo is the capital of Japan" are materially equivalent because they are both true, but we obviously cannot replace one with the other. Similarly, the statements "All spiders are poisonous" and "No spiders are poisonous" are materially equivalent simply because they are both false, and they certainly cannot replace one another!

But there are many circumstances in which we must express the relationship that does permit mutual replacement. Two statements can be equivalent in a sense much stronger than that of material equivalence; they may be equivalent in *meaning* as well as having the same truth value. If they do have the same meaning, any proposition that incorporates one of them could just as well incorporate the other; there will not be—there cannot then be—any case in which one of these statements is true while the other is false. Statements equivalent in this very strong sense we call *logically equivalent*.

Of course, any two statements that are logically equivalent will be materially equivalent as well, for they would obviously have to have the same truth value. Indeed, if two statements are logically equivalent, they are materially equivalent under *all* circumstances—and this explains the short but powerful definition of logical equivalence: **two statements are logically equivalent when the statement of their material equivalence is a tautology.** That is, the statement that they do have the same truth value is itself necessarily true. And this why we use, to express this very strong logical relationship, the three bar symbol with a small **T** immediately above it, $\overset{\text{T}}{=}$, indicating that the logical relationship is of such a nature that the material equivalence of the two statements is a tautology. And because material equivalence is a "biconditional" (the two statements implying one another) we may think of this symbol of logical equivalence, $\overset{\text{T}}{=}$, as expressing a tautological biconditional.

Some simple logical equivalences very commonly employed will make this relation, and its great power, very clear. It is a commonplace that $p$ and $\sim\sim p$ mean the same thing; "he is aware of that difficulty" and "he is not unaware of that difficulty" are two statements with the same content. In substance, either of these expressions may be replaced by the other because they both say the same thing. This principle of *double negation*, whose truth is obvious to all, may be exhibited on a truth table, where the material equivalence of two statement forms is shown to be a tautology, thus:

| $p$ | $\sim p$ | $\sim\sim p$ | $p \overset{\text{T}}{=} \sim\sim p$ |
|-----|----------|--------------|-------------------------------------|
| T | F | T | T |
| F | T | F | T |

This truth table proves that $p$ and $\sim\sim p$ are *logically equivalent*. This very useful logical equivalence, double negation, is symbolized thus:

$$p \overset{\text{T}}{=} \sim \sim p$$

The difference between *material equivalence* on the one hand and *logical equivalence* on the other hand is very great and very important. The former is a truth-functional connective, $\equiv$, which may be true or false depending only upon the truth or falsity of the elements it connects. But the latter, logical equivalence, $\overset{\text{T}}{=}$, is not a mere connective, and it expresses a relation between two statements that is not truth-functional. Two statements are logically equivalent only when it is absolutely impossible for them to have different truth values. But if they *always* have the same truth value, logically equivalent statements must have the same meaning, and in that case they may be substituted for one another in any truth-functional context without changing the truth value of that context. By contrast, two statements are materially equivalent if they merely *happen* to have the same truth value, even if there are no factual connections between them. Statements that are merely materially equivalent certainly may not be substituted for one another!

There are two well-known logical equivalences (*i.e.*, logically true biconditionals) of great importance because they express the interrelations among conjunction and disjunction, and their negations. Let us examine these two logical equivalences more closely.

First, what will serve to deny that a disjunction is true? Any disjunction $p \vee q$ asserts no more than that at least one of its two disjuncts is true. One cannot contradict it by asserting that at least one is false; we must (to deny it) assert that both disjuncts are false. Therefore, asserting the *negation of the disjunction* $(p \vee q)$ is logically equivalent to asserting the *conjunction of the negations of p and of q*. To show this on a truth table, we may formulate the biconditional, $\sim(p \vee q) \equiv (\sim p \bullet \sim q)$, place it at the top of its own column, and examine its truth value under all circumstances, that is, in each row.

| $p$ | $q$ | $p \vee q$ | $\sim(p \vee q)$ | $\sim p$ | $\sim q$ | $\sim p \bullet \sim q$ | $\sim(p \vee q) \equiv$ $(\sim p \bullet \sim q)$ |
|---|---|---|---|---|---|---|---|
| T | T | T | F | F | F | F | T |
| T | F | T | F | F | T | F | T |
| F | T | T | F | T | F | F | T |
| F | F | F | T | T | T | T | T |

Of course we see that, whatever the truth values of $p$ and of $q$, this biconditional must always be true. It is a tautology. Because the statement of that material equivalence *is* a tautology, we conclude that the two statements are logically equivalent. We have proved that

$$\sim(p \vee q) \stackrel{\mathsf{T}}{\equiv} (\sim p \bullet \sim q)$$

Similarly, since asserting the conjunction of $p$ and $q$ asserts that both are true, to contradict this assertion we need merely assert that at least one is false. Thus, asserting the negation of the conjunction, $(p \bullet q)$, is logically equivalent to asserting the disjunction of the negations of $p$ and of $q$. In symbols, the biconditional, $\sim(p \bullet q) \equiv (\sim p \vee \sim q)$ may be shown, on a truth table, to be a tautology. Such a table proves

$$\sim(p \bullet q) \stackrel{\mathsf{T}}{\equiv} (\sim p \vee \sim q)$$

These two tautologous biconditionals, or logical equivalences, are known as De Morgan's theorems, because they were formally stated by the mathematician and logician Augustus De Morgan (1806–1871). De Morgan's theorems can be formulated in English thus:

**(a)** The negation of the disjunction of two statements is logically equivalent to the conjunction of the negations of the two statements;

and

**(b)** The negation of the conjunction of two statements is logically equivalent to the disjunction of the negations of the two statements.

These theorems of De Morgan prove to be exceedingly useful.

Another important logical equivalence is very helpful when we seek to manipulate truth-functional connectives. Material implication, $\supset$, was defined earlier in this chapter (in section 8.3) as an abbreviated way of saying $\sim(p \bullet \sim q)$. That is, "$p$ materially implies $q$" simply means, by definition, that it is not the case that $p$ is true while $q$ is false. In this definition we see that the *definiens*, $\sim(p \bullet \sim q)$, is the denial of a conjunction. And by De Morgan's theorem we know that any such denial is logically equivalent to the disjunction of the denials of the conjuncts; that is, we know that $\sim(p \cdot \sim q)$ is logically equivalent to $(\sim p \vee \sim \sim q)$; and this expression in turn, applying the principle of double negation, is logically equivalent to $\sim p \vee q$. Logically equivalent expressions mean the same thing, and therefore the original *definiens* of the horseshoe, $\sim(p \cdot \sim q)$, may be replaced with no change of meaning by the simpler expression $\sim p \vee q$. This gives us a very useful *definition of material implication: $p \supset q$ is logically equivalent to $\sim p \vee q$*. In symbols we write:

$$(p \supset q) \stackrel{\mathrm{T}}{=} (\sim p \vee q)$$

This definition of material implication is widely relied upon in the formulation of logical statements and the analysis of arguments. Manipulation is often essential, and manipulation is more efficient when the statements we are working with have the same central connective. With the simple definition of the horseshoe we have just established, $(p \supset q) \stackrel{\mathrm{T}}{=} (\sim p \vee q)$, statements in which the horseshoe is the connective can be conveniently replaced by statements in which the wedge is the connective; and likewise, statements in disjunctive form may be readily replaced by statements in implicative form. When we seek to present a formal proof of the validity of deductive arguments, replacements of this kind prove very useful indeed.

## 8.7    THE PARADOXES OF MATERIAL IMPLICATION

There are two forms of statements, $p \supset (q \supset p)$ and $\sim p \supset (p \supset q)$, that are easily proved to be tautologies. Trivial as these statement forms may be in their symbolic formulation, when stated in ordinary English they seem surprising and even paradoxical. The first may be stated as "If a statement is true, then it is implied by any statement whatever." Since it is true that the earth is round, it follows that "The moon is made of green cheese implies that the earth is round"; and this is very curious indeed, especially since it also follows that "The moon is *not* made of green cheese implies that the earth is round." The second tautology may be stated as "If a statement is false, then it implies any statement whatever." Since it is false that the moon is made of green cheese, it follows that "The moon is made of green cheese implies that the earth is round"; and this is all the more curious when we realize that it also follows that "The moon is made of green cheese implies that the earth is *not* round."

These seem paradoxical because we believe that the shape of the earth and the matter of the moon are utterly irrelevant to each other, and we believe further that no statement, true or false, can really imply any other statement, false or true, to which it is utterly irrelevant. And yet truth tables establish that a false statement implies any statement, and that a true statement is implied by any statement. This paradox is easily resolved, however, when we acknowledge the ambiguity of the word "implies." In several senses of the word "implies," it is perfectly true that no contingent statement can imply any other contingent statement with unrelated subject matter. It is true in the case of *logical* implication and of *definitional* and *causal* implications. It may even be true of *decisional* implications, although here the notion of relevance may have to be construed more broadly.

But subject matter or *meaning* is strictly irrelevant to *material implication*, which is a truth function. Only truth and falsehood are relevant here. There is nothing paradoxical in stating that any disjunction is true which contains at least one true disjunct, and this fact is all that is asserted by statements of the forms $p \supset (\sim q \vee p)$ and $\sim p \supset (\sim p \vee q)$, which are logically equivalent to the "paradoxical" ones. We have already given a justification of treating material implication as *a* sense of "if–then," and of the logical expediency of translating *every* occurrence of "if–then" into the "$\supset$" notation. That justification was the fact that translating "if–then" into the "$\supset$" preserves the validity of all valid arguments of the type with which we are concerned in this part of our logical studies. There are other proposed symbolizations, adequate to other types of implication, but they belong to more advanced parts of logic, beyond the scope of this book.

## 8.8  THE THREE "LAWS OF THOUGHT"

**For Enrichment**   Some early thinkers, after having defined logic as "the science of the laws of thought," went on to assert that there are exactly three *basic* laws of thought, laws so fundamental that obedience to them is both the necessary and the sufficient condition of correct thinking. These three have traditionally been called:

- The principle of identity.
  This principle asserts that *if any statement is true, then it is true.* Using our notation we may rephrase it by saying that the principle of identity asserts that every statement of the form $p \supset p$ must be true, that every such statement is a tautology.
- The principle of noncontradiction.
  This principle asserts that *no statement can be both true and false.* Using our notation we may rephrase it by saying that the principle of noncontradiction asserts that every statement of the form $p \bullet \sim p$ must be false, that every such statement is self-contradictory.
- The principle of excluded middle.
  This principle asserts that *every statement is either true or false.* Using our notation we may rephrase it by saying that the principle of excluded middle asserts that every statement of the form $p \vee \sim p$ must be true, that every such statement is a tautology.

It is obvious that these three principles are indeed true, logically true—but the claim that they deserve a privileged status as the most fundamental laws of thought is doubtful. The first (identity) and the third (excluded middle) are tautologies, but there are many other tautologous forms whose truth is equally certain. And the second (noncontradiction) is by no means the only self-contradictory form of statement.

We do use these principles in completing truth tables. In the initial columns of each row of a table we place either a **T** or an **F**, being guided by the principle of excluded middle. Nowhere do we put both **T** and **F** together, being guided by the principle of noncontradiction. And once having put a **T** under a symbol in a given row, then (being guided by the principle of identity) when we encounter that symbol in other columns of that row we regard it as still being assigned a **T**. So we could regard the three laws of thought as principles governing the construction of truth tables.

Nevertheless, in regarding the entire system of deductive logic, these three principles are no more important or fruitful than many others. Indeed, there are tautologies that are more fruitful than they for purposes of deduction, and in that sense more important than these three. A more extended treatment of this point lies beyond the scope of this book.[16]

Some thinkers, believing themselves to have devised a new and different logic, have claimed that these three principles are in fact not true, and that obedience to them has been needlessly confining. But these criticisms have been based on misunderstandings.

The principle of identity has been attacked on the ground that things change, and are always changing. Thus, for example, statements that were true of the United States when it consisted of the 13 original states are no longer true of the United States today with 50 states. But this does not undermine the principle of identity. The sentence "There are only thirteen states in the United States" is incomplete, an elliptical formulation of the statement that "There were only 13 states in the United States *in 1790*"—and that statement is as true today as it was in 1790. When we confine our attention to complete, nonelliptical formulations of propositions, we see that their truth (or falsity) does not change over time. The principle of identity is true, and it does not interfere with our recognition of continuing change.

The principle of noncontradiction has been attacked by Hegelians and Marxists on the grounds that genuine contradiction is everywhere pervasive, that the world is replete with the inevitable conflict of contradictory forces. That there are conflicting forces in the real word is true, of course—but to call these conflicting forces "contradictory" is a loose and misleading use of that term. Labor unions and the private owners of industrial plants may indeed find themselves in conflict—but neither the owner nor the union is the "negation" or the "denial" or the "contradictory" of the other. The principle of contradiction, understood in the straightforward sense in which it is intended by logicians, is unobjectionable and perfectly true.

The principle of excluded middle has been the object of much criticism, on the grounds that it leads to a "two-valued orientation," which implies that

---

[16] For further discussion of these matters, the interested reader can consult I. M. Copi and J. A. Gould, eds., *Readings on Logic*, 2d ed., New York, Macmillan, 1972, part 2; and I. M. Copi and J. A. Gould, eds., *Contemporary Philosophical Logic*, New York, St. Martin's Press, 1978, part 8.

120

things in the world must be either "white or black," and which thereby hinders the realization of compromise and less than absolute gradations. This objection also arises from misunderstanding. Of course the statement "This is black" cannot be jointly true with the statement "This is white"—where "this" refers to exactly the same thing. But although these two statements cannot both be true, they can both be false. "This" may be neither black nor white; the two statements are *contraries*, not contradictory. The contradictory of the statement "This is white" is the statement "It is not the case that this is white" and (if "white" is used in precisely the same sense in both of these statements) one of them must be true and the other false. The principle of excluded middle is inescapable.

All three of these "laws of thought" are unobjectionable—so long as they are applied to statements containing unambiguous, nonelliptical, and precise terms. They may not deserve the honorific status assigned to them by some philosophers,[17] but they are indubitably true.

## Summary of Chapter 8

This chapter has presented the most fundamental concepts of modern symbolic logic.

In section 8.1, we explained the value of special symbols.

In section 8.2, we introduced and defined the symbols for **negation** (the curl: ~), and for the truth-functional connectives **conjunction** (the dot: •) and **disjunction** (the wedge: ∨). We also explained logical punctuation.

In section 8.3, we discussed conditional statements and defined the truth-functional connective **material implication** (the horseshoe: ⊃).

In section 8.4, we explained **the formal structure of arguments** and defined essential terms for dealing with **argument forms**. We gave a precise account of validity and invalidity as characteristics of argument forms and arguments. We explained **truth tables** and showed how the validity or invalidity of an argument form may be determined by use of a truth table.

In section 8.5, we explained **the formal structure of statements** and defined essential terms for dealing with **statement forms**. We introduced **tautologous, contradictory,** and **contingent statement forms** and defined a fourth truth-functional connective, **material equivalence** (three bars: ≡).

In section 8.6 we introduced and defined a powerful new relation, **logical equivalence,** using the symbol $\overset{\text{T}}{=}$. We explained why statements that are logically equivalent may be substituted for one another, while statements that are

---

[17] Plato appealed explicitly to the principle of noncontradiction in Book IV of his *Republic* (at nos. 436 and 439); Aristotle discussed all three of these principles in Books IV and XI of his *Metaphysics*. Of the principle of noncontradiction Aristotle wrote: "That the same attribute cannot at the same time belong and not belong to the same subject and in the same respect" is a principle "which everyone must have who understands anything that is," and which "every one must already have when he comes to a special study." It is, he concluded, "the most certain of all principles."

merely materially equivalent cannot replace one another. We introduced several logical equivalences of special importance: **De Morgan's theorems,** the **definition of material implication,** and **the principle of double negation.**

In section 8.7, we explained why the so-called **paradoxes of material implication** are thought to be paradoxes only because the nature of the connective we call material implication is often imperfectly understood.

In section 8.8, we discussed certain logical equivalences that have been thought by many to be fundamental in all reasoning: the principle of **identity,** the principle of **noncontradiction,** and the principle of the **excluded middle.**

*Unit II*

$$J \lor M$$
$$\sim M$$
$$\overline{\phantom{J \lor M}}$$
$$J$$
$$\sim J$$

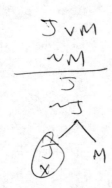

# Truth Trees

## Donald Nute

An argument consists of a set of claims where some of the claims are offered as reasons for accepting other of the claims. The claims given as support for other claims are called **premises** and the claims that are supported are called **conclusions**. Premises might provide stronger or weaker support for the conclusions they support. The truth of the premises might guarantee the truth of a conclusion, or they might only make the conclusion more likely or probable. When the premises guarantee the conclusion, when it is impossible that the premises could be true and the conclusion be false, the argument is called **deductively valid**. An example of a deductively valid argument is

    (1) Either John or Mary took the book. But Mary didn't take it. So John must have taken it.

The first two claims support the third claim. And if the first two claims are true, the third claim would have to be true also. An example of an argument that is persuasive but not deductively valid is

    (2) I don't think Harry saw *Love Story*. He doesn't like romantic movies.

Now it is certainly possible that Harry saw *Love Story* even though he doesn't like romantic movies, but the second claim here certainly gives us a good reason to think the first claim is true.

There are methods we can use to show that some arguments are deductively valid. These methods depend on the ways simpler sentences are included in more complex sentences in the premises and conclusions of these arguments. This is what is happening in (1) above. The first premise says that one of the two sentences, 'John took the book' and 'Mary took the book', is true. The second premise says that the second of these sentences is *not* true. So that means the first must be true - and that is our conclusion.

We can represent part of the structure of sentences by showing how they are built up from simpler sentences using **sentence connectives**. The sentence connectives we will use are ~ (not), & (and), ∨ (or), → (if-then), and ↔ (if-and-only-if). To test to see if an argument is deductively valid, we will try to see if there is any way the premises could be true while the conclusion is false. The method we will use to perform this test is called a **truth tree**. Basically, when we construct a truth tree for an argument we explore all the different combinations of truth values the atomic sentences used in the argument could have to see if any of them would make the premises true and the conclusion false.

We begin the truth tree by writing down the premises and the **negation** of the conclusion. For example, if we let J be 'John took the book' and we let M be 'Mary took the book', then we would begin a truth tree for argument (1) like this:

J ∨ M    first premise
~M       second premise
~J       negation of the conclusion

Then we extend the tree by processing sentences in the tree that are not single letters or negations of single letters. In this tree, the only sentence like that is the first sentence. We see that if J ∨ M is true, then either J is true or M is true. That lets us add two branches to our tree:

```
J ∨ M    √
  ~M
   ~J
  / \
 J   M
```

I have put a check mark beside J ∨ M to help me remember that I have already processed it. Now look at the left branch of the tree, the one that starts at the top with J ∨ M and ends at the bottom with J. Both J and ~J are in this branch. But both J and ~J can't be true. So we **close** this branch by putting an × below that branch.

```
J ∨ M    √
  ~M
   ~J
  / \
 J   M
×
```

But look at the right hand branch. It contains both M and ~M, and these can't both be true either. So we close that branch as well.

```
J ∨ M    √
  ~M
   ~J
  / \
 J   M
×   ×
```

But now every branch in our tree is closed. This means there is *no way* to make the premises of argument (1) true and the conclusion false at the same time. So argument (1) is deductively valid.

You probably didn't need to do a truth tree to see that argument (1) was deductively valid, but it is often difficult to tell whether more complex arguments are deductively valid. Truth trees give us a method for determining this, at least for a large family of arguments.

Before we look at more complex examples, we need to determine how we should process sentences in truth trees.

Let's begin with a sentence like ~ ~ P. An example would be, 'Its not true that Peter doesn't own a car.' But that means that Peter *does* own a car. So whenever we see a sentence of the form ~ ~ P in a truth tree, we can put a P at the bottom of each open branch in the tree and mark the sentence ~ ~ P with an exclamation point.

~~P   √
  P

$$\frac{\sim\sim P}{\begin{array}{c} P \\ \sim P \\ \wedge \\ P \\ x \end{array}}$$

We have already seen how to process a sentence of the form P V Q. We *split* each open branch, putting P at the end of each new left hand branch and Q at the end of each new right hand branch.

P ∨ Q   √
/   \
P   Q

If P & Q is true, then P is true and Q is true. So we extend each open branch in the tree by adding *both* P and Q.

P & Q   √
  P
  Q

Now consider this argument which includes both & and ∨.

(3) Either Jordan didn't play or the Bulls won. But the Bulls and the Hawks both lost. So Jordan didn't play.

We begin a truth tree for this argument like this:

 ~ J ∨ B    first premise
~ B & ~ H   second premise
  ~ ~ J     negation of the conclusion

Processing the first premise we get

 ~ J ∨ B   √
~ B & ~ H
  ~ ~ J
  /  \
~ J   B

We do not have both a letter and its negation in eitther branch; so both branches remain open. Next we process the second premise.

```
   ~ J ∨ B      √
  ~ B & ~ H     √
      ~ ~ J
      /    \
  ~ J      B
  ~B       ~B
  ~H       ~H
```

The right hand branch includes both B and ~ B; so we close it.

```
   ~ J ∨ B      √
  ~ B & ~ H     √
      ~ ~ J
      /    \
  ~ J      B
  ~B       ~B
  ~H       ~H
            ×
```

Finally, we process the negation of the conclusion.

```
   ~ J ∨ B      √
  ~ B & ~ H     √
      ~ ~ J     √
      /    \
  ~ J      B
  ~B       ~B
  ~H       ~H
   J        ×
```

But then the right branch includes both J and ~J; so we close it as well.

```
   ~ J ∨ B      √
  ~ B & ~ H     √
      ~ ~ J     √
      /    \
  ~ J      B
  ~B       ~B
  ~H       ~H
   J        ×
   ×
```

With every branch closed, there is no way the premises and the negation of the conclusion could all be true. So the argument is deductively valid.

The only way we can be sure a conditional (if-then statement) is false is if the antecedent is true and the consequent is false. So if either the antecedent is false or the consequent is true, then the conditional may be true. Thus, we process a conditional by splitting each open branch as follows:

$$P \rightarrow Q \quad \sqrt{}$$
```
  /   \
~ P    Q
```

A biconditional $P \leftrightarrow Q$ says that P and Q have the same truth value. So they must both be true or both be false.

$$P \leftrightarrow Q \quad \sqrt{}$$
```
 /    \
P     ~P
Q     ~Q
```

That takes care of all our connectives. Now we need to look at negations of connectives. For $P \vee Q$ to be true, only one of P and Q has to be true. So for $P \vee Q$ to be false, *both* P and Q must be false.

$$\sim (P \vee Q) \quad \sqrt{}$$
```
   ~ P
   ~Q
```

For P & Q to be true, both P and Q must be true. So for P & Q to be false, only one of P and Q has to be false.

$$\sim (P \,\&\, Q) \quad \sqrt{}$$
```
  /    \
~P     ~Q
```

The only way we can be sure a conditional is false is if the antecendent is true and the conclusion is false.

$$\sim (P \rightarrow Q) \quad \sqrt{}$$
```
   P
  ~ Q
```

And the only way a biconditional $P \leftrightarrow Q$ can be false is if P and Q have different truth values.

### 130

```
~ (P ↔ Q)     √
   /    \
   P    ~ P
  ~ Q    Q
```

So we have a total of nine rules for processing or **simplifying** sentences that occur in truth trees, rules for &, ∨, →, ↔, ~ ~, ~ &, ~ ∨, ~ →, and ~ ↔. With these nine rules, we can continue building a truth tree until every branch is closed or until every sentence in the tree that is not either a single sentence or the negation of a single sentence has been simplified. In the latter case, we can conclude that the sentence is not deductively valid **at the sentential level**. That does not mean, however, that it is not deductively valid. We will say more about that later.

Now let's consider another simple argument.

(4) If Betty had stolen Jim's money, then she would have run from the police officer and she would have had more than $500 in her possession. Betty did run from the police officer and she did have more than $500 in her possession. So she stole Jim's money.

The truth tree looks like this when we are finished:

```
first premise:              S → (R & M)    √
second premise:               R & M        √
negation of conclusion:         ~S
                            /      \
                          ~S      R & M    √
                          R         R
                          M         M
                                    R
                                    M
```

Notice that we have R and M twice in the right hand branch because we have two occurrences of R & M to process in this branch. We might have just put R and M once and marked both occurrences of R & M at the same time. Notice also that neither branch is closed. This means that the premise could be true and the conclusion false if Betty didn't steal the money but she ran from the police officer and had more than $500 with her for some other reason. (Perhaps she had taken the money from the bank to pay her rent and in the dim light she mistook the police officer for a mugger.) In any case, this shows that the argument is not decutively valid at the sentential level.

When we show that an argument is deductively valid at the sentential level, then we can be sure that it is impossible for the premises of the argument to be true while the conclusion is false. So if we accept the premises, we must also accept the conclusion. But if we show that an argument is *not* deductively valid at the sentential level, this does *not* guarantee that the argument is not deductively valid at some deeper level. Take for example this argument:

(1) All whales are mammals.
(2) Some sea creatures are whales.
(3) So some sea creatures are mammals.

Each of the sentences in this argument is simple; it is not a combination of other sentences. So the standard form for this argument is just

P
Q
∴ R

and the truth tree for the argument is just

P
Q
~ R

Since none of the sentences is compound, there is nothing to simplify. The truth tree has a single, open branch and the argument is *not* deductively at the sentential level. However, if you look at the argument carefully you should be able to see that if is in fact impossible for the premises to be true and the conclusion false. We need additional methods to analyze the deeper structure of arguments like this one, methods that go beyond the scope of this course.

## Guidelines for Symbolizing Arguments

Before you can construct a truth-tree for an argument, you need to represent the form of the argument using our five sentence connectives. Here are guidelines for doing this.

First we will consider kinds of sentences that should be symbolized using the negation symbol ~. Of course, you would use ~ to represent a sentence that had the word 'not' in it, but you would also use ~ for sentences with the phrases 'it is false that' or 'it is not the case that'. For example, if we use P to represent 'Peter lives on my street', then we would represent 'It is false that Peter lives on my street' as ~P. We also use ~ to represent sentences containing words with negative prefixes such as 'un' or 'im'. Using K to represent 'The source of the Nile was known in 1816', we would use ~K to represent 'The source of the Nile was unknown in 1916.' Finally, we sometimes use ~ to represent a negative concept even when no negative prefix is involved. Consider the argument, 'If Linda could distinguish red and green, she would not have problems reading traffic lights. But she does have problems reading traffic lights. So she must be red-green color blind.' Using D to represent 'Linda can distinguish red and green' and P to represent 'Linda has problems reading traffic lights', this argument has the form

D → ~P

P
So, ~D

Some words besides 'and' that we represent with & are 'but', 'yet', and 'although'. These words have the additional connotation that the assertion that comes after them is surprising or unexpected given the assertion that comes before them, but from the point of view of truth-trees they are treated exactly the same. For example, we would represent 'Peter was deeply in debt but he bought a new car' as D & C. We can also represent sentences with compound subjects and predicates using &. Where J is 'John lives in Atlanta' and M is 'Mary lives in Atlanta', we represent 'John and Mary live in Atlanta' as J & M. Where A is 'Bob visited Australia' and N is 'Bob visited New Zealand', we represent 'Bob visited Australia and New Zealand' as A & N.

We use ∨ to represent 'or', but we also use it to represent 'unless'. 'Quincy went to the movies or he went to the baseball game' and 'Quincy went to the movies unless he went to the baseball game' should be represented in exactly the same way: M ∨ B.

The disjunction symbol ∨ always means *inclusive* disjunction. That is, P ∨ Q indicates that P could be true or Q could be true or both P and Q could be true. But sometimes we want to represent *exclusive* or, meaning that one of P and Q is true but not both. Then we must augment the ∨. We would normally understand the sentence 'You or your ex-spouse may take a deduction for your dependent child' to mean one or the other of you may take the deduction, but you can't both take the deduction. We would symbolize this as (Y ∨ S) & ~(Y & S), that is, you may take the deduction or your ex-spouse may take the deduction but it is not the case that you can take the deduction *and* your ex-spouse can take the deduction.

We use P → Q to represent all of the following sentence forms:

If P, then Q.
If P, Q.
Q if P.
Q provided that P.
P only if Q.

It is worth taking a careful look at the last of these. We call the part of sentence that goes on the left side of the → symbol the *antecedent* of the conditional, and we call the part that goes on the right side the *consequent*. The word 'if' by itself marks the antecedent of a conditional, but the words 'only if' marks the consequent.

We also use → to represent *necessary* and *sufficient* conditions. Necessary conditions for something go in the consequent of a conditional and sufficient conditions go in the antecedent. So 'Good grades are a necessary condition for getting into medical school' becomes M → G and 'Being born in the United States is a sufficient condition for being a United States citizen' becomes 'B → C'.

We use ↔ to represent situations where the two assertions flanking the ↔ must both have the same truth value, that is, where both must be true or both must be false. So we use P ↔ Q to represent the following sentence forms:

P is a necessary condition for Q.
P if and only if Q.
P if but only if Q.
P just in case Q.

## Summary of Rules for Constructing True-Trees

| P & Q √ | P ∨ Q √ | P → Q √ | P ↔ Q √ |
|---------|---------|---------|---------|
| P | / \ | / \ | / \ |
| Q | P Q | ~P Q | P ~P |
| | | | Q ~Q |

| ~ (P & Q) √ | ~ (P ∨ Q) √ | ~ (P → Q) √ | ~ (P ↔ Q) √ | ~ ~ P √ |
|-------------|-------------|-------------|-------------|---------|
| / \ | ~P | P | / \ | P |
| ~P ~Q | ~Q | ~Q | P ~P | |
| | | | ~Q Q | |

## Truth Tree Exercises

Symbolize the following arguments and then construct truth-trees to determine if they are valid.

1. Mary took geometry and calculus in high school, but Linda didn't take geometry or calculus. If they had both gone to Lincoln High, they would both have taken calculus. So they didn't both go to Lincoln High.
2. Henry didn't fire the gun. Otherwise, he would have had gun powder residue on his hands. If he had gun powder residue on his hands, the paraffin test would have revealed it. But the paraffin test was negative.
3. A necessary condition for the car to start is a good battery. If the lights work and the horn works, then the battery is good. The lights and horn work. So the car will start.
4. If determinism is true, we can not do other than we do, hence we are not responsible for what we do. If indeterminism is true, then human actions are random, hence not free, hence we are not responsible for what we do. Either determinism or indeterminism is true. Therefore, we are not responsible for what we do.

5. People are different from animals either in kind or in degree. If we are different in kind, then there should be at least one characteristic we obviously have that animals don't. There is no obvious difference; therefore we must be different in degree. But if we are only different from animals in degree then we're essentially just animals.

6. I'm buying my mother a new watch for Christmas; but if I buy the watch, I can't afford the table saw my father has been wanting. If I can't get him the table saw, I can still get him books or a new jacket. If I get him books, I can afford a gift for my favorite aunt. If I buy him a jacket, I cannot. I want to give my aunt a Christmas present. So I will buy books for my father.

# Venn Diagrams

## Donald Nute

### Constructing Venn Diagrams

A Venn diagram provides a way to represent information about individuals and groups. In English, some of the kinds of information conveyed by Venn diagrams is expressed using quantifier terms such as `all', `some', and `none'. We use regions labeled with capital letters to represent groups and we use lowercase letters to represent individuals. Together, these components give us a visual representation of the relations we are interested in. By constructing a diagram that represents some initial set of relations, we can often immediately deduce other relations from the diagram. These include relations between groups as well as membership of particular individuals in groups.

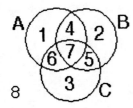

**Figure VENN-1**

The basic form of the Venn diagram is three intersecting circles inside a box. We have an example of this basic form in Figure VENN-1. In this diagram, each of the circles represents a group of individuals or objects that have some common property or characteristic. We can think of the circles as a fence drawn around these individuals. Each of the numbered regions formed by the intersection of the circles also represents a group. We normally label the circles with a capital letter that stands for the features the things in the circle have in common. Let A stand for Albanians, B stand for barbers, and C stand for cello players. Then in Figure VENN-1, anything in regions 1, 4, 6, and 7 is an Albanian, anything in regions 4 and 7 is an Albanian barber, and anything in region 7 is an Albanian barber that plays the cello. Notice that region 8 outside all the circles is where we would find those individuals that are not Albanians, barbers, or cello players.

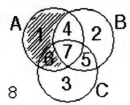

**Figure VENN-2**

We show that a region is empty by shading it. For example, in Figure VENN-2 we have shaded regions 1 and 6 to show that they are empty. What exactly does this mean in terms of our three properties? If regions 1 and 6 are empty, then anything in circle A must be in regions 4 and 7. But regions 4 and 7 are also inside circle B. So anything in circle A must also be in circle B. Or to put is another way, all Albanians are barbers.

This gives us a method for representing the information given in an English sentence of the form `All S are P', where S is the subject of the sentence and P is the predicate. We draw a Venn diagram and label one of the circles S and another P. Then we shade the part of the circle labeled S that is outside the circle labeled P. Sometimes, though, the subject of the English sentence is not represented by an entire circle. Take for example the sentence `All Albanian barbers play the cello'. There is no circle in our diagram representing Albanian barbers. Instead, they are represented by the two regions 4 and 7. What the English sentence says is that everything in these two regions is a cello player, i.e., is inside circle C. But region 4 is outside circle C. So to show that all Albanian barbers play the cello, we must shade region 4 as in Figure VENN-3. In general, then, to show that all S are P, we identify the region in the diagram corresponding to S (call this the S-region) and shade any part of this region that is outside the P-region.

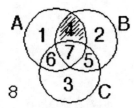

**Figure VENN-3**

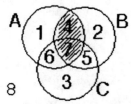

**Figure VENN-4**

What information do we represent if we shade regions 4 and 7 as in Figure VENN-4? It tells us that the intersection of the Albanian circle and the barber circle is empty. So no Albanians are barbers. Conversely, no barbers are Albanians. How would we then represent the information that no Albanian barbers are cello players? We would find the region that represents the Albanian barbers (i.e., the football-shaped region made up of regions 4 and 7) and shade the portion of that region where cello players might be found (i.e., the part inside circle C). In general, to represent an English sentence of the form `No S are P', we shade the intersection of the S-region and the P-region.

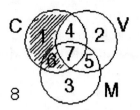

**Figure VENN-5**

People often find the word `only' confusing. Consider the sentence `Only citizens can vote'. How would we represent this in a Venn diagram? The first idea most people have is that we shade the part of the citizen-region outside the voter-region. Look at Figure VENN-5 where C stands for citizens, V for voters, and M for minors (in this case, persons under 18). If we follow our first instinct and shade all of the C-region outside the V-region, what we end up saying is that all citizens can vote, including minor citizens. There is no non-shaded part of the minor-citizen-region outside the voter-region. Something has gone wrong. It's true that only citizens can vote, but it certainly isn't true that all citizens (including minors) can vote. We have represented something that we did not intend to represent.

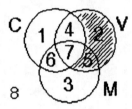

**Figure VENN-6**

Let's think about this further. If only citizens are voters, then all voters must be citizens. What we want to do, then, is shade all of the voter-region that is outside the citizen-region as in Figure VENN-6. And in general, to represent `Only S are P', you should shade all of the P-region outside the S-region. Perhaps the safest way to remember this is just to reverse an `only' and change it to an `all' whenever you see it: `Only S are P' is diagrammed the same way as `All P are S'.

Shading, then, is the operation we use to represent the information that some region of a Venn diagram is empty. But how do we show that a region is occupied? We will use letters to represent individuals and put those letters in the regions they occupy. Since we are using capital letters to represent properties or features of things, we will use lower case letters to represent individuals. Sometimes we will know something about a particular individual. We might know, for example, that George is a barber who plays the cello. We can use the letter g to represent George in a diagram. Since we know who g stands for, we say that it is a constant. Other times, we may only know that something or other is in a region, for example, that there must be Albanian barbers although we don't know who they are. Then we will use an x, y, or z as a variable that stands for one of these unknown Albanian barbers.

To show that George is a cello-playing barber, we need to put a g in every part of the cello-playing-barber-region, i.e., in every part of the intersection of circles B and C. So we put a g in regions 5 and 7. We also want to show that something is an Albanian barber; so we put x's in regions 4 and 7. The result is Figure VENN-7.

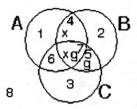

**Figure VENN-7**

From Figure VENN-7, we can't tell whether George is Albanian. He could be in either region 5 or 7. If he is in region 7, he is Albanian. But if he is in region 5, he is not. Suppose we learn that George and Ellen are not Albanian. We represent this new information about George by crossing out the g in region 7. But we don't have any e's in the diagram; so we need to find another way to show that Ellen is not Albanian. We do this by putting an e in each region outside circle A, i.e., in regions 2, 3, 5, and 8. The result of these changes is shown in Figure VENN-8.

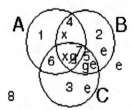

**Figure VENN-8**

We show that a region in a Venn diagram is empty, then, by shading that region. And we show that individuals either have or do not have various properties and features by adding constants or variables to the diagram or by crossing out constants and variables. We can also read information from a Venn diagram. We find out that English sentences using the quantifiers `all', `no', and `only' are true by noticing which regions of the diagram are shaded, and we find out that sentences using names or the quantifiers `some' and `not all' are true by noticing where constants and variables are located in the diagram.

Look again at Figure VENN-8. If we learn that no Albanians play the cello, we will shade the intersection of circles A and C. This gives Figure VENN-9 which represents the following information:

1. George is a cello-playing barber.
2. Some Albanians are barbers.
3. George and Ellen are not Albanians.
4. No Albanians play the cello.

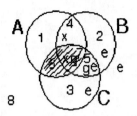

**Figure VENN-9**

But the diagram gives us more information. Notice that we have an x in the barber-region but no x in any non-shaded part of the cello-player-region. That means that there is someone who is a barber that does not play the cello, i.e., that some barbers do not play the cello. Can we also conclude that some cello players are not barbers? We see that there is an e in the cello-player-region 3, which is outside the barber-region. But there are also e's inside the barber region. We know that Ellen is in region 2, 3, 5, or 8, but we can't locate her any better than that. So we cannot conclude that some cell players are not barbers.

On the next two pages, we have a summary of these and other principles for representing information in Venn diagrams and for reading information from Venn diagrams. The only way to really get a feel for how we can use this method to form new conclusions from the information we have is by practicing. After the summaries of principles, you will find some exercises and practice quizzes. Notice that we can use a Venn diagram either to test whether an argument is reliable or to extract new information from the information we already have. So Venn diagrams are both a tool for evaluating arguments and a tool for problem solving.

## Summary of Principles for Constructing Venn Diagrams

| *To represent this statement in your diagram...* | *do this.* |
|---|---|
| 1. All S are P. | Shade all of the S-region outside the P-region. |
| 2. Some S are P. | Pick a letter near the end of the alphabet that does not occur in the diagram and write it in every part of the intersection of the S-region and the P-region. |
| 3. No S are P. | Shade the intersection of the S-region and the P-region. |
| 4. Some S are not P. | Pick a letter near the end of the alphabet that does not occur in the diagram and write it in every part of the S-region that is outside the P-region. |
| 5. Only S are P. | Shade every part of the P-region that is outside the S-region. |

| | |
|---|---|
| 6. Nothing is P. | Shade all of the P-region. |
| 7. c is a P. | If there are no c's in the diagram, write c in every part of the P-region. If there are c's in the diagram, blot out every c that is outside the P-region. |
| 8. c is not a P. | If there are no c's in the diagram, write c in every area that is not in P. Don't forget the region outside all the circles! If there are c's in the diagram, blot out every c that is inside the P-region. |

## Summary of Principles for Reading Venn Diagrams

| *This statement is guaranteed by a Venn diagram...* | *if the diagram satisfies this condition.* |
|---|---|
| 1. All S are P. | Every part of the S-region that is not also a part of the P-region is shaded. |
| 2. Some S is P. | There is a letter that occurs in the intersection of the S-region and the P-region that doesn't occur in any non-shaded area outside the intersection of the S-region and the P-region. |
| 3. No S is P. | The intersection of the S-region and the P-region is shaded. |
| 4. Some S is not P. | There is a letter that occurs only in the S-region that doesn't occur in any non-shaded part of the P-region. |
| 5. Only S are P. | Every part of the P-region that is not in the S-region is shaded. |
| 6. Nothing is P. | The entire P-region is shaded. |
| 7. c is a P. | c occurs in some non-shaded part of the P-region and doesn't occur in any non-shaded part of the diagram outside the P-region. |
| 8. c is not a P. | c occurs in some non-shaded part of the diagram but doesn't occur in any non-shaded part of the P-region. |

## Exercises on Venn Diagrams

Use Venn diagrams to determine whether the grounds guarantee the claims in the following arguments. To do this, represent the grounds in the Venn diagram, then see if the diagram guarantees the claim.

1. Only dragons breathe fire, and all dragons fly. So all flying dragons breathe fire.
2. Some sea creatures are mammals, and some mammals have well-developed social structures. So some sea creatures have well-developed social structures.
3. All flying mammals eat insects. Some mammals do not eat insects. So some mammals do not fly.
4. Bats are flying mammals. The Red Baron is a flying mammal. So the Red Baron is a bat.
5. Penguins are found only in Antarctica. No cichlasomas are found in Antarctica. So penguins are not cichlasomas.
6. All professional athletes are overpaid. Bruce Jenner is an athlete, but he is not a professional. So he is not overpaid.
7. No genius is tidy. Some children are geniuses. So some children are not tidy.
8. Only hard-workers pass this course. Some of my students are hard workers. So some of my students will pass this course.
9. None but the beautiful may join the club. I am not beautiful. All the snobs are in the club. So I am not a snob.
10. Tom and Dick are both singers, but only Tom sings opera. Only opera singers sing at the Metropolitan, and even some opera singers don't sing at the Metropolitan. So Dick doesn't sing at the Metropolitan.
11. All rich people drive big cars. A Cadillac is a big car. So Jones must be rich, because he drives a Cadillac.
12. Only flying mammals have sonar. My pet is a mammal and it doesn't have sonar. So it doesn't fly.
13. Some fish care for their young. No fish that care for their young are nothobranches. So some nothobranches are not fish.
14. All beautiful actresses are famous. Jane is beautiful, but she is not an actress. So Jane is not famous.
15. Some people like okra and some don't. People who like okra are strange. So not all people are strange (i.e., some people are not strange).
16. All poor people eat at McDonald's. Some people eat at McDonald's and some don't. So some people are poor.
17. Only actors live in Los Angeles. Some people who live in Los Angeles are rich. So some actors are rich.
18. Some students goof off. No student who goofs off passes my course. So some students do not pass my course.
19. Ivan is a Russian. All Russians who are not communists are traitors. Ivan is not a traitor. So Ivan is a communist.
20. Bradley was a philosopher. All philosophers are either idealists or realist. Bradley was not a realist, so he was an idealist.
21. Not all kangaroos are grey. Grey kangaroos are not endangered. So not all kangaroos are endangered.
22. All elephants and rhinos are pachyderms. Some pachyderms are not rhinos. So some rhinos are not elephants.
23. Some mushrooms are non-poisonous. Only death's cap mushrooms are poisonous. So some mushrooms are not death's cap mushrooms.

# Unit III

*In reality, all arguments from experience are founded on the similarity which we discover among natural objects, and by which we are induced to expect effects similar to those which we have found to follow from such objects.*
---David Hume

*Though analogy is often misleading, it is the least misleading thing we have.*
---Samuel Butler

*Analogies prove nothing, that is quite true, but they can make one feel more at home.*
---Sigmund Freud

# CHAPTER 11

# ANALOGY AND PROBABLE INFERENCE

## 11.1 ARGUMENT BY ANALOGY

The preceding chapters have dealt with deductive arguments, which are valid if their premisses establish their conclusions *demonstratively*, but invalid otherwise. There are very many good and important arguments, however, whose conclusions cannot be proved with certainty. Many causal connections in which we rightly place confidence can be established only with *probability*—though the degree of probability may be very high. Thus we can say without reservation that smoking is a cause of cancer, but we cannot ascribe to that knowledge the kind of certainty that we ascribe to our knowledge that the conclusion of a valid deductive argument is entailed by its premisses. On that deductive standard, one distinguished medical investigator observes, "No one will ever be able to *prove* that smoking causes cancer, or that anything causes anything. Theoretically, you can never *prove* anything."[1] Deductive certainty is, indeed, too high a standard to impose when evaluating our knowledge of facts about the world.

In this and the following chapters we turn to the analysis of arguments that are not claimed to demonstrate the truth of their conclusions as following necessarily from their premisses, but are intended merely to support their conclusions as *probable*, or probably true. Arguments of this latter kind are generally called *inductive*, and they are radically different from the deductive variety. The fundamental distinction between deduction and induction was discussed at some length in our opening chapter. Part Two of this book has been devoted to deduction; Part Three will be devoted to induction.

---

[1]Bert Vogelstein, "So, Smoking Causes Cancer: This is News?" *New York Times*, 27 October 1996. (Emphasis added.)

Of all inductive arguments there is one type that is most commonly used: argument by *analogy.* Two examples of analogical arguments are these:

Some people look on preemployment testing of teachers as unfair—a kind of double jeopardy. "Teachers are already college graduates," they say. "Why should they be tested?" That's easy. Lawyers are college graduates and graduates of professional school, too, but they have to take a bar exam. And a number of other professions ask prospective members to prove that they know their stuff by taking and passing examinations: accountants, actuaries, doctors, architects. There is no reason why teachers shouldn't be required to do this too.[2]

We may observe a very great similitude between this earth which we inhabit, and the other planets, Saturn, Jupiter, Mars, Venus, and Mercury. They all revolve round the sun, as the earth does, although at different distances and in different periods. They borrow all their light from the sun, as the earth does. Several of them are known to revolve around their axis like the earth, and by that means, must have a like succession of day and night. Some of them have moons, that serve to give them light in the absence of the sun, as our moon does to us. They are all, in their motions, subject to the same law of gravitation, as the earth is. From all this similitude, it is not unreasonable to think that those planets may, like our earth, be the habitation of various orders of living creatures. There is some probability in this conclusion from analogy.[3]

Most of our own everyday inferences are by analogy. Thus, I infer that a new computer will serve me well on the grounds that I got very good service from a computer earlier purchased from the same manufacturer. If a new book by a certain author is called to my attention, I infer that I will enjoy reading it on the basis of having read and enjoyed other books by that author. Analogy is at the basis of most of our ordinary reasonings from past experience to what the future will hold. Not an explicitly formulated argument, of course, but something very much like analogical inference is presumably involved in the conduct of the burned child who shuns the fire.

None of these arguments is certain or demonstratively valid. None of their conclusions follows with logical necessity from their premises. It is logically possible that what is appropriate for judging the employability of lawyers and doctors is not appropriate for judging the employability of teachers. It is logically possible that earth may be the only inhabited planet, that the new computer may not work well at all, and that I may find my favorite author's latest book to be intolerably dull. It is even logically possible that one fire may burn and not another. But no argument by analogy is intended to be mathematically certain. Analogical arguments are not to be classified as either valid or invalid. Probability is all that is claimed for them.

In addition to their frequent use in arguments, analogies very often are used nonargumentatively, for the purpose of lively description. The literary

---

[2]Albert Shanker, "Testing Teachers," *New York Times*, 8 January 1995.
[3]Thomas Reid, *Essays on the Intellectual Powers of Man*, Essay 1, 1785.

uses of analogy in metaphor and simile are tremendously helpful to the writer who strives to create a vivid picture in the reader's mind. For example:

> Life on this earth is not only without rational significance, but also apparently unintentional. The cosmic laws seem to have been set going for some purpose quite unrelated to human existence. Man is thus a sort of accidental by-product, as the sparks are an accidental by-product of the horseshoe a blacksmith fashions on his anvil. The sparks are far more brilliant than the horseshoe, but all the same they remain essentially meaningless.[4]

Analogy also is used in explanation, where something that may be unfamiliar to the reader is made somewhat more intelligible through being compared to something else, presumably more familiar, to which it has certain similarities. When the Director of the Genome Center at the Massachusetts Institute of Technology Dr. Eric Lander sought to explain the great eventual impact of the human genome project, analogy was one of the devices he used to enhance the understanding of those unfamiliar with genetic research:

> The genome project is wholly analogous to the creation of the periodic table in chemistry. Just as Mendeleev's arrangement of the chemical elements in the periodic table made coherent a previously unrelated mass of data, so the tens of thousands of genes in present-day organisms will all turn out to be made from combinations of a much smaller number of simpler genetic modules or elements, the primordial genes, so to speak.[5]

The use of analogies in description and explanation is not the same as their use in argument, though in some cases it may not be easy to decide which use is intended. But whether used argumentatively or otherwise, analogy is not difficult to define. **To draw an analogy between two or more entities is to indicate one or more respects in which they are similar.**

This explains what an analogy is, but there is still the problem of characterizing an argument by analogy. Let us examine a particular analogical argument and analyze its structure. Take the simplest of the examples cited thus far, the argument that my new computer will serve me well because my old computer, purchased from the same manufacturer, gave good service. The two things said to be similar are the two computers. There are three points of analogy involved, three respects in which the two entities are said to resemble each other: first, in being computers; second, in being purchased from the same manufacturer; and third, in serving me well.

The three points of analogy do not play identical roles in the argument, however. The first two occur in the premisses, whereas the third occurs both in the premisses and in the conclusion. In quite general terms, the given argument may be described as having premisses that assert, first, that two things are similar in two respects and, second, that one of those things has a further

---

[4]Bertrand Russell, *Religion and Science* (London, Oxford, 1949).
[5]Quoted in an interview in the *New York Times*, 10 September 1996.

characteristic, from which the conclusion is drawn that the other thing also has that further characteristic.

Analogical argument is one of the most fundamental tools of appellate courts. Rather than laying down strict rules or principles in advance, judges very often reason that because two cases—an earlier one that has been decided, and the case at hand to be decided—share relevant characteristics, they should share the same outcome. Thus, once it has been decided that members of the Ku Klux Klan may not be restrained from speaking, a court is likely to conclude by analogical reasoning that the Nazi Party cannot be stopped from parading.[6] This argument from precedent, when it is spelled out, will identify and emphasize those respects in which the older case and the current case are closely alike.

Not every analogical argument need concern exactly two things or exactly three different characteristics, of course. Thus the argument by Thomas Reid presented earlier, suggesting that other planets may well be inhabited, draws analogies among six things (the then-known planets) in some eight respects. Apart from these numerical differences, however, all analogical arguments have the same general structure or pattern. **Every analogical inference proceeds from the similarity of two or more things in one or more respects to the similarity of those things in some further respect.** Schematically, where $a$, $b$, $c$, and $d$ are any entities and $P$, $Q$, and $R$ are any attributes or "respects," an analogical argument may be represented as having the form

> $a$, $b$, $c$, $d$ all have the attributes $P$ and $Q$.
> $a$, $b$, $c$ all have the attribute $R$.
> Therefore $d$ probably has the attribute $R$.

In identifying, and especially in appraising, analogical arguments, it may be found helpful to recast them into this form.

### Exercises

All of the following passages contain analogies. Distinguish those that contain analogical arguments from those that make nonargumentative uses of analogy.

### Example:

1.   A Man ought no more to value himself for being wiser than a Woman, if he owes his Advantage to a better Education, than he ought to boast of his Courage for beating a Man when his hands were bound.

     —Mary Astell, *An Essay in Defence of the Female Sex*, 1721

---

[6]See Cass R. Sunstein, *Legal Reasoning and Political Conflict* (New York: Oxford University Press, 1996).

## Solution:

This is an analogical argument. The analogy drawn here is between beating a man when his hands are bound and being wiser than a woman as a consequence of a better education, one party having an enormous advantage in both cases. In the first case, it is plain that one with such an advantage ought not to boast of his courage; in the second case (this argument concludes), it is equally inappropriate for one with such an advantage to boast of his relative wisdom.

2. "I'm not anti-Semitic, I'm just anti-Zionist" is the equivalent of "I'm not anti-American, I just think the United States shouldn't exist."

   —Benjamin Netanyahu, *A Place Among the Nations*,
   (Bantam Books, 1993)

3. Marriage is in the same state as the Church: Both are becoming functionally defunct, as their preachers go about heralding a revival, eagerly chalking up converts in a day of dread. And just as God has been pronounced dead quite often but has this sneaky way of resurrecting himself, so everyone debunks marriage, yet ends up married.

   —Shulamith Firestone, *The Dialectic of Sex:*
   *The Case for Feminist Revolution*

4. It is true that science has become so specialized, even a good education in basic science does not prepare one to be expert in all science. But the same is true of nonscientific pursuits. That historians, for example, have become experts in particular periods or areas (the history of the military, perhaps, or of science or economics) has not dissuaded us from teaching history.

   —Bruce J. Sobol, *Current Issues and Enduring Questions*
   (Boston: St. Martin's Press, 1990)

*5. Studies show that girls get better grades in high school and college than boys—yet only about 35 percent of National Merit Scholarship winners are girls. The Executive Director of FairTest contends that the "inequity is due solely to gender bias in the test used to select eligible students." But the spokeswoman for the National Merit Scholarship Corporation, Elaine Detweiler, replies "We don't really know why girls do worse on the exams. To blame the test for the difference between how boys and girls perform is like blaming a yardstick that boys are taller than girls."

   —"Merit Test Defended," *Los Angeles Times*, 26 May 1993

6. The famous chemist and biologist, Justus von Liebig, dismissed the germ theory with a shrug of the shoulders, regarding Pasteur's view that microbes could cause fermentation as ridiculous and naive as the opinion of a child "who would explain the rapidity of

the Rhine current by attributing it to the violent movement of the many millwheels at Maintz."

—René Dubos, *Pasteur and Modern Science*

7. Talking about Christianity without saying anything about sin is like discussing gardening without saying anything about weeds.

—The Rev. Lord Soper, quoted in the *New York Times*, 24 Dec 1998

8. Men and women may have different reproductive strategies, but neither can be considered inferior or superior to the other, any more than a bird's wings can be considered superior or inferior to a fish's fins.

—David M. Buss, "Where is Fancy Bred? In the Genes or in the Head?" the *New York Times*, 1 June 1999

9. "This is a matter of national spirit," said Marjorie Wilson, coordinator of the Kangaroo Protection Cooperative, an Australian wildlife group. "We believe here that we have enough meat in this country to satisfy people without them having to eat their national symbol. You Americans don't cook your bald eagles, do you?"

—"Battling over a National Symbol," *New York Times*, 10 July 1995

*10. One sure thing is that melting sea ice cannot be implicated in the coastal flooding that many global warming models have projected. Just as melting ice cubes do not cause a glass of water to overflow, melting sea ice does not increase oceanic volume. Any future rise in sea level would result from glaciers melting on land, of which there has been little evidence to date.

—Walter Gibbs, "Research Predicts Summer Doom for Northern Icecap," *New York Times*, 11 July 2000.

11. Thomas Henry Huxley, Charles Darwin's nineteenth-century disciple, presented this analogy: "Consciousness would appear to be related to the mechanism of the body simply as a collateral product of its working and to be completely without any power of modifying that working, as the steam whistle which accompanies the work of a locomotive is without influence upon its machinery."

12. The Elgin Marbles—17 figures and 56 panels that once decorated the Parthenon, on the Acropolis in Athens—were taken from the Parthenon in 1801 by Thomas Bruce, the seventh Earl of Elgin, and brought to the British Museum, in London. The Greeks say that he stole them; the British say that they were properly acquired, by purchase. Some Britons have urged that the Marbles be returned to Greece in time for the Olympic Games to be held in Athens in 2004. Said one of the leaders of the Labor Party: "The Parthenon without the Elgin Marbles is like a smile missing a tooth."

13. The Feminists decided to examine the institution of marriage as it is set up by law in order to find out whether or not it did operate in

women's favor. It became increasingly clear to us that the institution of marriage "protects" women in the same way that the institution of slavery was said to "protect" blacks—that is, that the word "protection" in this case is simply a euphemism for oppression.

—Sheila Cronan, "Marriage," in Anne Koedt, Ellen Levine, and Anita Rapone, eds., *Radical Feminism*

14. Wittgenstein used to compare thinking with swimming: just as in swimming our bodies have a natural tendency to float on the surface so that it requires great physical exertion to plunge to the bottom, so in thinking it requires great mental exertion to force our minds away from the superficial, down into the depth of a philosophical problem.

—George Pitcher, *The Philosophy of Wittgenstein*

*15. A person without a goal is like a computer without a program. And that's an ugly piece of furniture.

—Steve Danish, "Getting a Life," *New York Times*, March 1998

16. The quest for usable energy from fusion involves the use of interlocked magnetic fields to contain very hot (180 million degrees Fahrenheit) and highly compressed (to a density 20 times that of lead) electrically charged plasma (a kind of gas) within a vacuum chamber. The plasma must never touch the solid walls of its container, for if it does it instantly loses its heat and can never be coaxed into undergoing fusion. One scientific report put the problem this way:

Everything depends on keeping the plasma's magnetic bottle tightly stoppered. . . . [but] confining a dollop of super-hot compressed plasma has proved to be harder than compressing and shaping a blob of jelly using only rubber bands. Each clever idea of the plasma physicists for solving this problem has been matched by a new challenge.

—Malcolm W. Browne, "Reviving the Quest to Tame the Energy of the Stars," *New York Times*, 8 June 1999.

17. It is important that we make clear at this point what definition is and what can be attained by means of it. It seems frequently to be credited with a creative power; but all it accomplishes is that something is marked out in sharp relief and designated by a name. Just as the geographer does not create a sea when he draws boundary lines and says: the part of the ocean's surface bounded by these lines I am going to call the Yellow Sea, so too the mathematician cannot really create anything by his defining.

—Gottlob Frege, *The Basic Laws of Arithmetic*

18. Children in school are like children at the doctor's. He can talk himself blue in the face about how much good his medicine is going to do them; all they think of is how much it will hurt or how bad it will taste. Given their own way, they would have none of it.

So the valiant and resolute band of travelers I thought I was leading toward a much hoped-for destination turned out instead to be more like convicts in a chain gang, forced under threat of punishment to move along a rough path leading nobody knew where and down which they could see hardly more than a few steps ahead. School feels like this to children: it is a place where *they* make you go and where *they* tell you to do things and where *they* try to make your life unpleasant if you don't do them or don't do them right.

—John Holt, *How Children Fail*

19. I simply can't imagine the world will ever be normal again for us. I do talk about "after the war," but it's as if I were talking about a castle in the air, something that can never come true.

I see the eight of us in the Annex as if we were a patch of blue sky surrounded by menacing black clouds. The perfectly round spot on which we're standing is still safe, but the clouds are moving in on us, and the ring between us and the approaching danger is being pulled tighter and tighter. We're surrounded by darkness and danger, and in our desperate search for a way out we keep bumping into each other. We look at the fighting down below and the peace and beauty up above. In the meantime, we've been cut off by the dark mass of clouds, so that we can go neither up nor down. It looms before us like an impenetrable wall, trying to crush us, but not yet able to. I can only cry out and implore, "Oh, ring, ring, open wide and let us out!"

—Anne Frank, from *The Diary of a Young Girl*, 8 November 1943

*20. Unfortunately, the diary [of H. L. Mencken] reveals a man who was shockingly anti-Semitic and racist, to the point where his stature as a giant of American letters may be in danger. . . . I would draw a comparison with Richard Wagner, a virulent anti-Semite. One can still listen to Wagner's operas and appreciate their artistic beauty. The work is separated from the man. Or is it?

—Gwinn Owens, "Mencken—Getting a Bum Rap?"
*New York Times*, 13 December 1989

## 11.2 APPRAISING ANALOGICAL ARGUMENTS

No argument by analogy is ever deductively valid, in the sense of having its conclusion follow from its premises with logical necessity, but some analogical arguments are more cogent than others. Analogical arguments are evaluated as better or worse depending on the degree of probability with which their conclusions may be affirmed.

Two commonplace examples will help us to see what serves to make analogical arguments more (or less) effective. Suppose you choose to purchase a given pair of shoes because other pairs like it have given you satisfaction in the past; and suppose you select a dog of a given breed because other dogs of that same breed have exhibited the characteristics that you prize. In both cases analogical arguments have been relied upon. To appraise the strength of these sample arguments, and indeed all analogical arguments, six criteria may be distinguished.

1. **Number of entities.** If my past experience with shoes of a certain kind is limited to only one pair that I wore and liked, I will be disappointed with an apparently similar pair that I find flawed in unexpected ways. But if I have repeatedly purchased shoes just like those, I may reasonably suppose that the next pair will be as good as the ones worn earlier. Several experiences of the same kind with the same item will support the conclusion— that the purchase will be satisfying—much more than will a single instance. Each instance may be thought of as an additional entity, and the *number* of entities is the first criterion in evaluating an analogical argument.

   *In general, the larger the number of entities—that is, cases in our past experience—the stronger the argument.* But there is no simple ratio between that number and the probability of the conclusion. Six happy experiences with golden retrievers, intelligent and sweet-tempered dogs, will lead one to conclude that the next golden retriever will be intelligent and sweet-tempered also. But the conclusion of the analogical argument having six instances in its premisses will not be exactly three times as probable as a similar argument with two such instances in its premisses. Increasing the number of entities is important, but other factors enter as well.

2. **Variety of the instances in the premisses.** If my previous purchases of those good shoes had been both from a department store and a specialty store, and had been made both in New York and in California, by both mail order and direct sale, I may be confident that it is the shoes themselves and not their seller that accounts for my satisfaction. If my previous golden retrievers were both males and females, acquired both as puppies from breeders and as adults from the humane society, I may be more confident that it is their breed—not their sex or age or source—that accounts for my earlier satisfaction.

   We understand this criterion intuitively: *The more dissimilar the instances mentioned only in the premisses of the analogical argument, the stronger is the argument.*

3. **Number of similar respects.** Among the instances in the premisses there may have been various similarities: perhaps the shoes were of the same style, had the same price, were made of the same sort of leather; perhaps the dogs were of the same breed, came from the same breeder at the same age, and so on. All the respects in which the instances in the premisses are like one another, and also like the instance in the conclusion, increase the probability that the instance in the conclusion will have that further attribute at which the argument is aimed—giving great satisfaction in the case of the new shoes, being of a sweet disposition in the case of a new dog.

   This criterion also is rooted in common sense: *The greater the number of respects in which the entity in the conclusion is similar to the entities in the premisses, the more probable is that conclusion.* But again, of course, there is no simple numerical ratio between that conclusion and the number of similar respects identified.

4. **Relevance.** As important as the *number* of respects shared is the *kind* of respects in which the instances in the premisses are like the instance in the conclusion. If the new pair of shoes, like the previous pairs, is purchased on a Tuesday, that is a likeness that will have no bearing on the satisfaction they give; but if the new pair, like all the previous pairs, had the same manufacturer, that will of course count heavily. *Respects add to the force of the argument when they are relevant* (as style of shoe, and price, and material surely are)—*and a single highly relevant factor contributes more to the argument than a host of irrelevant similarities.*

There will sometimes be disagreement about which attributes really are relevant in establishing the likelihood of our conclusion. But the *meaning* of relevance itself is not in dispute. One attribute is relevant to another when it is connected to that other, when there is some kind of *causal relation* between them. That is why identifying causal connections of one kind or another is critical in analogical arguments, and why establishing such connections is often crucial in determining the admissibility of evidence, as relevant or irrelevant, in a court of law.

Analogical arguments can be probable whether they go from cause to effect or from effect to cause. They can even be probable when the attribute in the premiss is neither the cause nor the effect of the conclusion's attribute, provided both are the effect of the same cause. A doctor, noting the presence of a certain symptom in her patient, may predict another symptom accurately not because either symptom is the cause of the other, but because they are jointly caused by the same disorder. The color of a manufactured product is most often irrelevant to function, but it may serve as a relevant respect in an argument when that color is very unusual, and shared by the entities in the premisses and the conclusion. The color itself may contribute nothing to the function of the product—but it may serve in argument if it is known to be an attribute of the manufacturing process of a unique producer.

The causal connections that are the key to the evaluation of analogical arguments can be discovered only empirically, by observation and experiment. The general theory of empirical investigation is the central concern of inductive logic, and will be discussed at length in the chapters that follow.

5. **Disanalogies.** A disanalogy is a point of difference, a respect in which the case we are reasoning about in our conclusion is distinguishable from the cases upon which the argument is based. Returning to the example of the shoes: if the pair we plan to buy looks like those we had earlier owned, but is in fact much cheaper and made by a different company, those disanalogies will give us reason to doubt the satisfaction they will provide.

What was earlier said about relevance is important here also. Disanalogies undermine analogical arguments when the points of difference identified are relevant, causally connected to the outcome we are seeking. Investors often purchase shares of a stock mutual fund on the basis of its successful "track record," reasoning that since earlier purchases resulted in capital appreciation, a future purchase will do so as well. But if we learn that the person who had managed the fund during the period of its profitability has just been replaced, we confront a disanalogy substantially reducing the strength of that analogical argument.

*Disanalogies weaken analogical arguments.* They will therefore be commonly employed in *attacking* an analogical argument. As critics we may try to show that the case in the conclusion is different in important ways from the earlier cases, and that what was true of them is not likely to be true of it. In the law, where the uses of analogy are pervasive, some earlier case (or cases) will commonly be offered to a court as a precedent for deciding the case at hand. The argument is analogical. Opposing counsel will seek to *distinguish* the case at hand from the earlier cases; that is, counsel will seek to show that because there is some critical difference between the facts in the case at hand, and the facts in those earlier cases, they do not serve as good precedents in the present matter. If the differences are great, if the disanalogy is indeed critical, it may succeed in demolishing the analogical argument that had been put forward.

Because disanalogies are the primary weapon against an analogical argument, whatever can ward off any potential disanalogies will strengthen that argument. This explains why variety among the instances in the premisses adds force to an argument, as noted previously in the second criterion. The more the instances in the premisses vary from one to another, the less likely it is that the critic can point to some disanalogy between all of them and the conclusion that will weaken the argument. To illustrate: Kim Kumar comes to a university as a first year student; ten others from her secondary school had successfully completed studies at the same university. We may argue analogically that she is likely to succeed as well. If all those other students are similar to one another in some respect that bears upon college study but differ from Kim in that respect, that disanalogy will undermine the argument for Kim's success. But if we learn that the ten successful predecessors varied among themselves in many ways—in economic background, in family relations, in religious affiliation, and so on, those differences among them ward off such potential disanalogies. The argument for Kim's success is fortified—as we saw earlier—if the other students from her school serving as premisses in the argument do not resemble each other closely, but exhibit substantial variety.

A confusion must be avoided: The principle that disanalogies weaken analogical arguments is to be contrasted with the principle that differences among the premisses strengthen such arguments. In the former, the differences are between the instances in the premisses and the instance in the conclusion; in the latter differences are among the instances in the premisses only. A disanalogy is a difference between the cases with which we have had experience and the case about which a conclusion is being drawn. That conclusion (we may say in presenting the disanalogy as refutation) is not warranted because circumstances in the critical case are not similar to circumstances in earlier cases. The analogy is said to be "strained" or "does not hold." But when we point to dissimilarities among the premisses we are strengthening the argument by saying, in effect, that the analogy has wide force, that it holds in cases like this and in other cases, and that therefore the respects in which the instances in the premisses vary are not relevant to the matter with which the conclusion is concerned.

In sum: Disanalogies undermine an analogical argument; dissimilarities among the premisses reinforce it. And both considerations are tied to the question of relevance: Disanalogies tend to show that there are relevant respects in which the case in the conclusion differs from those in the premisses; dissimilarities among the premisses tend to show that what might have been thought causally relevant to the attribute of interest is not really relevant at all.

Note that the very first criterion identified, pertaining to the *number* of entities among which the analogy is said to hold, is also linked to relevance. The greater the number of instances appealed to, the greater the number of dissimilarities likely to obtain among them. Increasing the number of entities is therefore desirable—but as the number of entities increases, the impact of each additional case is reduced, since the dissimilarity it may provide is the more likely to have been provided by earlier instances—in which case it will add little or nothing to the protection of the conclusion from damaging disanalogies.

6. **Claim that the conclusion makes.** Every argument makes the claim that its premisses give reasons to accept its conclusion. It is easy to see that the more one claims, the greater the burden of sustaining that claim, and that is obviously true for every analogical argument. The *modesty of the conclusion relative to the premisses* is critical in determining the merit of the inference.

If my friend gets 30 miles to the gallon from his new car, I may infer that were I to acquire a car of the same make and model I would get at least 20 miles to the gallon; that conclusion is modest and therefore very probable. Were my conclusion much bolder—say, that I would get at least 29 miles to the gallon—it would be less well supported by the evidence I have. In general, *the more modest the claim the less burden is placed upon the premisses and the stronger the argument; the bolder the claim the greater is burden on the premisses and the weaker the argument.*

An analogical argument is strengthened by reducing the claim made on the basis of the premisses affirmed, or by retaining the claim unchanged while supporting it with additional or more powerful premisses. Likewise, an analogical argument is weakened if its conclusion is made bolder while its premisses remain unchanged, or if the claim remains unchanged while the evidence in its support is found to exhibit greater frailty.

## Exercises

I. For each of the following arguments by analogy, six additional premisses are suggested. For each of these alternative premisses, decide whether its addition would make the resulting argument more or less probable. Identify the criterion of appraisal that justifies this judgment, and explain how that criterion applies to the given case.

**Example:**

1.  An investor has purchased one hundred shares of oil stock every December for the past five years. In every case the value of the stock has appreciated by about 15 percent a year, and it has paid regular dividends of about 8 percent a year on the price at which she bought it. This December she decides to buy another hundred shares of oil stock, reasoning that she will probably receive modest earnings while watching the value of her new purchase increase over the years.

    a.  Suppose that she had always purchased stock in eastern oil companies before, and plans to purchase stock in an eastern oil company this year too.

    b.  Suppose that she had purchased oil stocks every December for the past 15 years, instead of for only 5 years.

    c.  Suppose that the oil stocks previously purchased had gone up by 30 percent a year, instead of only 15 percent.

    d.  Suppose that her previous purchases of oil stock had been in foreign companies as well as in eastern, southern, and western American oil companies.

    e.  Suppose she learns that OPEC has decided to meet every month instead of every six months.

    f.  Suppose she discovers that tobacco stocks have just raised their dividend payments.

**Solution:**

    a.  More probable. **Number of similar respects.** The change provides an additional respect in which the instance in the conclusion is the same as those in the premisses.

    b.  More probable. **Number of entities.** With this change the number of entities in the premisses is substantially increased.

    c.  More probable. **Claim made by the conclusion.** With this change in the premisses, the conclusion, although unchanged, is now, relatively speaking, substantially more modest.

    d.  More probable. **Variety among the premisses.** With this change, the dissimilarity among the instances in the premisses is clearly established.

    e.  Less probable. **Disanalogy.** With this change in the premisses, a significant difference between the instance in the conclusion and the instances in the premisses is introduced.

    f.  Neither. **Relevance.** It is unlikely that the dividends paid by tobacco companies would have any relevance to the profitability of oil companies or the price of their shares.

2.  A faithful alumnus, heartened by State's winning its last four football games, decides to bet his money that State will win its next game, too.

    a.  Suppose that since the last game, State's outstanding quarterback was injured in practice and hospitalized for the remainder of the season.

    b.  Suppose that two of the last four games were played away, and that two of them were home games.

    c. Suppose that, just before the game, it is announced that a member of State's Chemistry Department has been awarded a Nobel Prize.

    d. Suppose that State had won its last *six* games rather than only four of them.

    e. Suppose that it has rained hard during each of the four preceding games, and that rain is forecast for next Saturday too.

    f. Suppose that each of the last four games was won by a margin of at least four touchdowns.

3. Although she was bored by the last few foreign films she saw, Charlene agrees to go to see another one this evening, fully expecting to be bored again.

    a. Suppose that Charlene also was bored by the last few American movies she saw.

    b. Suppose that the star of this evening's film has recently been accused of bigamy.

    c. Suppose that the last few foreign films seen by Charlene were Italian, and that tonight's film is Italian as well.

    d. Suppose that Charlene was so bored by the other foreign films that she actually fell asleep during the performance.

    e. Suppose that the last few foreign films she saw included an Italian, a French, an English, and a Swedish film.

    f. Suppose that tonight's film is a mystery, whereas all of those she saw before were comedies.

4. Bill has taken three history courses and found them very stimulating and valuable. So he signs up for another one, confidently expecting that it too will be worthwhile.

    a. Suppose that his previous history courses were in ancient history, modern European history, and American history.

    b. Suppose that his previous history courses had all been taught by the same professor that is scheduled to teach the present one.

    c. Suppose that his previous history courses all had been taught by Professor Smith, and the present one is taught by Professor Jones.

    d. Suppose that Bill had found his three previous history courses to be the most exciting intellectual experiences of his life.

    e. Suppose that his previous history courses had all met at 9 A.M., and that the present one is scheduled to meet at 9 A.M. also.

    f. Suppose that, in addition to the three history courses previously taken, Bill also had taken and enjoyed courses in anthropology, economics, political science, and sociology.

*5. Dr. Brown has stayed at the Queen's Hotel every fall for the past six years on her annual visit to New York, and she has been quite satisfied with her accommodations there. On her visit to New York this fall, Dr. Brown goes again to the Queen's Hotel, confidently expecting to enjoy her stay there again.

    a. Suppose that when she stayed at the Queen's Hotel before, she had occupied a single room twice, shared a double room twice, and twice occupied a suite.

b. Suppose that last spring a new manager had been put in charge of the Queen's Hotel.

c. Suppose that she had occupied a suite on all of her previous trips and is assigned a suite this time as well.

d. Suppose that on her previous trips she had come to New York by train, but this time she flew.

e. Suppose that, when she stayed at the Queen's Hotel before, her quarters had been the most luxurious she had ever known.

f. Suppose that she had stayed at the Queen's Hotel three times a year for the past six years.

II. Analyze the structures of the analogical arguments in the following passages, and evaluate them in terms of the six criteria that have been explained.

*1. If you cut up a large diamond into little bits, it will entirely lose the value it had as a whole; and an army divided up into small bodies of soldiers, loses all its strength. So a great intellect sinks to the level of an ordinary one, as soon as it is interrupted and disturbed, its attention distracted and drawn off from the matter in hand: for its superiority depends upon its power of concentration—of bringing all its strength to bear upon one theme, in the same way as a concave mirror collects into one point all the rays of light that strike upon it.

—Arthur Schopenhauer, "On Noise"

2. Every species of plant or animal is determined by a pool of germ plasm that has been most carefully selected over a period of hundreds of millions of years. We can understand now why it is that mutations in these carefully selected organisms almost invariably are detrimental. The situation can be suggested by a statement made by Dr. J. B. S. Haldane: My clock is not keeping perfect time. It is conceivable that it will run better if I shoot a bullet through it; but it is much more probable that it will stop altogether. Professor George Beadle, in this connection, has asked "What is the chance that a typographical error would improve *Hamlet?*"

—Linus Pauling, *No More War!*

3. Look round the world: contemplate the whole and every part of it: you will find it to be nothing but one great machine, subdivided into an infinite number of lesser machines, which again admit of subdivisions, to a degree beyond what human senses and faculties can trace and explain. All these various machines, and even their most minute parts, are adjusted to each other with an accuracy, which ravishes into admiration all men, who have ever contemplated them. The curious adapting of means to ends, throughout all nature, resembles exactly, though it much exceeds, the production of human contrivance; of human design, thought, wisdom, and intelligence. Since therefore the effects resemble each other, we are led to infer, by

all the rules of analogy, that the causes also resemble; and that the Author of Nature is somewhat similar to the mind of men; though possessed of much larger faculties, proportioned to the grandeur of the work, which he has executed. By this argument *a posteriori*, and by this argument alone, do we prove at once the existence of a Deity, and his similarity to human mind and intelligence.

—David Hume, *Dialogues Concerning Natural Religion*, 1779

4. The philosopher Metrodorus of Chios, who lived in the fourth century B.C., was greatly interested in the heavenly bodies. He wrote: "To consider the Earth as the only populated world in infinite space is as absurd as to assert that in an entire field of millet, only one grain will grow."

*5. To the casual observer porpoises and sharks are kinds of fish. They are streamlined, good swimmers, and live in the sea. To the zoologist who examines these animals more closely, the shark has gills, cold blood, and scales; the porpoise has lungs, warm blood, and hair. The porpoise is fundamentally more like man than like the shark and belongs, with man, to the mammals—a group that nurses its young with milk. Having decided that the porpoise is a mammal, the zoologist can, without further examination, predict that the animal will have a four-chambered heart, bones of a particular type, and a certain general pattern of nerves and blood vessels. Without using a microscope the zoologist can say with reasonable confidence that the red blood cells in the blood of the porpoise will lack nuclei. This ability to generalize about animal structure depends upon a system for organizing the vast amount of knowledge about animals.

—Ralph Buchsbaum, *Animals without Backbones*

6. The body is the substance of the soul; the soul is the functioning of the body. . . . The relationship of the soul to its substance is like that of sharpness to a knife, while the relationship of the body to its functioning is like that of a knife to sharpness. What is called sharpness is not the same as the knife, and what is called the knife is not the same as sharpness. Nevertheless, there can be no knife if the sharpness is discarded, nor sharpness if the knife is discarded. I have never heard of sharpness surviving if the knife is destroyed, so how can it be admitted that the soul can remain if the body is annihilated?

—Fan Chen, *Essay on the Extinction of the Soul*, in Fung Yu-Lan, *A History of Chinese Philosophy*

7. If a single cell, under appropriate conditions, becomes a person in the space of a few years, there can surely be no difficulty in understanding how, under appropriate conditions, a cell may, in the course of untold millions of years, give origin to the human race.

—Herbert Spencer, *Principles of Biology*

8. An electron is no more (and no less) hypothetical than a star. Nowadays we count electrons one by one in a Geiger counter, as we count the stars one by one on a photographic plate. In what sense can an electron be called more unobservable than a star? I am not sure whether I ought to say that I have seen an electron; but I have just the same doubt whether I have seen a star. If I have seen one, I have seen the other. I have seen a small disc of light surrounded by diffraction rings which has not the least resemblance to what a star is supposed to be; but the name "star" is given to the object in the physical world which some hundreds of years ago started a chain of causation which has resulted in this particular light-pattern. Similarly in a Wilson expansion chamber I have seen a trail not in the least resembling what an electron is supposed to be; but the name "electron" is given to the object in the physical world which has caused this trail to appear. How can it possibly be maintained that a hypothesis is introduced in one case and not in the other?

   —Arthur Eddington, *New Pathways in Science*

9. Just as the bottom of a bucket containing water is pressed more heavily by the weight of the water when it is full than when it is half empty, and the more heavily the deeper the water is, similarly the high places of the earth, such as the summits of mountains, are less heavily pressed than the lowlands are by the weight of the mass of the air. This is because there is more air above the lowlands than above the mountain tops; for all the air along a mountain side presses upon the lowlands but not upon the summit, being above the one but below the other.

   —Blaise Pascal, *Treatise on the Weight of the Mass of the Air*

*10. Suppose that someone tells me that he has had a tooth extracted without an anaesthetic, and I express my sympathy, and suppose that I am then asked, "How do you know that it hurt him?" I might reasonably reply, "Well, I know that it would hurt me. I have been to the dentist and know how painful it is to have a tooth stopped [filled] without an anaesthetic, let alone taken out. And he has the same sort of nervous system as I have. I infer, therefore, that in these conditions he felt considerable pain, just as I should myself."

   —Alfred J. Ayer, "One's Knowledge of Other Minds," *Theoria*, 1953

11. Now if we survey the universe, so far as it falls under our knowledge, it bears a great resemblance to an animal or organized body and seems actuated with a like principle of life and motion. A continual circulation of matter in it produces no disorder: a continual waste in every part is incessantly repaired; the closest sympathy is perceived throughout the entire system: and each part or member, in performing its proper offices, operates both to its own

preservation and to that of the whole. The world, therefore, I infer, is an animal, and the Deity is the *soul* of the world, actuating it, and actuated by it.

—David Hume, *Dialogues Concerning Natural Religion*

12. One cannot require that everything shall be defined, any more than one can require that a chemist shall decompose every substance. What is simple cannot be decomposed, and what is logically simple cannot have a proper definition.

—Gottlob Frege, "On Concept and Object"

13. Most endangered or threatened species in the United States find suitable habitat on private land, and the destruction of habitat is widely recognized as the leading cause of extinctions. For these reasons, protecting wildlife without regulating the use of private land has been compared by biologists to playing the piano with just the black keys.

—John H. Cushman, Jr., "Environmentalists Gain a Victory,"
*New York Times*, 30 June 1995

14. Opposing legislation that would restrict handgun ownership in the United Kingdom, the husband of Queen Elizabeth II reasoned as follows:

> Look, if a cricketer, for instance, suddenly decided to go into a school and batter a lot of people to death with a cricket bat, which he could do very easily, are you going to ban cricket bats?

—Prince Philip, the duke of Edinburgh, in an interview
on the BBC, 19 December 1996

*15. . . . The simplest form of the theological argument from design [was] once well known under the name "Paley's watch." Paley's form of it was just this: "If we found by chance a watch or other piece of intricate mechanism we should infer that it had been made by someone. But all around us we do find intricate pieces of natural mechanism, and the processes of the universe are seen to move together in complex relations; we should therefore infer that these too have a Maker."

—B. A. D. Williams, "Metaphysical Arguments,"
in D. F. Pears, ed., *The Nature of Metaphysics*

## 11.3 REFUTATION BY LOGICAL ANALOGY

"You should say what you mean," [said the March Hare, reproving Alice sharply.]
 "I do," Alice hastily replied; "at least—at least I mean
what I say—that's the same thing, you know."
 "Not the same thing a bit!" said the Hatter.
"Why, you might just as well say that 'I see what I
eat' is the same thing as 'I eat what I see'!"

> "You might just as well say," added the March Hare, "that 'I like what I get' is the same thing as 'I get what I like'!"
>
> "You might just as well say," added the Dormouse, which seemed to be talking in its sleep, "that 'I breathe when I sleep' is the same thing as 'I sleep when I breathe'!"
>
> "It *is* the same thing with you," said the Hatter, and here the conversation dropped.
>
> —Lewis Carroll, *Alice's Adventures in Wonderland*, chapter 7

The Hare, the Hatter, and the Dormouse all seek to refute Alice's claim—that meaning what you say is the same as saying what you mean—by using a *logical analogy*. The form of an argument, as distinct from its particular content, is the most important aspect of that argument from a logical point of view. Therefore, we often seek to demonstrate the weakness of a given argument by exhibiting another argument, known to be erroneous, that has the same logical form.

In the realm of deduction, a refuting analogy for a given argument is an argument having the same form as that of the given argument but whose premisses are known to be true and whose conclusion is known to be false. The refuting analogy is therefore known to be invalid, and the argument under attack, because it has the same form, is thus shown to be invalid as well. This is the same principle that underlies the testing of categorical syllogisms explained in section 6.2, and it also underlies the repeated emphasis upon the centrality of logical form, as explained in section 8.4.

In the realm of inductive argument, our present concern, the technique of refutation by logical analogy can also be used to great effect. Scientific, political, or economic arguments, not purporting to be deductive, may be countered by presenting other arguments having very similar design, whose conclusions are known to be false or are generally believed to be improbable. Inductive arguments differ fundamentally from deductive arguments in the character of the support claimed to be given to the conclusion by the premisses. But all arguments, inductive as well as deductive, may be said to have some underlying form or pattern. If, when confronted by an inductive argument we wish to attack, we can present another inductive argument having essentially the same form but one that is clearly flawed and whose conclusion is very doubtful, we throw similar doubt upon the conclusion of the argument under examination.

Consider the following illustration. One common objection to the legalization of assisted suicide is known as the *"slippery slope" argument*. It is essentially the argument that, once formal permission has been given to medical doctors to act in a certain way that is of questionable morality, that will lead to more and greater immoralities of the same general type. The first leniency ought to be avoided, the argument holds, because it must leave us insecure on a slope so slippery that our first step down cannot be our last. To this argument a contemporary critic responds as follows:

> The slippery slope argument, although influential, is hard to deal with rationally. It suggests that, once we allow doctors to shorten the life of patients who request it,

doctors could and would wantonly kill burdensome patients who do not want to die. This suggestion is not justified.... Physicians often prescribe drugs which, in doses greater than prescribed, would kill the patient. No one fears that the actual doses prescribed will lead to their use of lethal doses. No one objects to such prescriptions in fear of a "slippery slope." Authorizing physicians to assist in shortening the life of patients who request this assistance no more implies authority to shorten the life of patients who want to prolong it, than authority for surgery to remove the gall bladder implies authority to remove the patient's heart.[7]

This is an excellent example of refutation by logical analogy in the inductive sphere. The argument under attack is first presented: If we give physicians the authority to help patients to end their own lives, some will use that authority wantonly and abusively. Therefore, that argument concludes, we ought not take even the first step down that road; we should refuse to give to any doctor the authority to help any patient end his own life.

To this argument a refuting analogy is offered, allegedly of the same form, which relies upon common knowledge, inductively acquired, about the behavior of physicians: We do give physicians authority to take action that could be used abusively. We give physicians the authority to prescribe dangerous drugs which in low doses may be helpful, knowing that they then *could* prescribe those drugs in high doses that would kill their patients. But the fact that such abusive uses of the authority to prescribe such drugs could be the outcome, does not for a moment cause us to regret that such authority has been granted. So it may be seen that the argument which proceeds from the *possible* abuse of authority to its *likely* abuse is (this refutation suggests), at least in so far as the argument is applied to medical doctors, not very persuasive.

The passage quoted above offers a second refutation by analogy, very similar in form: Giving physicians the authority to assist patients who request help in shortening their own lives will lead (according to the argument under attack) to the giving of authority to shorten the lives of patients who really want their lives prolonged. In this case the slippery slope is taken to be one on which not physicians alone, but also the authorizing legislature, will slide.

An allegedly refuting analogy is again presented: Authority now is commonly given to physicians to remove some bodily organ with the consent of the patient. It would be absurd to conclude (the analogy suggests) that this authorization would lead anyone, legislator or physician, to suppose that the granting of such authority includes the right to remove some *other* vital organ concerning which no consent has been given.

In disputation of this kind the focus is upon argument *form*. Defenders of the slippery slope argument are likely to respond to attacks such as those we have cited by contending that the allegedly refuting analogies are not successful, because their form does not correctly mirror the form of the original argument pre-

---

[7]Ernest van den Haag, "Make Mine Hemlock," *National Review,* 12 June 1995.

sented. The controversy no doubt will continue. But the logical technique in question is of great interest: Where an argument does have the same form as that of another under attack, and where that argument offered as a responding analogy is plainly bad, the argument under attack surely is damaged.

The presentation of a refutation by logical analogy is often signaled, in the inductive as in the deductive sphere, by the appearance of some revealing phrase: "you might just as well say," or some other words having that same sense. In the passage quoted above, the telltale phrase, prefacing the (allegedly) damaging analogy there, is "no more implies . . . than . . . ." A slightly different set of words is used in the refuting analogy of a scholar attacking the argument that because Islamic culture had been brought to the country of Chad from without, it is no more than a veneer there. "Chad [you say] has only an 'Islamic overlay.' One could as sensibly say that France has only a 'Christian overlay.'"[8]

When the point of the refuting analogy is manifest, no introductory phrases may be needed. The former governor of Mississippi, Kirk Fordice, argued that "It is a simple fact that the United States is a Christian nation," because "Christianity is the predominant religion in America." The journalist Michael Kinsley, with whom he was debating on television, responded with these telling analogies: "Women are a majority in this country. Does that make us a female country? Or does it make us a white country because most people in this country are white?"[9]

## Exercises

Each of the following is intended to be a refutation by logical analogy. Identify the argument being refuted in each and the refuting analogy, and decide whether they do indeed have the same argument form.

1. Steve Brill, founder of Court TV, has no doubt that cameras belong in the courtroom, and answers some critics in the following way: "Some lawyers and judges say that TV coverage makes the system look bad. They confuse the messenger with the message. If press coverage of something makes it look bad, that is a reason to have the press coverage. That criticism is like saying that because journalists were allowed to be with the troops in Vietnam, the Vietnam War was ruined."

   —Steve Brill, "Trial: A Starting Place for Reform,"
   *Ann Arbor News*, 12 June 1995

2. The whole history of bolshevism, both before and after the October revolution, is full of instances of maneuvering, temporizing and compromising with other parties, bourgeois

---

[8]Bassam K. Abed, in a letter to the *New York Times*, 26 June 1988.
[9]"Evangelical Update," the *New York Times*, 21 November 1992.

parties included! To carry on a war for the overthrow of the international bourgeoisie, a war which is a hundred times more difficult, prolonged and complicated than the most stubborn of ordinary wars between states, and to refuse beforehand to maneuver, to utilize the conflict of interests (even though temporary) among one's enemies, to refuse to temporize and compromise with possible (even though transitory, unstable, vacillating and conditional) allies—is this not ridiculous in the extreme? Is it not as though, when making a difficult ascent of an unexplored and hitherto inaccessible mountain, we were to refuse beforehand ever to move in zigzags, ever to retrace our steps, ever to abandon the course once selected to try others?

—V. I. Lenin, *"Left Wing" Communism: An Infantile Disorder*, 1920

3. To suggest that because early statute writers in the United States were Christians it is therefore a Christian state is like saying that because ancient Romans believed in a pantheon of gods Europeans should today bow at the feet of statues of Jupiter and Juno.

—Jeremy Gilbert, "The Roots of U.S. Law Lead to Rome," *New York Times*, 23 April 1997

4. The argument against new highways is given forceful statement by three distinguished urban planners: The authors write: "The only long term solutions to traffic are public transit and coordinated land use." New highways, they argue, bring "induced traffic." So building more highways will only cause more traffic congestion, not less.[10]

   A highly critical reviewer responds to this argument as follows: "This is nonsense. . . . Long lines at a grocery store would not prompt anyone to say, "Well, we can't build any more grocery stores. That would only bring out more customers." Building more highways wouldn't lure cars. The cars come anyway."[11]

*5. America's supply of timber has been increasing for decades, and the nation's forests have three times more wood today than in 1920. "We're not running out of wood, so why do we worry so much about recycling paper?" asks Jerry Taylor, the director of natural research studies at the Cato Institute. "Paper is an agricultural product, made from trees grown specifically for paper production. Acting to conserve trees by recycling paper

---

[10]A. Duany, E. Plater-Zyberk, and J. Speck, *Suburban Nation: The Rise of Sprawl and the Decline of the American Dream* (North Point, 2000).

[11]F. Barnes, "Suburban Beauty: Why Sprawl Works," *The Weekly Standard*, 22 May 2000.

is like acting to conserve cornstalks by cutting back on corn consumption."

—John Tierney, "Recycling Is Garbage,"
*New York Times Magazine,* 30 June 1996

6. In 1996, heated controversy arose between the states of New Jersey and New York over formal possession of Ellis Island, located at the mouth of the Hudson River near the New Jersey shore, a tiny speck of land on which so many tens of thousands of immigrants to the United States first touched American soil. An essay defending New York's claim to the historic island appeared in the *New York Times* on 23 July 1996. The following letter appeared in the same newspaper four days later:

> Clyde Haberman is right that almost every immigrant who passed through Ellis Island was bound for New York, not New Jersey. But this fact does not determine where the island is. A significant number of passengers arriving at Newark International Airport are also on their way to New York, but it would be hard to argue that New York thus has a claim on the airport. Cincinnati International Airport is in Covington, Kentucky, and presumably, few travelers are on their way to sparsely populated northern Kentucky. Would Mr. Haberman suggest that the airport belongs to Ohio?

7. I'm getting tired of assertions like those of Rep. Ernest Istook, Jr.— "As prayer has gone out of schools, guns, knives, drugs, and gangs have come in"—with the unsupported implication that there is some causal connection between these events. This is the *post hoc ergo propter hoc* fallacy . . . We could just as well say, "After we threw God out of the schools, we put a man on the moon." Students may or may not need more faith, but Congress could certainly use more reason."

—Douglas E. McNeil, "School-Prayer Fallacy,"
*New York Times,* 10 June 1998

8. The big question is not whether we are a biological species; it's whether that is all we are. For E. O. Wilson in his book *Consilience,* the case is closed. "Virtually all contemporary scientists and philosophers expert on the subject agree that the mind, which comprises consciousness and rational process, is the brain at work. . . . The brain and its satellite glands have now been probed to the point where no particular site remains that can reasonably be supposed to harbor a nonphysical mind."

This is on a par with Nikita Krushchev's announcement that Yuri Gagarin, the first human visitor to space, had failed to locate God. Does Wilson really suppose that if there were an immaterial component to the mind it would show up in a brain scan?

—Stephen M. Barr, "Mindless Science," *The Weekly Standard*, 6 April 1998

9. Artificial human minds will never be made (we are told) because "artificial intelligence investigation is based on advanced solid-state physics, whereas the humble human brain is a viable semiliquid system!" That is no more reassuring than the suggestion that automobiles could never replace horses because they are made of metal, while the humble horse is a viable organic system with legs of flesh and bone.

—Michael D. Rohr, *New York Times*, 27 March 1998.

*10. Modern political rhetoric [Ronald Dworkin argues] "is now extremely repetitive," and a good bit of it could be dispensed with—by law. "Every European democracy does this," the world's most highly regarded legal philosopher points out, "and Europeans are amazed that we do not."

Europeans are also amazed that we bathe as frequently as we do. What the hell kind of argument is that?

—David Tell, "Silencing Free Speech in the Name of Reform" *The Weekly Standard*, 25 November 1996

## Summary of Chapter 11

In this chapter we began the analysis of inductive arguments, of which analogical arguments are one of the most common kinds.

In section 11.1, we explained argument by analogy. An **analogy is a likeness or comparison;** we draw an analogy when we indicate one or more respects in which two or more entities are similar. An **argument by analogy is an argument in which the similarity of two or more entities in one or more respects is used as the premiss(es); its conclusion is that those entities are similar in some further respect.** Not all analogies are used for purposes of argument; they also may serve some literary effect, or for purposes of explanation. **Because analogical arguments are** *inductive*, **not deductive, the terms "validity" and "invalidity" do not apply to them. The conclusion of an analogical argument, like the conclusion of every inductive argument, has** *some degree of probability,* **but is not claimed to be certain.**

In section 11.2, we explained **six criteria** used in determining whether the premisses of an analogical argument render its conclusion more or less probable. These are:

1. The *number of entities* between which the analogy is said to hold
2. The *variety,* or *degree of dissimilarity,* among those entities or instances mentioned only in the premisses

3. The *number of respects* in which the entities involved are said to be analogous
4. The *relevance* of the respects mentioned in the premisses to the further respect mentioned in the conclusion
5. The *number and importance of disanalogies* between the instances mentioned only in the premisses and the instance mentioned in the conclusion
6. The *modesty (or boldness)* of the conclusion relative to the premisses

In section 11.3, we explained **refutation by logical analogy,** an effective method of refuting both inductive and deductive arguments. To show that a given argument is mistaken, one may present another obviously mistaken argument that is very similar in form to the argument under attack.

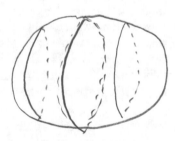

① # of entities
② Variety
③ Relevance
④ # of Disanoly5y
⑤ Boldness
⑥ # of respects

# Defeasible Reasoning

## Donald Nute

### Defeasible Rules

Sometimes we can be sure that a particular conclusion follows from the information available to us, but most of the time we cannot. One reason for this is that most of the time our reasoning depends on rules of thumb that apply in the usual or normal case but that do not apply in unusual cases. When we have a situation that fits one of these rules of thumb, we are justified in applying the rule and at least tentatively drawing a conclusion - unless we have evidence that the situation is an exception to the rule. When we have this kind of evidence to the contrary, we say that it *defeats* the rule of thumb in the particular case. Because they can be defeated, we call these rules of thumb *defeasible.*  → Rules of thumb, defeated by the Contrary

Let's consider a few examples having to do with a kitchen sink. We believe that if we turn the faucet, water will come out of it. We believe that the water will be safe to drink. We believe that if we turn the right handle the water will be cold, and if we turn the left handle the water will become hot in a few seconds. We believe that the water will run out the drain in the sink. These are some of the things we believe about kitchen sinks. None of them is certain.

Suppose you haven't paid the water bill since you left for summer vacation, or that the drain was stopped up last night, or that you heard on the radio that the river has overflowed into the water treatment plant. Will you apply all of the rules of thumb we mentioned in the preceding paragraph to this sink? Probably not. Each of these bits of information will defeat some of the rules about kitchen sinks that you routinely accept. In each of these cases we have a competing rule. If you haven't paid the water bill in a couple of months, may not come out of the faucet. If the drain was stopped up last night, water may not go down it today. If river water has flowed into the water purification plant, the water that comes from the faucet may not be safe to drink. Each of these defeasible rules can defeat one of the earlier ones.

We are going to look at how we reason defeasibly. In particular, we are going to look at the way we sort things out when we have competing rules of thumb that apply to the same situation. The simplest kinds of cases can be represented in a diagram called a simple *defeasible logic graph* or *d-graph.* More complicated examples require a more complicated d-graph than those we will consider. All d-graphs are knowledge representation schemes that can be used both for evaluating arguments and for problem solving.

### The Defeasible Reasoning Game

We are going to look at some examples involving reasoning with defeasible rules. Suppose you are on a quiz show. At the beginning of the show, you are given $100, then you are asked some questions. You can answer each question 'yes', 'no', or 'I haven't been given enough information to answer the question.' You win $10 for each correct answer and lose $10 for each incorrect answer. How would you answer the following questions?

1. Cichlids and chromides are kinds of fish. Cichlids normally live in fresh water and chromides normally do not live in fresh water. If a fish is both a cichlid and a chromide, does it live in fresh water?
2. A chromide is a kind of cichlid. Given this plus the information in the first question, if a fish is both a cichlid and a chromide, does it live in fresh water?
3. Animals with scales are typically reptiles. Animals that bear their young live are typically mammals. But no mammals are reptiles. If an animal with scales bears its young live, is it a mammal?
4. Someone who was born in Pennsylvania was born in the United States. Someone who speaks Pennsylvania Dutch normally was born in Pennsylvania. Someone who has a Swedish driver's license normally was not born in the United States. If someone with a Swedish driver's license speaks Pennsylvania Dutch, were they born in the United States?
5. A nautilus is a cephalopod. If something does not have a shell, then it typically is not a nautilus. Animals with tentacles normally are cephalopods. If an animal has both tentacles and a shell, is it a nautilus?
6. If an animal has both tentacles and a shell, is it a cephalopod?
7. Libertarians are conservatives, and conservatives normally belong to the Republican party. But libertarians normally do not belong to the Republican party. Members of the Republican party normally support bush, but libertarians normally do not support Bush. If some libertarian is a member of the Republican party, do they support Bush?
8. Starships can go faster than the speed of light. But a starship with a flawed dilithium crystal might not be able to go faster than the speed of light. However, a starship with a flawed dilithium crystal that goes through a worm hole could go faster than the speed of light. The Enterprise is a starship and its dilithium crystal is flawed. Can the Enterprise go faster than the speed of light?

---

## Defeasible Graphs

The purpose of the Defeasible Reasoning Game is to impress upon you how difficult it may be to figure out the right conclusions to draw from fairly simple sets of evidence when defeasible inference rules are involved. Now we will develop some tools to help us sort out this kind of information.

The tool we will develop a simple defeasible graph or d-graph. The kinds of information that can be represented in simple d-graphs are similar to some of the kinds of information that can be represented in a Venn diagram. For example, we can use a Venn diagram to represent the claim that all birds fly. But we know that many birds do not fly. Yet if we were paid by a zoo to build an enclosure for birds, then unless we were told specifically that the bird was a penguin or some other kind of flightless bird, we would put a top on the enclosure. If the zoo claimed that we should not charge so much for the enclosure because it is for kiwis and we wasted money on materials for the top, we would respond that we should have been told that the enclosure was for a flightless bird when it was ordered. Notice that we wouldn't automatically put a top on an enclosure for wildebeest, wolverines, or warthogs.

We can distinguish between a strict inference rule and a defeasible one. All penguins are birds and birds typically fly. The rule that penguins are birds is strict and could not possibly have any exceptions; the rule that birds fly is defeasible and has exceptions. We will use capital letters to represent different kinds of things and we will use arrows to indicate that we can infer membership in one group from membership in another. We will use a single arrow (--->) for strict inference rules and a double arrow (===>) for defeasible inference rules. So our penguin rule becomes **P--->B** and our flight rule becomes **B==>F**. We also have negative rules. For example, no birds are mammals (strict) and penguins normally don't fly (defeasible). We use arrows with lines through them for these cases: **B-/->M** and **P=/=>F** respectively. So we have representations for both the strict and the defeasible readings of the rules we express in English using the quantifiers `all', `only', and `no'.

When we represent a rule as defeasible, we tacitly acknowledge that it may have exceptions. **B==>F** tells us that being a bird is a good reason, but not a conclusive reason, for thinking something can fly. If we find out something is a penguin, we have a good reason for thinking that it can't fly. But suppose we later find out that a bird is sick. This casts doubt on its ability to fly, but we don't want to go so far as to say that a sick bird typically *can't* fly. Instead, we should say that a sick bird *might not* fly. We call a principle like this an undercutting defeater and we represent it using a wiggly arrow (~~~>) or a wiggly arrow with a line through it (~/~>). Of course, any bird might not fly. But being a bird is not a reason to doubt that something can fly while being a sick bird is. We will only want to represent an undercutting defeater in our diagrams if we think it provides a good reason to doubt that one kind of thing is also another kind of thing.

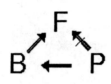

We can combine several strict rules, defeasible rules, and defeaters together to form a diagram. We call such a diagram a *defeasible graph* or *d-graph*. The letters in the diagram are called *nodes* and the arrows are called *links* or *rules*. In Figure 1, we have the diagram for the bird example we have been discussing. We have three nodes (B, P, and F) and three links, two defeasible and one strict.

**Figure 1**

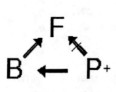

Once we have constructed an diagram, we can use it to reason about the properties an individual has or the groups an individual belongs to. Our reasoning must begin with some initial information about the individual. For example, we might learn that Opus is a penguin. Then to reason about what other properties Opus might have or what other groups Opus might belong to, we first put + beside P in our diagram as in Figure 2. What we need to develop are methods for deciding what other nodes we might be able to mark with + to indicate the individual has the property associated with the node, − to indicate that the individual does not have the property, or ? to indicate that we can't tell from our information whether or not the individual has the property.

**Figure 2**

We will call the node that a link points *from* the *tail* of the link, and we will call the node a link points *to* the *head* of the link. For example, the link P--->B in Figure 2 has **P** as its tail and **B** as its head. A link is *supported* if it has + by its tail. A link is *failed* if it has − or ? by its tail. Starting with some initial set of nodes marked +, we put markers beside other nodes according to certain principles we will develop. This process is called *propagation of markers*. Often a node gets marked when we *propagate a link*. When we propagate a positive link (a link that does not have a bar through it,) we put + beside its head. When we propagate a negative link (a link that does have a bar through it,) we put − beside its head. At any stage in the process of propagating markers in a d-graph, a particular link may be supported, failed, or neither. Only supported links can be propagated, and we never propagate undercutting defeaters.

We always propagate supported *strict* links, and we always propagate supported *defeasible* links unless they have *competitors*. The supported strict link going from **P** to **B** in Figure 2 has no competitor; so we propagate it to produce Figure 3. Two supported defeasible links are competitors when they would give us evidence for conflicting conclusions if both were supported. If two defeasible links have the same head but one is positive and the other is negative, then they compete. For example, the supported links **B===>F** and **P=|=>F** in Figure 3 would give us a reason to think that something both does and does not.

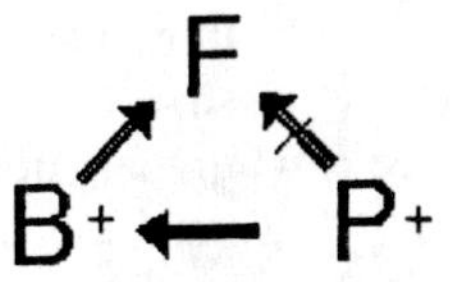

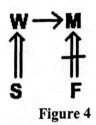

**Figure 3**

If a strict link is strictly supported, then we always propagate it. So if a positive strict link and a negative strict link are both supported and have the same head, we will mark their common head both + and −. But this means that the same statement is both true and false, which is impossible. Our d-graph is contradictory. We stop investigating the d-graph at this point. It is unreliable unless we can eliminate the contradiction.

Here is another way two defeasible links can compete. Suppose you are at the zoo looking at an animal in a cage. The sign on the cage says, 'wombat'. Of course, if the sign says that the animal is a wombat then that is a reason to think it is a wombat. You know that mammals normally do not have feathers, and the animal in the cage appears to have feathers. So you have a reason to think the animal is a wombat and a reason to think that it is not a mammal. But by definition, a wombat is a kind of mammal. So the **S===>W** link and the **F=|=>M** link compete. Figure 4 shows the d-graph for this example. We can generalize on the condition that makes these two links competitors: If there is a path of positive strict links going from a node **P** to a node **Q**, then any positive defeasible link that has **P** as its head will compete with any negative defeasible link that has **Q** as its head.

And Figure 5 shows a third and final way two defeasible links can compete. Birds are not reptiles, but an animal with feathers is normally a bird and an animal with a heat-seeking organ in its head is normally a reptile (specifically, a pit viper.) So if we were told that a particular animal had feathers and also had a heat-seeking organ in its head, we would have evidence that it was a bird and that it was a reptile. Since it can't be both, our evidence is at odds. The links **F===>B** and **H===>R** compete. More generally, if we have a path of strict links from node **P** to node **Q**, the last link in the path is negative, and all the other links in the path are positive, then any positive defeasible link that has **P** as its head will compete with any positive defeasible link that has **Q** as its head.

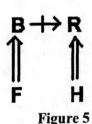

**Figure 4**

**Figure 5**

A defeasible link competes with an undercutting defeater in exactly the same cases where it would compete with another defeasible link.

When defeasible links compete, or when defeasible links compete with undercutting defeaters, we first need to determine whether the competing links are supported before we can decide what marker to put at the heads of the links. If all but one of the links is failed (has − or ? by its source), then we propagate the single supported link. If competing links are both supported, then we may be able to use specificity to adjudicate between the links. This is what we do automatically in the Opus example.

We know that a penguin is a special kind of bird. Thus, penguins might not have some property that birds ordinarily have. In particular, we know that a penguin is a flightless bird. In Figure 3, the information that a penguin is a special kind of bird is clearly represented by the strict link from **P** to **B**. When we have two competing links as we do in Figure 3 and we can tell that one of the links is more specific than the other, we propagate the more specific link. Notice that this only applies if both links are defeasible. A strict link always defeats a defeasible link. We will say more about specificity below.

When all else fails, we mark a node ?.

We will put these considerations together to produce a procedure for propagating markers through a simple d-graph. The procedure has five steps, but some of these steps may be repeated several times.

### Algorithm for Marking Simple Defeasible Graphs

1.  A leaf node is one that does not have any arrows pointing toward it. Put ? beside every leaf node that is not already marked. Go to 2.

2.  Propagate every supported strict link that has not already been propagated. Go to 3.

3.  Is any node marked both + and −? If so, stop; the diagram is contradictory and unreliable. Otherwise, go to 4.

4.  Is there a supported defeasible link whose head is not marked, all of its strict competitors are failed, all of its non-strict competitors are either supported or failed, and it is more specific than all of its supported non-strict competitors? If so, propagate the link and go to 2. Otherwise, go to 5.

5.  Is there an unmarked node such that every link having that node as head is marked? If so, mark the node ? and go to 2. Otherwise, stop. You have marked every node that you can mark.

When is one link more specific than another? Suppose the first link we are considering has **A** as its tail and the other has **B** as its tail. Here is how we check to see if the link with **A** as its tail is more specific than the link with **B** as its tail. First, we check to see if **A** *forces* **B** in our d-graph.

1.  Check to see if there is a path made up entirely of ---> and ===> links going from **A** to **B**. If there isn't, we will say that **A** *does not force* **B** in the d-graph. If there is, go to step 2.

2.       Make a copy of the d-graph where only **A** is marked +. Propagate markers through this copy. If **B** does not get marked + in the copy, then **A** *does not force* **B** in the d-graph. If **B** does not get marked +, then **A** *forces* **B** in the d-graph.

Next, check to see if **B** forces **A** in the d-graph. If **A** forces **B** but **B** does not force **A**, then the link with **A** as its tail is more specific than the link with **B** as its tail. If **B** forces **A** but **A** does not force **B**, then the link with **B** as its tail is more specific than the link with **A** as its tail. In every other case, neither link is more specific than the other.

After we have propagated markers through a d-graph, we interpret the diagram to say that the individual we are reasoning about belongs to all the groups represented by letters with + beside them and belongs to none of the groups with − beside them. The diagram leaves unresolved whether the thing belongs to those groups represented by letters with ? beside them.

Defeasible graphs can be used to evaluate arguments. An argument has conclusions and a premise. If all of these can be interpreted as claims about groups that something belongs to or as strict or defeasible rules about how membership in one group follows from membership in another group, then the argument lends itself to evaluation by this method. We use the premises of the argument to build the diagram and to decide which letters are marked with + initially. To be fair, we may need to add some links to represent commonly accepted information that is not explicitly stated in the argument. (For example, we might add a strict link showing that penguins are birds even if this wasn't explicitly stated.) Then we propagate markers in the diagram. If the conclusion is that the thing being considered belongs to some particular group of things and the letter corresponding to that group of things has a + beside it when we are through, then the argument is persuasive so far as it goes. But we must always remember that some of our links may be defeasible. It is possible that some information not included in the argument would give us reason to doubt the conclusion of the argument or some of the intermediate steps to the conclusion. If we are aware of such counter-evidence, we should add the corresponding information to our original diagram and propagate markers again. With the new information added, we may no longer get + beside the critical conclusion. So an argument that has *prima facie* strength may fall apart when we consider other relevant information. This additional evidence would *rebut* the argument.

Defeasible graphs can also be used for problem solving. In this kind of situation, we have questions instead of conclusions. We construct a d-graph that represents our initial inference rules and information about the groups a thing belongs to. Then we propagate markers and look at what we have. We may discover conclusions that we can draw that surprise us and that are independent of the specific question with which we began.

One last consideration in constructing d-graphs is when to use a strict link and when to use a defeasible link. A link should only be strict if it is *impossible* for something to be a member of the class at the tail of the link without also being in the class at the head of the link (or not being in the class at the head of the link in the case of a negative link.) For example, it is impossible for something to be a square and not be a rectangle. This is because of the way squares and rectangles are *defined*. Similarly, it is impossible for something to be a bachelor and also be married. So we use a strict link **A** ---> **B** when by definition anything that is an **A** must also be a **B**, and we use a strict link **A** -|-> **B** when by definition anything that is an **A** cannot be a **B**.

It is also impossible for something to be a platypus without being a mammal or for something to be made of mercury without being made of metal. Now this is not entirely a matter of definition. When the platypus was discovered by Europeans, it was not obvious that the animal was a mammal. And mercury, being liquid at room temperature, does not have all the properties we intuitively associate with metals. The terms 'platypus', 'mammal', 'mercury', and 'metal' are what we call *natural kind terms*. These are terms that refer to natural groupings of objects. Natural kind terms include terms for biological species, biological genera, biological families, and other biological groups. They also include terms for elements like mercury and gold, and for some other substances or kinds of substances like water and metal. Terms like 'democrat', 'vehicle', 'furniture', or 'flier' are not natural kind terms. Someone is or is not a democrat as a matter of choice. Vehicles and furniture include diverse objects that do not make a natural grouping. If you slide down a mountain on a cello a lá James Bond, then the cello becomes a vehicle. If you put a large rock on your deck and sit on it, then it becomes furniture. And fliers include birds, bats, bumble bees, airplanes, and many other things. So the notion of a natural kind or of a natural kind term is hard to precisely define but relatively easy to understand. In any case, when a claim is made that something belonging to one natural kind does or does not belong to another natural kind, we interpret that claim as *strict* and represent it in a d-graph by a strict link.

There is yet another way a link might be strict. Anyone who lives in Atlanta *must* live in Georgia, and anyone who was born before World War II *must* have been born before Bill Clinton was elected President. These two relationships are necessary because of spatial and temporal regularities.

So we should make a link strict if the connections between its head and its tail follows from definition, states a relation between two natural kinds, or depends on a spatial or temporal regularity. Otherwise, we should make a link defeasible. But what about cases like "Penguins don't fly" or "Whales live in the sea"? We don't know of any exceptions to these claims. So shouldn't they be strict? The answer is no. It's not a matter of definition that penguins don't fly or that whales live in the sea, and we certainly don't want to say that fliers or sea creatures are a natural kind. Suppose we carefully bred a group of penguins for large wings and 'flight' muscles. Could we eventually develop a super-penguin that could fly? Perhaps. Would these birds still be penguins? They would be if they could still interbreed with our ordinary, flightless penguins. So even though perhaps no actual penguins fly, it is not impossible that there could be a penguin that could fly. Furthermore, we think penguins evolved from birds that did fly and whales evolved from creatures that lived on the land. There is a fossil whale called *Ambulocetus natans* that apparently lived on land but hunted in the sea. So it is not even true, much less necessary, that all whales live in the sea. The point of this kind of example is that, no matter how tempting it may be, we should not make a link strict unless its strictness is a consequence of a definition, it is a link between natural kind terms, or it depends on a spatial or temporal regularity of the sort we have discussed.

**Exercise on Defeasible Rules and Specificity**

1.  What is the difference between a strict rule and a defeasible rule? Give an example of both a strict rule and a defeasible rule about bananas.

2.  Which of the following rules are strict and which are defeasible?
    a.  Cats like milk.
    b.  No bachelor is married.
    c.  Anyone with a dependent child under the age of 18 who pays more than half of the child's support is entitled to a tax deduction.
    d.  Doctors make more money than plumbers.
    e.  Eating green apples will give you indigestion.
    f.  Congressmen live in Washington, DC.
    g.  Congressmen are legislators.
    h.  Cadillacs are expensive.
    i.  Toyotas come from Japan.
    j.  People who drive Mercedes are rich.
    k.  Tigers are cats.
    l.  Tigers have stripes.
    m.  Gold is yellow.
    n.  Gold is an element.
    o.  Gold is a metal.

**Exercises on Defeasible Reasoning**

Construct d-graphs for all the examples in the Defeasible Reasoning Game. Do you get the same answers that you did when you first played the game?

Construct d-graphs using the following information. Do not add any information to that given in each example. Put a + next to the nodes indicated, then put +, −, or ? next to all the other nodes.

1.   (N)othos(+) are (K)illifish. Killifish and (R)ice fish are (T)op minnows. Nothos normally lay their eggs in (M)ud. Top minnows normally do not lay their eggs in mud.

2.   Technically, a (P)orpoise(+) is a kind of (W)hale, and whales are (M)ammals. Porpoises live in the (S)ea and the typical sea creature is not a mammal.

3.   Of course, both (R)oyal(+) elephants and (A)frican(+) elephants are (E)lephants. (E)lephants are normally (G)ray, but royal elephants typically are not gray.

4.   (T)rout and (B)ass(+) are (F)ish. Fish are (C)old-blooded. Cold-blooded animals are (N)on-mammals. Non-mammals are not (F)ur-bearing.

5.   (W)hales(+) are (M)ammals and mammals normally (B)reathe air. Whales are also (S)ea-creatures and sea-creatures normally do not breathe air.

6.   Same as 5, but add the information that whales normally breathe air and that (H)umpbacks are whales. Then start with + beside humpback.

7.   (D)extrocephaloids(+) are normally (S)apioglutes and (M)alpeds(+) normally are not. (E)upeds and malpeds are (H)ypercorticals. Eupeds are normally (N)otopods, but hypercorticals are normally dextrocephaloids.

8.   (P)latypuses(+) are (M)ammals, but (Po)isonous animals normally are not mammals. Platypuses are poisonous animals.

9.   (C)onservatives(+) are normally (R)epublicans and Republicans normally are not (P)acifists. (S)upporters(+) of the Dukakis campaign normally are not Republicans. Typically, (Q)uakers(+) are pacifists.

10. People who (S)top smoking typically (E)at more. People who (C)ontract emphysema due to smoking(+) normally stop smoking but also have difficulty (G)aining weight. People who eat more usually gain weight.

11. (R)hodes Scholars(+) and college (G)ymnasts are college (A)thletes. Rhodes Scholars normally are not required to attend regular team (P)ractices. College athletes normally receive athletic (S)cholarships, and students on athletic scholarships normally are required to attend regular team practices.

*Unit IV*

*It is indeed not the least of the logician's tasks*
*to indicate the pitfalls laid by language*
*in the way of the thinker.*
—*Gottlob Frege*

*It would be a very good thing if every trick could receive*
*some short and obviously appropriate name, so that when*
*anyone used this or that particular trick, he could at once*
*be reproved for it.*
—*Arthur Schopenhauer*

CHAPTER 4

# FALLACIES

## 4.1 WHAT IS A FALLACY?

An argument, whatever its subject or sphere, is generally constructed in such a way as to prove its conclusion true. But any argument can fail to fulfill this purpose in two ways. One way it can fail is by assuming a false proposition as one of its premisses. We saw, in Chapter 1, that every argument involves the claim that the truth of its conclusion follows from, or is implied by, the truth of its premisses. So if its premisses are not true, the argument fails to establish the truth of its conclusion, even if the reasoning based on those premisses is correct. To test the truth or falsehood of premisses, however, is not the special responsibility of the logician; it is rather the task of inquiry in general, since premisses may deal with any subject matter whatever.

The other way in which an argument can fail to establish the truth of its conclusion is to rely upon premisses that do not imply the conclusion. Here we are in the special province of the logician, whose chief concern is the logical relations between premisses and conclusion. An argument whose premisses do not support its conclusion is one whose conclusion *could* be false *even if* all its premisses were true. In cases of this kind, the reasoning is bad, and the argument is said to be *fallacious.* A fallacy is an error in reasoning.

The word "fallacy," however, as logicians use it, designates not any mistaken inference or false belief, but *typical* errors, that is, mistakes that arise commonly in ordinary discourse and that devastate the arguments in which they appear. Each fallacy is a type of incorrect argument. An argument in which a mistake of a given type appears is said to *commit* that fallacy. Since each fallacy is a type, we can say of two or more different arguments that they contain or commit the same fallacy; that is, they exhibit the same kind of mistake in reasoning. An argument that contains or commits a fallacy of a given type may also be said to *be* a fallacy, that is, to be an example of that typical mistake.

There are many ways in which reasoning can go astray; that is, there are many *kinds* of mistakes in argument. It is customary to reserve the term "fallacy" for arguments that, although incorrect, are psychologically persuasive. Some arguments are so obviously incorrect as to deceive and persuade no one. But fallacies are dangerous because most of us are fooled by some of them on occasion. We therefore define a **fallacy** as **a type of argument that may seem to be correct, but that proves, on examination, not to be so.** It is profitable to study these mistaken arguments, because the traps they set can best be avoided when they are well understood. To be forewarned is to be forearmed!

Whether a given argument does in fact commit a fallacy may depend on the interpretation given to the terms used by its author. In a passage that appears to be fallacious, it may be difficult to determine out of context what meanings the author intended for the terms used. Sometimes the accusation of "Fallacy!" is unjustly leveled at a passage that was intended by its author to make a point missed by the critic—perhaps even to make a joke. We should bear such unavoidable complications in mind as we apply the analysis of fallacious argument to actual discourse. Our logical standards should be high, but our application of them to arguments in ordinary life should also be generous and fair.

How many different kinds of mistakes in arguments—different fallacies—may be distinguished? Aristotle, the first systematic logician, identified 13 types;[1] recently a listing of more than 100 has been developed![2] There is no precisely determinable number of fallacies, however, since much depends, in counting them, on the system of classification used. We distinguish 17 fallacies here—the most common and most deceptive mistakes in reasoning—divided into three large groups, called (a) fallacies of *relevance;* (b) fallacies of *presumption;* and (c) fallacies of *ambiguity.*[3]

The grouping of fallacies is always in some degree arbitrary, because mistakes of one kind will bear close similarities to, and sometimes overlap with, mistakes of another kind. The placement of a given fallacious passage in one

---

[1] Aristotle, *Sophistical Refutations.*

[2] The most voluminous list of fallacies we know appears in David H. Fischer's *Historians' Fallacies* (New York: Harper & Row, 1979); he discussed and named even more than the 112 different fallacies noted in his index. In *Fallacy: The Counterfeit of Argument* (Englewood Cliffs, NJ: Prentice-Hall, 1959), W. W. Fernside and W. B. Holther named and illustrated 51 fallacies. A historical and theoretical treatment of the topic was given by C. L. Hamblin in *Fallacies* (London: Methuen, 1970), and another excellent treatment of the topic is to be found in *Argument: The Logic of the Fallacies* (Scarborough, Ont.: McGraw-Hill Ryerson, 1982) by John Woods and Douglas Walton. Howard Kahane presented insightful criticism of the usual methods of classifying fallacies in "The Nature and Classification of Fallacies" in *Informal Logic,* edited by J. A. Blair and R. J. Johnson (Inverness, CA: Edgepress, 1980). All these books are warmly recommended to readers who wish to go more deeply into the subject of fallacies.

[3] Other fallacies, arising in special contexts, are discussed elsewhere in this book. Fallacies common in the misuse of syllogisms are explained in sections 6.4 and 7.7; fallacies common in symbolic logic are explained in section 8.4; some fallacies in causal reasoning are explained in Chapter 12; "the gambler's fallacy," committed in reasoning about probability, is explained in section 14.3. The kinds of mistakes made in reasoning are many and various; those discussed in this chapter are fallacies encountered in everyday, informal discourse.

specific group is also often disputable, because there may be more than one mistake of reasoning in that passage. If one remains mindful of this unavoidable imprecision, gaining an understanding of the essential features of each of the three major categories and the specific features of its several subcategories will be of much practical use. It enables one to detect the most troublesome errors in reasoning as they occur in ordinary discourse, and it promotes the logical sensitivity needed to detect related errors that may fall outside any one of these groupings.

## 4.2 FALLACIES OF RELEVANCE

**When an argument relies on premises that are not relevant to its conclusion, and that therefore cannot possibly establish its truth, the fallacy committed is one of** *relevance.* "*Irrelevance*" may perhaps better describe the problem, but the premises are often *psychologically* relevant to the conclusion, and this relevance explains their seeming correctness and persuasiveness. How psychological relevance can be confused with logical relevance can be explained in part by the different uses of language that we discussed in Chapter 2; the mechanics of these confusions will become clearer in the following analyses.

Latin names traditionally have been given to many fallacies; some of these—such as *ad hominem*—have become part of the English language. We will use here both the Latin and the English names.

### R1. The Argument from Ignorance: Argument *Ad Ignorantiam*

The argument *ad ignorantiam* (from ignorance) is the mistake that is committed **when it is argued that a proposition is true simply on the basis that it has not been proved false, or that it is false because it has not been proved true.** We realize, on reflection, that many false propositions have not yet been proved false, and many true propositions have not yet been proved true—and thus our ignorance of how to prove or disprove a proposition does not establish either truth or falsehood. This fallacious appeal to ignorance crops up most commonly in the misunderstandings incidental to developing science, where propositions whose truth cannot yet be established are mistakenly held to be false for that reason, and also in the world of pseudoscience, where propositions about psychic phenomena and the like are fallaciously held to be true because their falsehood has not been conclusively established.

Famous in the history of science is the argument *ad ignorantiam* given in criticism of Galileo, when he showed leading astronomers of his time the mountains and valleys on the moon that could be seen through his telescope. Some scholars of that age, absolutely convinced that the moon was a perfect sphere, as theology and Aristotelian science had long taught, argued against Galileo that, although we see what appear to be mountains and valleys, the moon is in fact a perfect sphere, because all its apparent irregularities are filled in by an invisible crystalline substance—an hypothesis that saves the perfection of the heavenly bodies and that Galileo could not prove false! Legend has it that Galileo, to expose the argument *ad ignorantiam*, offered another of the same kind as a caricature. Unable to prove the nonexistence of the transparent crystal supposedly filling the valleys, he put forward the equally probable hypothesis that there were, rising up from that invisible crystalline envelope, even greater mountain peaks—but made of crystal and thus invisible! And this hypothesis, he pointed out, his critics could not prove false.

Those who strongly oppose some great change are often tempted to argue against the change on the ground that it has not yet been proved workable or safe. Such proof is often impossible to provide in advance, and commonly the appeal of the objection is to ignorance mixed with fear. Such an appeal often takes the form of rhetorical questions that suggest, but do not flatly assert, that the proposed changes are full of unknown peril. Policy changes may be supported, as well as opposed, by an appeal to ignorance. When the federal government issued a waiver, in 1992, allowing Wisconsin to reduce the additional benefits it had been giving to welfare mothers for having more than one child, the governor of Wisconsin was asked if there was any evidence that unwed mothers were having additional children simply in order to gain the added income. His reply, *ad ignorantiam*, was this: "No, there isn't. There really isn't, but there is no evidence to the contrary, either."[4]

In some circumstances, of course, the fact that certain evidence or results have not been obtained, after they have been actively sought in ways calculated to reveal them, may have substantial argumentative force. New drugs being tested for safety, for example, are commonly given to rodents or other animal subjects for prolonged periods; the absence of any toxic effect on the animals is taken to be evidence (although not conclusive evidence) that the drug is probably not toxic to humans. Consumer protection often relies on evidence of this kind. In circumstances like these, we rely not on ignorance but on our knowledge, or conviction, that if the result we are concerned about were likely to arise, it would have arisen in some of the test cases. This use of the inability to prove something true supposes that investigators are highly skilled, and that they very probably would have uncovered the evidence sought had that been possible. Tragic mistakes sometimes are made in this sphere, but if the standard is set too high—if what is required is a conclusive proof of harmlessness that cannot ever be given—consumers will be denied what may prove to be valuable, even lifesaving, medical therapies.

Similarly, when a security investigation yields no evidence of improper conduct by the persons investigated, it would be wrong to conclude that the investigation has left us ignorant. A thorough investigation will properly result in their being "cleared." *Not* to draw a conclusion, in some cases, is as much a breach of correct reasoning as it would be to draw a mistaken conclusion.

The appeal to ignorance is common and often appropriate in a criminal court, where an accused person, in American jurisprudence and British common law, is presumed innocent until proved guilty. We adopt this principle because we recognize that the error of convicting the innocent is far more grave than that of acquitting the guilty—and thus the defense in a criminal case may

---

[4] "Wisconsin to Cut Welfare," *Ann Arbor News*, 11 April 1992.

legitimately claim that if the prosecution has not proved guilt beyond a reasonable doubt, the only verdict possible is not guilty. The U.S. Supreme Court strongly reaffirmed this standard of proof in these words:

> The reasonable-doubt standard . . . is a prime instrument for reducing the risk of convictions resting on factual error. The standard provides concrete substance for the presumption of innocence—that bedrock axiomatic and elementary principle whose enforcement lies at the foundation of the administration of our criminal law.[5]

But *this* appeal to ignorance succeeds only where innocence must be assumed in the absence of proof to the contrary; in other contexts, such an appeal is indeed an argument *ad ignorantiam*.

## R2. The Appeal to Inappropriate Authority: Argument *Ad Verecundiam*

In attempting to make up one's mind about some difficult or complicated question, it is entirely reasonable to be guided by the judgment of an acknowledged expert. When we argue that a given conclusion is correct on the ground that an expert authority has come to that judgment, we commit no fallacy. Indeed, such recourse to authority is necessary for most of us on very many matters. Of course, an expert's judgment constitutes no conclusive proof; experts disagree, and even in agreement they may err; but expert opinion surely is one reasonable way to support a conclusion.

The fallacy *ad verecundiam* arises **when the appeal is made to parties having no legitimate claim to authority in the matter at hand.** Thus, in an argument about morality, an appeal to the opinions of Darwin, a towering authority in biology, would be fallacious, as would be an appeal to the opinions of a great artist such as Picasso to settle an economic dispute.[6] But care must be taken in determining whose authority is reasonably to be relied on, and whose rejected. While Picasso was not an economist, his judgment might plausibly be given some weight in a dispute pertaining to the economic value of an artistic masterpiece; and if the role of biology in moral questions were in dispute, Darwin might indeed be an appropriate authority.

The most blatant examples of misplaced appeals to authority appear in advertising "testimonials." We are urged to drive an automobile of a given make because a famous golfer or tennis player affirms its superiority; we are urged to drink a beverage of a certain brand because some movie star or football coach expresses enthusiasm about it. Wherever the truth of some proposition is asserted on the basis of the authority of one who has no special competence in that sphere, the appeal to misplaced authority is the fallacy committed.

---

[5] Justice Brennan, writing for the Court, *In re Winship*, 397 U.S. 358, 1970.

[6] Fulton J. Sheen, a well-known Catholic bishop, remarked that it would be as fatuous for Albert Einstein to make judgments about God as it would be for Sheen to make judgments about relativity theory. "Both us," Sheen wrote, "would be talking about something we know nothing about." Cited by Laurence A. Marschall, in *The Sciences*, August 2000.

This appears to be a simpleminded mistake that is easy to avoid, but there are circumstances in which the fallacious appeal is tempting, and therefore intellectually dangerous. Here are two examples. In the sphere of international relations, in which weapons and war unhappily play a major role, one opinion or another is commonly supported by appealing to those whose special competence lies in the technical design or construction of weapons. Physicists such as Robert Oppenheimer or Edward Teller, for example, may indeed have had the knowledge to give authoritative judgments regarding how certain weapons can (or cannot) function; but their knowledge in this sphere does not give them special wisdom in determining broad political goals. An appeal to the strong judgment of a distinguished physicist as to the wisdom of ratifying some international treaty would be an argument *ad verecundiam*. Similarly, we admire the depth and insight of great fiction—say, in the novels of Alexander Solzhenitsyn or Saul Bellow—but to resort to their judgment in determining the real culprit in some political dispute would be an appeal *ad verecundiam*.[7]

Many persons offer themselves, or are presented by others, as "experts" in one field or another; yet determining whose authority is truly worthy to be relied upon is often a difficult matter. Suppose we want to know whether some proposition, $p$, is true. Suppose that some person, A, is alleged to be an expert about $p$, or propositions like $p$, and A says that $p$ is true. What are the conditions under which A's saying so really gives us good reason to accept the truth of $p$? In real cases the answer depends, of course, upon what $p$ asserts, and on the relation between A and propositions like $p$. In general, the question we must answer is this: Is A, by virtue of knowledge, experience, training, or general circumstances, more able than we, who are discussing the matter, to judge whether or not $p$ is true? If so, A's judgment has some value as evidence for us regarding the truth of $p$—although, of course, A's judgment may be weak evidence, perhaps more than counterbalanced by other considerations and perhaps outweighed by the testimony of still others who also have more knowledge about $p$ than do we.

The argument *ad verecundiam* is an appeal to one who has no claim greater than our own to judge the truth of $p$. Even one who does have a legitimate claim to authority may well prove mistaken, of course, and we may later regret our choice of experts. But if the experts we chose deserved their reputation for knowledge about things like $p$ (whatever $p$ may be), it was no fallacy to rely upon them even if they erred. Our mistake becomes one of reasoning (a fallacy) when our conclusion is based upon the verdict of an authority having no rational claim to expertise in that matter.[8]

---

[7] The name was originated by John Locke, whose criticism was directed chiefly at those who think that citing learned authorities is enough to win any argument, who think it "a breach of modesty for others to derogate any way from it, and question authority," and who "style it impudence in anyone who shall stand out against them." That argument Locke named *ad verecundiam*—literally, an appeal to the *modesty* of those who might be so bold as to oppose authority (J. Locke, *An Essay Concerning Human Understanding*, 1690).

[8] For an extended and penetrating analysis of the argument *ad verecundiam*, see Jim Mackenzie, "Authority," *Journal of Philosophy of Education* 22 (1988).

## R3. Argument *Ad Hominem*

The phrase *ad hominem* translates into "against the person." It names **a fallacious attack in which the thrust is directed, not at a conclusion, but at the person who asserts or defends it.** This fallacy has two major forms, because there are two major ways in which the attack can be personalized.

### A. *Argument* **Ad Hominen,** *Abusive*

Participants in strenuous argument sometimes disparage the character of their opponents, deny their intelligence or reasonableness, question their integrity, and so on. But the character of an individual is logically irrelevant to the truth or falsehood of what that person says, or to the correctness or incorrectness of that person's reasoning. To contend that proposals are bad, or assertions false, because they are proposed or asserted by "radicals" or "extremists" is a typical example of the fallacy *ad hominem,* abusive.

Abusive premises are irrelevant; they may nevertheless persuade by the psychological process of transference. Where an attitude of disapproval toward a person can be evoked, the field of emotional disapproval may be extended so as to include disagreement with the assertions that person makes.

A bitter controversy among several contemporary American philosophers illustrates this fallacious attack. One of the disputants wrote:

> It is one thing to be attacked by an honorable opponent in an honorable way. This happens all the time in philosophy. But in my view Sommers's intellectual methods are dishonest. She ignores the most elementary protocols of philosophical disputation.[9]

The target of this accusation replied:

> One dishonest and unworthy tactic used by several of my detractors is to attribute to me complaints I never made and then to dismiss the "complaints" as "irresponsible and evidence of my reckless unfairness."[10]

The merits of the positions of the conflicting parties are not illuminated by argument of this character.

*Ad hominem* abuse has very many variations. The opponent may be abused for being of a certain persuasion, an "isolationist" or an "interventionist," a member of the "radical right" or of the "loony left," or the like. When an argument *ad hominem,* abusive, takes the form of attacking the source or genesis of the opposing position—not relevant to its truth, of course—it may be called the "genetic fallacy."

A conclusion, or its proponent, may at times be condemned because the view is also defended by persons widely believed to be of bad character. Socrates was convicted of impiety at his notorious trial partly because of his association with persons widely known to have been disloyal to Athens and

---

[9] Sandra Lee Bartky, *Proceedings of the American Philosophical Association* 65 (June 1992), 56.
[10] Christina Sommers, *Proceedings of the American Philosophical Association* 65 (June 1992), 79.

rapacious in conduct. And, in 1997, Clyde Collins Snow, called a racist because of the conclusions he reached as a forensic scientist, replied as follows:

> In the past decade my work devoted to the investigation of the disappearance, torture, and extrajudicial execution of human rights victims in many countries has often made me the target of public criticism and official outrage. To date, however, none of my critics has called me a racist. Among my detractors have been apologists for the brutal military junta in Argentina, representatives of General Pinochet's military in Chile, the Guatemalan Defense Minister, and Serbian government spokesmen. Thus Mr. Goodman [Snow's accuser] finds himself in interesting company.[11]

Unfair accusation is an exceedingly common form of personal abuse; *guilt by association* is another pattern of abuse, less widespread but equally fallacious.

In legal proceedings it is sometimes appropriate to exhibit the unreliability of the person giving testimony, to "impeach the witness." If dishonesty in other matters can be shown and credibility thus undermined, such impeachment, in that context, may not be fallacious. But it is never enough simply to assert that the witness lied; a pattern of dishonesty or duplicity must be exhibited, or inconsistencies with past testimony revealed. And even in this special context, the attack on character cannot establish the *falsehood* of the testimony given; that inference would be fallacious.

### B. Argument Ad Hominem, *Circumstantial*

In the circumstantial form of the *ad hominem* fallacy, it is the irrelevance of the connection between the belief held and the circumstances of those holding it that gives rise to the mistake. The *circumstances* of one who makes (or rejects) some claim have no bearing on the truth of that claim.

Thus it may be argued fallaciously that *consistency* obliges an opponent to accept (or reject) some conclusion merely because of that person's employment, or nationality, or political affiliation, or other circumstances. It may be unfairly suggested that a clergyman must accept a given proposition because its denial would be incompatible with the Scriptures. Or it may be claimed that political candidates must support a given policy because it is explicitly propounded in the platform of their party. Such argument is irrelevant to the *truth* of the proposition in question; it simply urges that some persons' circumstances require its acceptance. Hunters, accused of the needless slaughter of unoffending animals, sometimes reply by noting that their critics eat the flesh of harmless cattle. Such a reply is plainly *ad hominem;* the fact that the critic eats meat does not even begin to prove that it is right for the hunter to kill animals for amusement. The Latin term *tu quoque* (meaning "you're another" or, more loosely, "look who's talking") is sometimes used to name this variety of circumstantial *ad hominem* argument.

While the circumstances of the opponent may not be the issue in a serious argument, calling attention to them may be psychologically effective in winning assent, or in persuading others. But however persuasive it may prove, argument of this kind is essentially fallacious.

---

[11] " 'Kind' Racism," *The Sciences,* June, 1997.

Circumstantial *ad hominem* arguments are sometimes used to suggest that the opponents' conclusion should be rejected because their judgment is warped, dictated by their special situation rather than by reasoning or evidence. But an argument that is favorable to some group deserves discussion on its merits; it is fallacious to attack it simply on the ground that it is presented by a member of that group and is therefore self-serving. The arguments in favor of a protective tariff (for example) may be bad, but they are not bad because they are presented by a manufacturer who benefits from such tariffs.

One argument of this kind, called "poisoning the well," is particularly perverse. The incident that gave rise to the name illustrates the argument forcefully. The British novelist and clergyman Charles Kingsley, attacking the famous Catholic intellectual John Henry Cardinal Newman, argued thus: Cardinal Newman's claims were not to be trusted because, as a Roman Catholic priest (Kingsley alleged), Newman's first loyalty was not to the truth. Newman countered that this *ad hominem* attack made it impossible for him and indeed for all Catholics to advance their arguments, since anything that they might say to defend themselves would then be undermined by others' alleging that, after all, truth was not their first concern. Kingsley, said Cardinal Newman, had poisoned the well of discourse.

Between the abusive and the circumstantial varieties of argument *ad hominem* there is a clear connection: the circumstantial may be regarded as a special case of the abusive. When a circumstantial *ad hominem* argument explicitly or implicitly charges the opponents with *inconsistency* (among their beliefs, or between what they profess and what they practice), that is clearly one kind of abuse. When a circumstantial *ad hominem* argument charges the opponents with a lack of trustworthiness by virtue of group membership or conviction, that is an accusation of *prejudice* in defense of self-interest and is clearly also an abuse. Whether of one form or the other, *ad hominem* arguments are directed fallaciously at the person of the adversary.

## R4.  The Appeal to Emotion: Argument *Ad Populum*

This common fallacy and the two that follow it are so evidently fallacious that they require little explanation. In each case, the premises plainly are not relevant to the conclusion and are deliberately chosen as instruments to manipulate the beliefs of the listener or reader.

The argument *ad populum*, the appeal to emotion (literally "to the people," and by implication to the mob's easily aroused emotions) is the device of every propagandist and demagogue. It is fallacious because it **replaces the laborious task of presenting evidence and rational argument with expressive language and other devices calculated to excite enthusiasm, excitement, anger, or hate.** The speeches of Adolph Hitler, which whipped up his German listeners to a state of patriotic frenzy, may be taken as a classic example. Love of country is an honorable emotion. The manipulation of one's audience by appealing inappropriately to that love is intellectually disreputable—leading to Samuel Johnson's caustic observation that "Patriotism is the last refuge of a scoundrel."

The heaviest reliance on arguments *ad populum* is to be found in commercial advertising, where its use has been elevated almost to the status of a fine art. The products advertised are associated, explicitly or slyly, with things that we yearn for or that excite us favorably. Breakfast cereal is associated with trim youthfulness, athletic prowess, and vibrant good health; whiskey is associated with luxury and achievement, and beer with high adventure; the automobile is associated with romance, riches, and sex. The men depicted using the advertised product are generally handsome and distinguished, the women sophisticated and charming—or hardly dressed at all. So clever and persistent are the ballyhoo artists of our time that we are all influenced to some degree, in spite of our resolution to resist. Almost every imaginable device may be used to command our attention, even to penetrate our subconscious thoughts. We are manipulated by relentless appeals to emotion of every kind.

The mere association of the product and the emotion is, by itself, no argument, but an argument *ad populum* commonly lies not far beneath the surface. When advertisers make claims about their products designed to win our emotional approval, and when it is suggested that we ought to make some purchase *because* the item in question is "sexy" or "best-selling" or is associated with wealth or power, the implicit claim that this conclusion follows from such premises is plainly fallacious.

Some instances of the argument *ad populum* are brazen. Here are the exact words of a recent advertisement on ABC-TV:

> Why are so many people attracted to the Pontiac Grand Prix? It could be that so many people are attracted to the Grand Prix because—so many people are attracted to the Grand Prix!

The appeal to popular enthusiasms can be particularly pernicious in the context of public polling, where the known emotive impact (negative or positive) of certain words and phrases[12] makes possible questions designed to yield the responses sought. What, for example, is the attitude of the American public toward tax cuts and federal spending in the light of an impending budget surplus? That depends on how you ask. The question was presented to large random population samples in January 2000—with two different wordings:[13]

> Variant 1: "Should a large portion [of the money in the coming surplus] be used for a tax cut, or should it be used to fund new government programs?"

To this wording of the question, 60 percent of the sample answered "tax cut," while 25 percent answered "new programs." Not surprising: "New government programs" are distinctly unappealing to many.

---

[12] See the discussion of emotive words in section 2.4.

[13] "How Use the Coming Surplus?" *New York Times* (reporting an investigation by the Pew Research Center), 30 January 2000.

Variant 2: "Should a large portion [of the money in the coming surplus] be used for a tax cut, or should it be spent on programs for education, the environment, health care, crime fighting, and military defense?"

To this wording of the question 22 percent of the sample answered "tax cut," and 69 percent answered "new programs." Again not surprising: "education, health care, crime fighting," and so on, are words and phrases known to have substantial popular appeal.

The popular acceptance of a policy does not show it to be wise, of course; nor does the fact that many people hold a given opinion prove it to be true. Bertrand Russell condemned such argument in language that is almost too vigorous:

> The fact that an opinion has been widely held is no evidence whatever that it is not utterly absurd; indeed, in view of the silliness of the majority of mankind, a wide-spread belief is more likely to be foolish than sensible.[14]

## R5.  The Appeal to Pity: Argument *Ad Misericordiam*

The appeal to pity (*misericordiam* meaning literally "a pitying heart") may be viewed as **a special case of the appeal to emotion, in which the altruism and mercy of the audience are the special emotions appealed to.** The attorney for a plaintiff, seeking compensatory damages for an injury, often arranges to have the client's disability revealed in the courtroom in some heartrending way.[15] And in criminal trials, although jury sympathy has no bearing whatever on the guilt or innocence of the accused, effective defense attorneys often appeal to the pity of the jury. Sometimes that appeal is made obliquely. At his trial in Athens, Socrates referred with disdain to other defendants who had appeared before their juries accompanied by their children and families, seeking to be acquitted by evoking pity. Socrates continued:

> …I, who am probably in danger of my life, will do none of these things. The contrast may occur to his [each juror's] mind, and he may be set against me, and vote in anger because he is displeased at me on this account. Now if there be such a person among you—mind, I do not say that there is—to him I may fairly reply: My friend, I am a man, and like other men, a creature of flesh and blood, and not "of wood or stone" as Homer says; and I have a family, yes, and sons, O Athenians, three in number, one almost a man, and two others who are still young; and yet I will not bring any of them here to petition you for acquittal.[16]

There are many ways to pull heart strings, and virtually all are tried. The argument *ad misericordiam* is ridiculed in the story of the trial of a youth accused of the murder of his mother and father with an ax. Confronted with overwhelming proof of his guilt, he pleaded for leniency on the grounds that he was now an orphan.

---

[14] Bertrand Russell, *Marriage and Morals* (New York: Liveright, 1929).

[15] There is more than anecdotal evidence to support the conclusion that the appeal *ad misericordium* pays off in court. See the findings reported in *The New England Journal of Medicine*, recounted in Exercise 7, section 12.2(5).

[16] Plato, *Apology*, 34; Jowett translation.

### R6. The Appeal to Force: Argument *Ad Baculum*

**The appeal to force, to cause the acceptance of some conclusion,** seems at first sight to be so obvious a fallacy as to need no discussion at all. The use or threat of "strong-arm methods" to coerce opponents would seem to be a last resort— a useful expedient when evidence or rational methods fail. "Might makes right" is hardly a subtle principle.

The force threatened need not be physical, of course. Two professors of law at Boise State University recently published (in a law journal of the University of Denver) an article harshly critical of the Boise Cascade Corporation, one of the world's largest producers of paper and wood products. Subsequently, the University issued a formal "errata" notice that "this article has been retracted for its lack of scholarship and false content."

Did Boise Cascade threaten the University with a lawsuit? "Well," said the University's general counsel, " 'threaten' is an interesting word. Let's just say they pointed out that the objections they raised did rise to the level of being actionable." The University, it turns out, had received a highlighted copy of the article in question from the general counsel of Boise Cascade, with a letter saying, "I have been advised to proceed with litigation against Denver University if any of these highlighted areas are republished by Denver University in any form."[17]

But there are occasions when appeals *ad baculum* (literally, "to the stick") are used with more subtlety. The arguer may not threaten directly and yet may convey a veiled threat, or a possible threat in a form calculated to win the assent (or at least the support) of those imperiled. When the attorney general in the Reagan administration was under strong attack in the press for misconduct, the White House chief of staff at the time, Howard Baker, opened one meeting of his staff by saying:

> The President continues to have confidence in the Attorney General and I have confidence in the Attorney General and you ought to have confidence in the Attorney General, because we work for the President and because that's the way things are. And if anyone has a different view of that, or any different motive, ambition, or intention, he can tell me about it because we're going to have to discuss your status.[18]

One may say that nobody is fooled by argument of this sort; the threatened party may *behave* appropriately but need not, in the end, accept the *truth* of the conclusion insisted upon. To this it was answered, by representatives of twentieth-century Italian fascism, that real persuasion can come through many different instruments, of which reason is one and the blackjack is another. But once the opponent is truly persuaded, they held, the instrument of persuasion may be forgotten. That fascist view appears to guide many of the governments of the globe to this day; but the argument *ad baculum*—reliance on the club, or on the threat of force in any form—is by reason unacceptable. The appeal to force is the abandonment of reason.

---

[17] Peter Monaghan, "A Journal Article is Expunged and Its Authors Cry Foul," *The Chronicle of Higher Education*, 8 December 2000.

[18] "White House Orders Silence on Meese," *Washington Post*, 29 April 1988.

# R7.  Irrelevant Conclusion: *Ignoratio Elenchi*

The fallacy of *ignoratio elenchi* (literally, mistaken proof) is committed **when an argument purporting to establish a particular conclusion is instead directed to proving a different conclusion.** The premises "miss the point"; the reasoning may seem plausible in itself, and yet the argument misfires as a defense of the conclusion in dispute. Arguments in the sphere of social legislation frequently commit this fallacy; a program of a particular kind, designed to achieve some larger objective that is widely shared, is supported by premises that do provide reasons to share the larger end, but that tell us nothing relevant about the specific program under consideration. Sometimes this approach is deliberate; sometimes it is the result of a passionate concern for the larger objective, which blinds some advocates of the more specific proposal to the irrelevance of their premisses.

For example, particular tax reforms sometimes are defended by an emphasis on the need to reduce budget deficits—when the real issue is the fairness or yield of the specific tax measure proposed. Or special programs proposed to support the building industry, or the automobile industry, may be defended with premises that show the need for assistance but do not support the need for the kind or amount of assistance the program at issue would provide. When the issue is the wisdom of developing a new and very expensive weapon system, the premises will miss the point if they simply underscore the need for a strong national defense. Whether the weapon system proposed is the one really needed is likely to be the key question. Objectives that are stated in very general terms—national security, good housing, a balanced budget—are easy to endorse; the hard questions are likely to be: Will this particular measure promote the end sought, and if so, will it do so better—more efficiently or more effectively—than the available alternatives? Bypassing these questions, by obscuring the issue with attractive generalizations about some larger or different end, commits the *ignoratio elenchi.*

How do such arguments ever fool anyone? Often they succeed by distracting attention. By urging with enthusiasm the need for the objective defended by the premises, the advocate may succeed in transferring that enthusiasm, in the minds of the audience, to the specific means fallaciously supported. The *ignoratio elenchi* also may prove effective when it is framed in highly emotional language that conceals the misfire with an *ad populum* appeal. But emotion is not the essence of this fallacy; even if the language used be cool and neutral, it is an *ignoratio elenchi* when its real thrust is a conclusion different from the one it purports to defend.

It may be said that every fallacy of relevance is, in a sense, an *ignoratio elenchi.* But as we use this term, it is the fallacy in which the argument misses the point without necessarily making one of those other mistakes—an *ad hominem* attack, or an *ad populum* appeal—that often characterize fallacies in which the premises are not relevant to the conclusion.

Political campaigns often give rise to the fallacy of irrelevant conclusion. As a candidate for the presidency of the United States in 2000, George W. Bush indicated that he was planning to grant a reprieve (under his authority as governor of Texas) to a man convicted of murder and scheduled for execution. Asked why he was telegraphing his intentions before making a final decision, he replied:

> I believe this is a case where it's important for me to send a signal about what I may do because it's a case where we're dealing with a man's innocence or guilt.[19]

The term *non sequitur* is also often applied to fallacies of relevance. That expression means no more than that the stated conclusion *does not follow from* its premiss or premisses, but it is most commonly applied when the gap between premisses and conclusion is very wide, and the claim that the conclusion does follow is a rather obvious blunder. In a speech in Chicago in 1854, Abraham Lincoln said:

> It was a great trick among some public speakers to hurl a naked absurdity at their audience, with such confidence that they should be puzzled to know if the speaker didn't see some point of great magnitude in it which entirely escaped their observation. A neatly varnished sophism would be readily penetrated, but a great, rough *non sequitur* was sometimes twice as dangerous as a well polished fallacy.[20]

But there are times when the claim that the argument presented is a *non sequitur* may itself be open to dispute. Consider this report of a historic "legal fiasco":

> The prisoner pleaded guilty. He then said he had made a mistake, and the judge allowed him to change his plea to not guilty. The case was tried. The jury acquitted. "Prisoner," said Mr. Justice Hawkins, "a few minutes ago you said you were a thief. Now the jury say you are a liar. Consequently you are discharged."[21]

## Exercises

I.     Identify and explain the fallacies of relevance in the following passages.

   *1.     A national organization called In Defense of Animals registered protest, in 1996, against alleged cruelty to animals being sold live or slaughtered in Chinese markets in San Francisco. Patricia Briggs, who brought the complaint to the city's Animal Welfare Commission, said: "The time of the crustaceans is coming. You'd think people wouldn't care about lobsters, because they aren't cuddly and fuzzy and they have these vacant looks and they don't vocalize. But you'd be surprised how many people care." To which response was given by Astella Kung, proprietor of Ming Kee Game Birds, where fowl are sold live: "How about the homeless people? Why don't the animal people use their energy to care for those people? They have no homes! They are hungry!"

               —"Cuisine Raises Debate on Cruelty and Culture," *New York Times*, 26 August 1996.

---

[19] "Bush Expected to Grant a Stay of an Execution," *New York Times*, 1 June 2000.
[20] *The Collected Works of Abraham Lincoln*, R. R. Basler, ed., vol. 2, p. 283.
[21] Stephen Tumim, *Great Legal Fiascos* (London: Arthur Barker, 1985).

2. Nietzsche was personally more philosophical than his philosophy. His talk about power, harshness, and superb immorality was the hobby of a harmless young scholar and constitutional invalid.

—George Santayana, *Egotism in German Philosophy*

3. Mr. Farrakhan, the Black Muslim leader, citing the example of Israel, said black Americans should also be able to form a country of their own on the African continent, and said he plans to ask African leaders to "carve out a territory for all people in the diaspora." He said black Americans should also be granted dual citizenship by all African countries. "We want dual citizenship," he said, "and because we don't know where we came from, we want dual citizenship everywhere."

—Kenneth Noble, "U.S. Blacks and Africans Meet to Forge Stronger Ties," *New York Times*, 27 May 1993

4. However, it matters very little now what the king of England either says or does; he hath wickedly broken through every moral and human obligation, trampled nature and conscience beneath his feet, and by a steady and constitutional spirit of insolence and cruelty procured for himself an universal hatred.

—Thomas Paine, *Common Sense*

*5. As the war in the Persian Gulf began to appear unavoidable in the late fall of 1990, Michael Moore gave a speech at the Law School of the University of Michigan condemning any American military action against the Iraqi regime of Saddam Hussein. "The day that Bush and so-called U.N. forces invade, this campus has got to be shut down. People have to take a significant stand. It's going to have to be stopped." A student asked him what he thought America should do in the light of the probability that Saddam Hussein had or was acquiring nuclear weapons. Moore replied:

"What should we do about Israel? They have the bomb. Does Hussein have the bomb? What if he did? It keeps eyes off the depression we're heading toward or we're already in. It keeps the focus off the Palestinian cause. It does a lot of things to prevent the pickle Bush was almost finding himself in."

—*The Michigan Daily*, 29 November 1990

6. On the Senate floor in 1950, Joe McCarthy announced that he had penetrated "Truman's iron curtain of secrecy." He had 81 case histories of persons whom he considered to be Communists in the State Department. Of Case 40, he said, "I do not have much information on this except the general statement of the agency that there is nothing in the files to disprove his Communist connections."

—Richard H. Rovere, *Senator Joe McCarthy*

196

7. In a scientific journal of very high repute appeared, quite recently, the following judgment of an industrial injury:

Summary: Whereas we cannot unequivocally eliminate other causes for the neuropsychiatric deficits noted in this case, the fact that no air samples were gathered at the worksite and no blood or urine measures were obtained at the time of exposure leads us to conclude that there is compelling evidence that this patient's workplace exposure eventuated in cerebral damage.

—"Lead Poisoning in an Oil-Pipeline Maintenance Worker," *Archives of Environmental Health*, vol. 50, no. 5, p. 391, 1995.

8. Radosh [Prof. Ronald Radosh] experienced a metaphysical lurch in 1973 during a radical junket to Cuba when his little group of revolutionary tourists were taken to one of Castro's mental hospitals and saw one ward filled with patients who had been recently lobotomized. He was disturbed enough to voice his concerns to the American tour guide who looked at him deeply for a moment and then said, "Ron, we have to understand the difference between capitalist lobotomies and socialist lobotomies."

—Peter Collier, "The Suppression of Ronald Radosh," *The Weekly Standard*, 10 June 1996

9. To ignore the possibility that America was discovered by Africans because these explorers are "unknown" is irresponsible and arrogant. If we are unaware of an event, does that mean it never happened?

—Andrew J. Perrin, "To Search for Truth," *New York Times*, 16 November 1990

*10. When we had got to this point in the argument, and everyone saw that the definition of justice had been completely upset, Thrasymachus, instead of replying to me, said: "Tell me, Socrates, have you got a nurse?"

"Why do you ask such a question," I said, "when you ought rather to be answering?"

"Because she leaves you to snivel, and never wipes your nose; she has not even taught you to know the shepherd from the sheep."

—Plato, *The Republic*

11. According to R. Grunberger, author of *A Social History of the Third Reich*, Nazi publishers used to send the following notice to German readers who let their subscriptions lapse: "Our paper certainly deserves the support of every German. We shall continue to forward copies of it to you, and hope that you will not want to expose yourself to unfortunate consequences in the case of cancellation."

12. I also admit that there are people for whom even the reality of the external world [is] a grave problem. My answer is that I do not address *them*, but that I presuppose a minimum of reason in my readers.

> —Paul Feyerabend, "Materialism and the Mind-Body Problem,"
> *The Review of Metaphysics*

13. But can you doubt that air has weight when you have the clear testimony of Aristotle affirming that all the elements have weight including air, and excepting only fire?

> —Galileo Galilei, *Dialogues Concerning Two New Sciences*

14. Like an armed warrior, like a plumed knight, James G. Blaine marched down the halls of the American Congress and threw his shining lances full and fair against the brazen foreheads of every defamer of his country and maligner of its honor.

    For the Republican party to desert this gallant man now is worse than if an army should desert their general upon the field of battle.

> —Robert G. Ingersoll, nominating speech at
> the Republican National Convention, 1876

*15. I was seven years old when the first election campaign, which I can remember, took place in my district. At that time we still had no political parties, so the announcement of this campaign was received with very little interest. But popular feeling ran high when it was disclosed that one of the candidates was "the Prince." There was no need to add Christian and surname to realize which Prince was meant. He was the owner of the great estate formed by the arbitrary occupation of the vast tracts of land reclaimed in the previous century from the Lake of Fucino. About eight thousand families (that is, the majority of the local population) are still employed today in cultivating the estate's fourteen thousand hectares. The Prince was deigning to solicit "his" families for their vote so that he could become their deputy in parliament. The agents of the estate, who were working for the Prince, talked in impeccably liberal phrases: "Naturally," said they, "naturally, no one will be forced to vote for the Prince, that's understood; in the same way that no one, naturally, can force the Prince to allow people who don't vote for him to work on his land. This is the period of real liberty for everybody; you're free, and so is the Prince." The announcement of these "liberal" principles produced general and understandable consternation among the peasants. For, as may easily be guessed, the Prince was the most hated person in our part of the country.

> —Ignazio Silone, *The God That Failed*

II. Each of the following passages may be plausibly criticized by some who conclude that it contains a fallacy, but each will be defended by some who deny that the argument is fallacious. Discuss the merits of each argument and explain why you conclude that it does or does not contain a fallacy of relevance.

*1. Chairman of General Electric, Jack Welch, was challenged at a stockholder's meeting recently by a nun who argued that GE was responsible for the cleanup of the Hudson River where pollutants from GE's plants had for many years been allowed to collect. Welch flatly denied the company's responsibility, saying, "Sister, you have to stop this conversation. You owe it to God to be on the side of truth here."

—Elizabeth Kolbert, "The River," *The New Yorker*, 4 December 2000

2. Gender feminism is notoriously impossible to falsify: it chews up and digests all counterevidence, transmuting it into confirming evidence. The fact that most people, including most women, do not see the pervasive and tenacious system of male power only shows how thoroughly they have been socialized to perpetuate it. The more women who reject the gender feminist perspective, the more this proves them in thrall to the androcentric system. Nothing and no one can refute the hypothesis of the sex-gender system for those who . . . see it so clearly "everywhere."

—Christina Sommers, *Proceedings of the American Philosophical Association*, June 1992

3. As the American Revolution began to appear likely, some Americans sought reconciliation with England; Thomas Paine opposed reconciliation bitterly. In *Common Sense* (1776), he wrote:

> . . . all those who espouse the doctrine of reconciliation may be included within the following descriptions. Interested men, who are not to be trusted, weak men who cannot see, prejudiced men who will not see, and a certain set of moderate men who think better of the European world than it deserves; and this last class, by an ill-judged deliberation, will be the cause of more calamities to this Continent than all the other three.

4. "But I observe," says Cleanthes, "with regard to you, Philo, and all speculative sceptics, that your doctrine and practice are as much at variance in the most abstruse points of theory as in the conduct of common life."

—David Hume, *Dialogues Concerning Natural Religion*

*5. A press release from the National Education Association (NEA) begins with the following statement. "America's teachers see smaller classes as the most critical element in doing a better job, a survey by the NEA indicates." . . . But the NEA, of course, is interested in having as many teachers in the schools as possible. For example, in a 3,000-pupil school system with 30 pupils assigned to each class, the teaching staff would be approximately 100. But if class size were changed to 25 the total number of teachers would rise to 120. And in a time of shrinking enrollments, that is a way to keep teachers on the public payroll. . . .

It is unfortunate that an organization with the professional reputation the National Education Association enjoys should be so self-serving.

—Cynthia Parsons, *Christian Science Monitor Service*

6. Consider genetically engineered fish. Scientists hope that fish that contain new growth hormones will grow bigger and faster than normal fish. Other scientists are developing fish that could be introduced into cold, northern waters, where they cannot now survive. The intention is to boost fish production for food. The economic benefits may be obvious, but not the risks. Does this make the risks reasonable?

—Edward Bruggemann, "Genetic Engineering Needs Strict Regulation," *New York Times*, 24 March 1992

7. ANYTUS: "Socrates, I think that you are too ready to speak evil of men: and, if you will take my advice, I would recommend you to be careful. Perhaps there is no city in which it is not easier to do men harm than to do them good, and this is certainly the case at Athens, as I believe that you know."

—Plato, *Meno*

8. The Greek historian Thucydides, in his *History of the Peloponnesian War*, gave the following account of an Athenian's appeal to representatives of the small island of Melos, to join Athens in its war against Sparta:

> You know as well as we do that, in the logic of human nature, right only comes into question where there is a balance of power, while it is might that determines what the strong exhort and the weak concede....Your strongest weapons are hopes yet unrealized, while the weapons in your hands are somewhat inadequate for holding out against the forces already arranged against you....Reflect that you are taking a decision for your country, a country whose fate hangs upon a single decision right or wrong.

9. In that melancholy book *The Future of an Illusion*, Dr. Freud, himself one of the last great theorists of the European capitalist class, has stated with simple clarity the impossibility of religious belief for the educated man of today.

—John Strachey, *The Coming Struggle for Power*

*10. The classic trap for any revolutionary is always "What's your alternative?" But even if you *could* provide the interrogator with a blueprint, this does not mean he would use it; in most cases he is not sincere in wanting to know.

—Shulamith Firestone, *The Dialectic of Sex: The Case for Feminist Revolution*

## 4.3 FALLACIES OF PRESUMPTION

Some mistakes in everyday reasoning are the consequence of an unjustified assumption, often suggested by the formulation of the argument. The reader, or listener, or even the author of the passage may be caused—through oversight or by deliberate design—to assume the truth of some unproved and unwarranted proposition. When such dubious assumptions buried in the argument are crucial for the support of the conclusion, the argument is bad and can be very misleading. **Unwarranted leaps of this kind are called *fallacies of presumption.***

In fallacious arguments of this kind the premises are, again, often not relevant to the conclusion. Indeed, in most fallacies there is a gap, an irrelevance between premises and conclusion. But the fallacies of presumption exhibit a special kind of mistake: the tacit supposition of what has not been given support and may even be insupportable. To expose such a fallacy, it is usually sufficient to call attention to that smuggled assumption, and to its doubtfulness or falsity.

### P1.  Complex Question

One of the most common fallacies of presumption is this: **asking a question in such a way as to presuppose the truth of some conclusion buried in that question.** The question itself is likely to be rhetorical, no answer being genuinely sought. But putting the question seriously, thereby introducing its presupposition surreptitiously, often achieves the questioner's purpose—fallaciously.

Thus an executive of a utility company may ask, "Why is the private development of resources so much more efficient than any government-owned enterprise?"—*assuming* the greater efficiency of the private sector. Or a homeowner may ask, regarding a proposed increase in the property tax, "How can you expect the majority of the voters, who rent but don't own property and don't have to pay the tax, to care if the tax burden of others is made even more unfair?"—assuming both that the burden of the proposed tax is unfair, and that those who rent rather than own their own homes are not affected by tax increases on property. Since assumptions like these are not openly asserted, the questioners evade the need to defend them forthrightly.

The complex question often is a deceitful device. The speaker may pose some question, then answer it or strongly suggest the answer with the truth of the premiss that had been buried in the question simply assumed. A letter-writer asks: "If America's booming economy depends on people's using consumer credit beyond their means, thus creating poverty, do we really have a healthy economy?"[22] But the role and the results of consumer credit remain to be addressed.

One critic of research in genetics hides his assumptions in this question: "What are the consequences of reducing the world's gene pool to patented intellectual property, controlled by a handful of life-science corporations?"[23] The "consequences" asked about are never actually discussed; they are only a de-

---

[22] Barbara Commins, "The Slide into Poverty," *New York Times,* 10 September 2000.

[23] Jeremy Rifkin, "Issues in Genetic Research," *The Chronicle of Higher Education,* 3 July 1998.

vice with which the reader may be frightened by the assumptions of the question—that the world's gene pool is soon likely to be reduced to patented intellectual property, and that a handful of corporations will soon control that gene pool. But establishing the plausibility of such threats requires much more than asking questions designed to presuppose them.

The appearance of a question in an editorial or headline often has the purpose of suggesting the truth of the unstated assumptions on which it is built: JUDGE TOOK BRIBE? This technique is a common mark of what is called "yellow journalism." And in debate, whenever a question is accompanied by the aggressive demand that it be answered "yes or no," there is reason to suspect that the question is "loaded," that it is unfairly complex.

The mistake that underlies the fallacy of complex question also underlies a common problem in parliamentary procedure. Deliberative bodies sometimes confront a motion that, although not intended deceptively, is covertly complex. In such circumstances there is a need, before discussion, to simplify the issues confronting the body. This accounts for the privileged position, in parliamentary procedure governed by *Robert's Rules of Order* or like manuals, of the motion to *divide the question*. For example, a motion that the body "postpone for one year" action on some controversial matter may wisely be divided into the decision to postpone action, and *if* that is done, then to determine the length of the postponement. Some members may support the postponement itself, yet find the one-year period intolerably long; if the opportunity to divide the question were not given priority, the body might be maneuvered into taking action on a motion that, because of its complexity, cannot be decided intelligently. A presiding officer, having the duty to promote a fully rational debate, may solicit the motion to divide the question before beginning the substantive discussion.

Egregious examples of the fallacy of the complex question arise in dialogue or cross-examination in which one party poses a question that is complex, a second party answers the question, and the first party then draws a fallacious inference for which that answer was the ground. For example:

LAWYER: The figures seem to indicate that your sales increased as a result of these misleading advertisements. Is that correct?

WITNESS: They did not!

LAWYER: But you do admit, then, that your advertising was misleading. How long have you been engaging in practices like these?

When a question is complex, and all of its presuppositions are to be denied, they must be denied individually. The denial of only one presupposition may lead to the assumption of the truth of the other. In law, this has been called "the negative pregnant." Here is an illustration from a notorious murder trial:

Q: Lizzie, did you not take an axe and whack your mother forty times, and then whack your father forty-one times when faced with the prospect of cold mutton stew?

A: Not true. We were to eat brussel sprouts fondue that day.

## P2. False Cause

It is obvious that any reasoning that relies on treating as the cause of some thing or event what is not really its cause must be seriously mistaken. But often we are tempted to suppose, or led to suppose, that we understand some specific cause-and-effect relation when in fact we do not. The nature of the connection between cause and effect, and how we determine whether such a connection is present or absent, are central problems of inductive logic and scientific method. These problems are discussed in detail in Part Three of this book. Presuming the reality of a causal connection that does not really exist is a common mistake; in Latin the mistake is called the fallacy of *non causa pro causa;* we call it simply the fallacy of false cause.

Whether the causal connection alleged is indeed mistaken may sometimes be a matter in dispute. Some college faculty members, it has been argued, grade leniently because they fear that rigorous grading will cause lowered evaluations of them by their students, and would do damage to their careers. Gradual "grade inflation" is said to be the result of this fear. One college professor wrote this:

> Course evaluation forms [completed by students] are now required in many institutions, and salaries are influenced by the results. When I joined the University of Michigan 30 years ago, my salary was higher than that of any member of the anthropology department who is still active today. My standards for grading have not followed the trend toward inflation. Student complaints about grades have increased, and now my salary is at the bottom of the professorial list.[24]

Do you think the author of this passage commits the fallacy of false cause?

It sometimes happens that we presume that one event is caused by another because it *follows* that other closely in time. We know, of course, that mere temporal succession does not establish a causal connection, but it is easy to be fooled. If an aggressive move in foreign policy is followed by a distantly related international event for which we had been aiming, some may mistakenly conclude that the aggressive policy was the cause of that event. In primitive science such mistakes were common; we now reject as absurd the claim that beating drums is the cause of the sun's reappearance after an eclipse, despite the undeniable evidence that every time drums have been beaten during an eclipse the sun subsequently did reappear.

Mistakes in reasoning of this kind remain widespread: Unusual weather conditions are blamed on some unrelated celestial phenomenon that happened to precede them; an infection really caused by a virus is thought to be caused by a chill wind or wet feet, and so on. This variety of false cause is called the fallacy of *post hoc ergo propter hoc* ("after the thing, therefore because of the thing"); an example of it appeared in a recent letter to the *New York Times,* in which the correspondent wrote:

> The death penalty in the United States has given us the highest crime rate and greatest number of prisoners per 100,000 population in the industrialized world.[25]

---

[24] C. Loring Brace, "Faculty is Powerless," *New York Times,* 24 February 1998.

[25] Harvey I, "Death Penalty Ethics." *New York Times,* 13 February 1996.

*Post hoc ergo propter hoc* is an easy fallacy to detect when it is blatant, but even the best of scientists and statesmen are on occasion misled.

## P3.  Begging the Question: *Petitio Principii*

**To beg the question is to assume the truth of what one seeks to prove, in the effort to prove it.** That would seem to be a silly mistake, evident to all—but how silly or obvious the mistake is depends largely on the way in which the premises of the argument are formulated. Their wording often obscures the fact that buried within one of the premises assumed lies the conclusion itself. This fallacy is illustrated by the following argument, reported long ago by the logician Richard Whately: "To allow every man unbounded freedom of speech must always be, on the whole, advantageous to the state; for it is highly conducive to the interests of the community that each individual should enjoy a liberty, perfectly unlimited, of expressing his sentiments."

Sometimes we fall into this mistake when, in the effort to establish our conclusion, we cast about in search of premises that will do the trick. Of course the conclusion itself, disguised in other language, certainly will do the trick! Most fallacies, we noted earlier, can be viewed in some light as fallacies of relevance— but the *petitio principii* cannot. The premises of the argument, in this case, are not irrelevant; they certainly do prove the conclusion—but they do so trivially. A *petitio principii* is always technically valid—but always worthless, as well.

This is another of those mistakes that often go unrecognized by those who commit them. The presumption buried in the premises may be obscured by confusing or unrecognized synonyms, or by a chain of intervening argument. Every *petitio* is a *circular argument*, but the circle that has been constructed may—if it is large or fuzzy—go quite undetected.

Powerful minds sometimes are snared by this fallacy, as is illustrated by a highly controversial issue in the history of philosophy. Logicians have long sought to establish the reliability of inductive procedures by establishing the truth of what is called the "principle of induction." This is the principle that the laws of nature will operate tomorrow as they operate today, that in basic ways nature is essentially uniform, and that therefore we may rely on past experience to guide our conduct in the future. "That the future will be essentially like the past" is the claim at issue, but this claim, never doubted in ordinary life, turns out to be very difficult to prove. Some thinkers have claimed that they could prove it by showing that, when we have in the past relied on the inductive principle, we have always found that this method has helped us to achieve our objectives. They ask, "Why conclude that the future will be like the past?" and answer, "Because it always has been like the past."

But as David Hume pointed out, this common argument is a *petitio*—it begs the question. For the point at issue is whether nature *will continue* to behave regularly; that it *has* done so in the past cannot serve as proof that it *will* do so in the future—unless one assumes the very principle that is here in question: that the future will be like the past. And so Hume, granting that in the past the future has been like the past, asked the telling question with which philosophers still tussle: How can we know that future futures will be like past futures? They *may* be so, of course, but we may not *assume* that they will be for the sake of *proving* that they will.[26]

## P4. and P5.   Accident and Converse Accident

The fallacies of accident and converse accident arise as a result of the careless, or deliberately deceptive, use of generalizations. In most important affairs, and especially in political or moral argument, we rely on statements of how things generally are, how people generally behave, and the like. But even where general claims are entirely plausible, we must be careful not to apply them to particular cases mechanically or rigidly. Circumstances alter cases; a generalization that is true by and large may not apply in a given case, for good reasons having to do with the special (or "accidental") circumstances of that case. **When we presume the applicability of a generalization to individual cases that it does not properly govern, we commit the fallacy of** *accident*. When we do the reverse, and carelessly or by design **presume that what is true of a particular case is true of the great run of cases, we commit the fallacy of** *converse accident*.

Experience teaches us that generalizations, even those widely applicable and useful, often have exceptions against which we must be on guard. In the law, principles that are sound in general sometimes have very specifically identified exceptions. For example, the rule that hearsay testimony may not be accepted as evidence in court is not applicable when the party whose oral communications are reported is dead, or when the party reporting the hearsay does so in conflict with his own best interest. Almost every good rule has appropriate exceptions; we are likely to argue fallaciously when we reason on the supposition that some rule applies with universal force.

In a dialogue with the young Euthydemus, who planned to become a statesman, Socrates drew from Euthydemus a commitment to many of the conventionally accepted moral truths: that it is wrong to deceive, unjust to steal, and so on. Then Socrates (as recounted by Xenophon in his report of the dialogue) presented a series of hypothetical cases in which Euthydemus reluctantly agreed that it would appear right to deceive (to rescue our compatriots) and just to steal (to save a friend's life), and so on. To all those who may try to decide specific and complicated issues by appealing mechanically to general rules, the fallacy of accident is a genuine and serious threat. The logician H. W. B. Joseph observed that "there is no fallacy more insidious than that of treating a statement which in many connections is not misleading as if it were true always and without qualification."

Accident is the fallacy we commit when we move carelessly or too quickly *from* a generalization; converse accident is the fallacy we commit when we move carelessly or too quickly *to* a generalization. We are all familiar with those who draw conclusions about all persons in a given category because of what may be true about one or a few persons in that category; we know, and

---

[26] See David Hume, "Sceptical Doubts Concerning the Operations of the Understanding," in *An Enquiry Concerning Human Understanding,* sec. 4 (1747).

need to remember, that although a certain drug or food may be harmless in some circumstance, it is not therefore harmless in all circumstances. For example: Eating deep-fried foods has a generally adverse impact on one's cholesterol level, but that bad outcome may not arise in some persons. The owner of a "fish and chips" shop in England recently defended the healthfulness of his deep-fried cookery with this argument:

> Take my son, Martyn. He's been eating fish and chips his whole life, and he just had a cholesterol test, and his level is below the national average. What better proof could there be than a frier's son?[27]

Converse accident is a kind of fallacious reasoning whose error is plain to everyone once that error has been exposed; yet it may serve as a convenient deception, on which many persons are tempted to rely when they argue inattentively or with great passion.

## Exercises

Identify and explain any fallacies of presumption found in the following passages.

*1. My generation was taught about the dangers of social diseases, how they were contracted, and the value of abstinence. Our schools did not teach us about contraception. They did not pass out condoms, as many of today's schools do. And not one of the girls in any of my classes, not even in college, became pregnant out of wedlock. It wasn't until people began teaching the children about contraceptives that our problems with pregnancy began.

—Frank Webster, "No Sex Education, No Sex," *Insight,*
17 November 1997

2. A national mailing in 1992, soliciting funds by People for the Ethical Treatment of Animals (PETA), contains a survey in which questions are to be answered yes or no. Two of the questions asked are these:

"Do you realize that the vast majority of painful animal experimentation has no relation at all to human survival or the elimination of disease?"

"Are you aware that product testing on animals does *not* keep unsafe products off the market?"

3. If you want a life full of sexual pleasures, don't graduate from college. A study to be published next month in *American Demographics* magazine shows that people with the most education have the least amount of sex.

—*The Chronicle of Higher Education,* 15 January 1998

---

[27] John Bedder, reported in "Fried and Salty, Yessir, Matey, but Truly English," *New York Times,* 9 March 1993.

4. There is no surprise in discovering that acupuncture can relieve pain and nausea. It will probably also be found to work on anxiety, insomnia, and itching, because these are all conditions in which placebos work. Acupuncture works by suggestion, a mechanism whose effects on humans are well known.

   The danger in using such placebo methods is that they will be applied by people inadequately trained in medicine in cases where essential preliminary work has not been done and where a correct diagnosis has not been established.

   —Fred Levit, M.D., "Acupuncture is Alchemy, Not Medicine," *New York Times*, 12 November 1997

*5. In a motion picture featuring the famous French comedian Sacha Guitry, some thieves are arguing over division of seven pearls worth a king's ransom. One of them hands two to the man on his right, then two to the man on his left. "I," he says, "will keep three." The man on his right says, "How come you keep three?" "Because I am the leader." "Oh. But how come you are the leader?" "Because I have more pearls."

6. ". . . I've always reckoned that looking at the new moon over your left shoulder is one of the carelessest and foolishest things a body can do. Old Hank Bunker done it once, and bragged about it; and in less than two years he got drunk and fell off of the shot tower, and spread himself out so that he was just a kind of a layer, as you may say; and they slid him edgeways between two barn doors for a coffin, and buried him so, so they say, but I didn't see it. Pap told me. But anyway it all come of looking at the moon that way, like a fool."

   —Mark Twain, *The Adventures of Huckleberry Finn*

7. Former Senator Robert Packwood of Oregon became so angry at the state's leading newspaper, the Portland *Oregonian*, that in response to a request from that paper for a quote he offered this: "Since I quit talking to the *Oregonian*, my business has prospered beyond all measure. I assume that my business has prospered because I don't talk to the Oregonian. Therefore I will continue that policy. Thanks."

   —*New York Times*, 7 February 1999

8. There is no such thing as knowledge which cannot be carried into practice, for such knowledge is really no knowledge at all.

   —Wang Shou-Jen, *Record of Instructions*

9. In 1960 this great country had the finest public schools in the world. After 35 years and spending billions of dollars of Federal money, our public schools rank near the bottom of the industrialized world. What happened? The Federal Government intruded

into public education. We now have the largest number of functional illiterates in the industrialized world.

—Ross Perot, 14 September 1996, in a speech to the Christian Coalition in
Washington, DC, during the presidential campaign of 1996

*10.  Hiroyuki Suzuki was formerly a member of the Sakaume gumi, an independent crime family in Japan known for its role in gambling. Mr. Suzuki's wife Mariko broke her kneecap, and when Mariko went to church the next Sunday, the minister put his hands on her broken knee and pronounced it healed. She walked away from church that day. Mr. Suzuki regarded her religion as a silly waste of time—but he was fascinated by the recovery of her knee. "In gambling," he said, "you use dice. Dice are made from bone. If God could heal her bone, I figured he could probably assist my dice and make me the best dice thrower in all of Japan." Mr. Suzuki's gambling skills did improve, enabling him to pay off his debts. He now says his allegiance is to Jesus.

—Stephanie Strom, "He Watched Over His Rackets,"
*New York Times*, 22 June 1999.

## 4.4  FALLACIES OF AMBIGUITY

The meaning of words or phrases may shift as a result of inattention, or may be deliberately manipulated within the course of an argument. A term may have one sense in a premiss, but quite a different sense in the conclusion. When the inference drawn depends upon such changes it is, of course, fallacious. Mistakes of this kind are called "fallacies of ambiguity" or sometimes "sophisms." The deliberate use of such devices is usually crude and readily detected—but at times the ambiguity may be obscure, the error accidental, the fallacy subtle. Five varieties are distinguished in the following.

### A1.  Equivocation

Most words have more than one literal meaning, and most of the time we have no difficulty in keeping those meanings apart by noting the context and using our good sense when reading and listening. **Yet when we confuse the several meanings of a word or phrase—accidentally or deliberately—we are using the word equivocally. If we do that in the context of an argument, we commit the fallacy of** *equivocation.*

Sometimes the equivocation is obvious and absurd and is used in a joking line or passage. Lewis Carroll's account of the adventures of Alice in *Through the Looking Glass* is replete with clever and amusing equivocations. One of them goes like this:

"Who did you pass on the road?" the King went on, holding his hand out to the messenger for some hay.

"Nobody," said the messenger.

"Quite right," said the King; "this young lady saw him too. So of course Nobody walks slower than you."

The equivocation in this passage is in fact rather subtle. As it is first used here, the word "nobody" simply means "no person." But reference is then made using a pronoun ("him"), as though that word ("nobody") had *named* a person. And when subsequently the same word is capitalized and plainly used as a name ("Nobody"), it putatively names a person having a characteristic (not being passed on the road) derived from the first use of the word. Equivocation is sometimes the tool of wit—and Lewis Carroll was a very witty logician.[28]

Equivocal arguments are always fallacious, but they are not always silly or comic, as will be seen in the example discussed in the following excerpt:

> There is an ambiguity in the phrase "have faith in" that helps to make faith look respectable. When a man says that he has faith in the president he is assuming that it is obvious and known to everybody that there is a president, that the president exists, and he is asserting his confidence that the president will do good work on the whole. But, if a man says he has faith in telepathy, he does not mean that he is confident that telepathy will do good work on the whole, but that he believes that telepathy really occurs sometimes, that telepathy exists. Thus the phrase "to have faith in *x*" sometimes means to be confident that good work will be done by *x*, who is assumed or known to exist, but at other times means to believe that *x* exists. Which does it mean in the phrase "have faith in God"? It means ambiguously both; and the self-evidence of what it means in the one sense recommends what it means in the other sense. If there is a perfectly powerful and good god it is self-evidently reasonable to believe that he will do good. In this sense "have faith in God" is a reasonable exhortation. But it insinuates the other sense, namely "believe that there is a perfectly powerful and good god, no matter what the evidence." Thus the reasonableness of trusting God if he exists is used to make it seem also reasonable to believe that he exists.[29]

One kind of equivocation deserves special mention. This is the mistake that arises from the misuse of "relative" terms, which have different meaning in different contexts. For example, the word "tall" is a relative word; a tall man and a tall building are in quite different categories. A tall man is one who is taller than most men, a tall building is one that is taller than most buildings. Certain forms of argument that are valid for nonrelative terms break down when relative terms are substituted for them. The argument "an elephant is an animal; therefore a gray elephant is a gray animal" is perfectly valid. The word "gray" is a nonrelative term. But the argument "an elephant is an animal; therefore a small elephant is a small animal" is ridiculous. The point here is that "small" is a relative term: a small elephant is a very large animal. The fallacy is one of equivocation with regard to the relative term "small." Not all equivocation on relative terms is so obvious, however. The word "good" is a relative term and

---

[28] This passage from *Alice in Wonderland* very probably inspired David Powers, who formally changed his name to Absolutely Nobody, and ran as an independent candidate for lieutenant governor of the State of Oregon. His campaign slogan was: "Hi, I'm Absolutely Nobody. Vote for me." In the general election of 1992, he drew 7 percent of the vote.

[29] Richard Robinson, *An Atheist's Values* (Oxford University Press, Oxford, 1964), p. 121.

is frequently equivocated on when it is argued, for example, that so-and-so is a good general and would therefore be a good president, or is a good scholar and must therefore be a good teacher.

## A2. Amphiboly

The fallacy of amphiboly occurs when one is arguing from premisses whose formulations are ambiguous because of their grammatical construction. The word "amphiboly" is derived from the Greek, its meaning in essence being "two in a lump," or the "doubleness" of a lump. **A statement is amphibolous when its meaning is indeterminate because of the loose or awkward way in which its words are combined.** An amphibolous statement may be true in one interpretation and false in another. **When it is stated as premiss with the interpretation that makes it true, and a conclusion is drawn from it on the interpretation that makes it false, then the fallacy of amphiboly has been committed.**

In guiding electoral politics, amphiboly can mislead as well as confuse. During the 1990s, while he sat in the U.S. House of Representatives as a Democrat from California, Congressman Tony Coelho is reported to have said: "Women prefer Democrats to men." Amphibolous statements make dangerous premisses—but they are seldom encountered in serious discourse.

What grammarians call "dangling" participles and phrases often present amphiboly of an entertaining sort, as in "The farmer blew out his brains after taking affectionate farewell of his family with a shotgun." And tidbits in *The New Yorker* make acid fun of writers and editors who overlook careless amphiboly:

> "Leaking badly, manned by a skeleton crew, one infirmity after another overtakes the little ship." (The *Herald Tribune,* book section)
> Those game little infirmities![30]

## A3. Accent

An argument may prove deceptive, and invalid, when the shift of meaning within it arises from changes in the emphasis given to its words or parts. **When a premiss relies for its apparent meaning on one possible emphasis, but a conclusion is drawn from it that relies on the meaning of the same words accented differently, the fallacy of *accent* is committed.**

Consider, as illustration, the different meanings that can be given to the statement

> *We should* not *speak* ill of *our friends.*

At least five distinct meanings—or more?—can be given to those eight words, depending on which one of them is emphasized. When read without any undue stresses the injunction is perfectly sound. If the conclusion is drawn from it, however, that we should feel free to speak ill of someone who is *not* our friend, this conclusion follows only if the premiss has the meaning it acquires

---

[30] *The New Yorker,* 8 November, 1958.

when its last word is accented. But when the last word of the sentence is accented, it is no longer acceptable as a moral rule; it then has a different meaning, and it is, in fact, a different premiss. The argument is a case of the fallacy of accent. So, too, would be the argument that drew from the same premiss the conclusion that we are free to *work* ill on our friends if only we do not speak it—and similarly with the other fallacious inferences that suggest themselves.

A phrase or passage can often be understood correctly only in its context, which makes clear the *sense* in which it is intended. The fallacy of accent may be construed broadly to include the distortion produced by pulling a quoted passage out of its context, putting it in another context, and there drawing a conclusion that could never have been drawn in the original context. This business of quoting out of context is sometimes done with deliberate craftiness. In the presidential election campaign of 1996 the Democratic vice-presidential candidate, Al Gore, was quoted by a Republican press aide as having said that "there is no proven link between smoking and lung cancer." Those were indeed Mr. Gore's exact words, uttered during a television interview in 1992. But they were only part of a sentence. In that interview, Mr. Gore's full statement was that some tobacco company scientists *"will claim with a straight face that* there is no proven link between smoking and lung cancer. . . . But the weight of the evidence accepted by the overwhelming preponderance of scientists is, yes, smoking does cause lung cancer."[31]

The omission of the words "will claim with a straight face" and of Gore's express conviction that cancer is caused by smoking, unfairly reversed the sense of the passage from which the quotation was pulled. The argument suggested by the abbreviated quotation, having the apparent conclusion that Mr. Gore seriously doubts the causal link between smoking and cancer, is an egregious example of the fallacy of accent.

Similarly, the deliberate omission of some qualification made by an author that plays a key role in giving the meaning intended for some written passage may be a damaging use of accent. In a critical essay about conservative thinkers, Sidney Blumenthal (1985) wrote about one such thinker, Gregory A. Fossedal, that "On the right, Fossedal is widely regarded as his generation's most promising journalist." A 1989 advertisement for a later book by Mr. Fossedal contained several "blurbs," including this one attributed to Mr. Blumenthal: "Many consider Fossedal the most promising journalist of his generation." The omission of the critic's phrase "on the right" very greatly distorts the sense of the original passage, leading the reader to draw a mistaken conclusion about the critic's judgment of the author. Mr. Blumenthal was understandably infuriated.[32]

Similarly, a theater critic who says of a new play that it is far from the funniest appearing on Broadway this year may be quoted in an ad for the play: "Funniest appearing on Broadway this year!" To avoid such distortions, and the fallacies of accent that may be built upon them, the responsible writer must be

---

[31] *New York Times,* 18 June 1996.

[32] "You Write the Facts, I'll Write the Blurbs," *New York Times,* 18 April 1989. The original passage appeared in the *Washington Post,* 22 November, 1985; the offending advertisement appeared in *The New Republic* in March 1989. Mr. Fossedal subsequently apologized to Mr. Blumenthal.

scrupulously accurate in quotation, always indicating whether italics were in the original, indicating (with dots) whether passages have been omitted, and so on.

Physical manipulation of print or pictures is commonly used to mislead deliberately through accent. Sensational words in large letters appear in the headlines of newspaper reports, deliberately suggesting mistaken conclusions to those who glance hastily at the account. Later in the report the headline is likely to be qualified by other words in much smaller letters. To avoid being tricked, by news reports or in contracts, one is well advised to give careful attention to "the small print." In political propaganda the misleading choice of a sensational heading or the use of a clipped photograph, in what purports to be a factual report, will use accent shrewdly so as to encourage the drawing of conclusions known by the propagandist to be false. An account that may not be an outright lie may yet distort by accent in ways that are deliberately manipulative or dishonest.

In advertising, such practices are hardly rare. A remarkably low price often appears in very large letters, followed by "and up" in tiny print. Wonderful bargains in airplane fares are followed by an asterisk, with a distant footnote explaining that the price is available only three months in advance for flights on Thursdays following a full moon, or that there may be other "applicable restrictions." Costly items with well-known brand names are advertised at very low prices, with a small note elsewhere in the ad that "prices listed are for limited quantities in stock." Readers are drawn into the store but are likely to be unable to make the purchase at the advertised price. Accented passages, by themselves, are not strictly fallacies; they become embedded in fallacies when one interpretation of a phrase, flowing from its accent, is relied upon to suggest a conclusion (*e.g.*, that the plane ticket or brand item can be advantageously purchased at the listed price) that is very doubtful when account is taken of the misleading accent.

Even the literal truth can be made use of, through manipulation of its placement, to deceive with accent. Disgusted with his first mate who was repeatedly inebriated on duty, the captain of a ship noted in the ship's logbook, almost every day, "The mate was drunk today." The angry mate took his revenge. Keeping the log himself on a day when the captain was ill, the mate recorded, "The captain was sober today."

## A4. Composition

The term "fallacy of composition" is applied to both of two closely related types of invalid argument. The first may be described as **reasoning fallaciously from the attributes of the parts of a whole to the attributes of the whole itself.** A particularly flagrant example would be to argue that, since every part of a certain machine is light in weight, the machine "as a whole" is light in weight. The error here is manifest when we recognize that a very heavy machine may consist of a very large number of lightweight parts. Not all examples of this kind of fallacious composition are so obvious, however. Some are misleading. One may hear it seriously argued that, since each scene of a certain play is a model of artistic perfection, the play as a whole is artistically perfect. But this is as much a fallacy of composition as it would be to argue that, since every ship is ready for battle, the whole fleet must be ready for battle.

The other type of composition fallacy is strictly parallel to that just described. **Here, the fallacious reasoning is from attributes of the individual elements or members of a collection to attributes of the collection or totality of those elements.** For example, it would be fallacious to argue that because a bus uses more gasoline than an automobile, therefore all buses use more gasoline than all automobiles. This version of the fallacy of composition turns on a confusion between the "distributive" and the "collective" use of general terms. Thus, although college students may enroll in no more than six different classes each semester, it is also true that college students enroll in hundreds of different classes each semester. This verbal conflict is easily resolved. It may be true of college students, distributively, that each of them may enroll in no more than six classes each semester. This is a distributive use of the term "college students," in that we are speaking of college students taken *singly*. But it is true of college students, taken collectively, that they enroll in hundreds of different classes each semester. This is a collective use of the term "college students" in that we are speaking of college students all together, as a totality. Thus, buses use more gasoline than automobiles, distributively, but collectively automobiles use more gasoline than buses, because there are so many more of them.

This second kind of composition fallacy may be defined as "the invalid inference that what may truly be predicated of a term distributively may also be truly predicated of the term collectively." Thus, the atomic bombs dropped during World War II did more damage than did the ordinary bombs dropped—but only distributively. The matter is exactly reversed when the two kinds of bombs are considered collectively, because there were so many more conventional bombs dropped than atomic ones. Ignoring this distinction in an argument would permit the fallacy of composition.

These two varieties of composition, although parallel, are really distinct because of the difference between a mere collection of elements and a whole constructed out of those elements. Thus, a mere collection of parts is no machine; a mere collection of bricks is neither a house nor a wall. A whole, such as a machine, a house, or a wall, has its parts organized or arranged in certain definite ways. And since organized wholes and mere collections are distinct, so are the two versions of the composition fallacy, one proceeding invalidly to wholes from their parts, the other proceeding invalidly to collections from their members or elements.

## A5. Division

The fallacy of division is simply the reverse of the fallacy of composition. In it the same confusion is present, but the inference proceeds in the opposite direction. As in the case of composition, two varieties of the fallacy of division may be distinguished. **The first kind of division consists in arguing fallaciously that what is true of a whole must also be true of its parts.** To argue that, since a certain corporation is very important and Mr. Doe is an official of that corporation, therefore Mr. Doe is very important, is to commit the fallacy of division. This first variety of the division fallacy would be committed in any such argument, as in moving from the premiss that a certain machine is heavy, or complicated, or valuable, to the conclusion that this or any other part of the machine must be heavy, or complicated, or valuable. To argue that a student must have a large room because it is located in a large dormitory would be still another instance of the first kind of fallacy of division.

**The second type of division fallacy is committed when one argues from the attributes of a collection of elements to the attributes of the elements themselves.** To argue that, since university students study medicine, law, engineering, dentistry, and architecture, therefore each, or even any, university student studies medicine, law, engineering, dentistry, and architecture would be to commit the second kind of division fallacy. It is true that university students, collectively, study all these various subjects, but it is false that university students, distributively, do so. Instances of this fallacy of division often look like valid arguments, for what is true of a class distributively is certainly true of each and every member. Thus the argument

> Dogs are carnivorous.
> Afghan hounds are dogs.
> Therefore Afghan hounds are carnivorous.

is perfectly valid. Closely resembling this argument is another,

> Dogs are frequently encountered in the streets.
> Afghan hounds are dogs.
> Therefore Afghan hounds are frequently encountered in the streets.

which is invalid, committing the fallacy of division. Some instances of division are obviously jokes, as when the classical example of valid argumentation

> Humans are mortal.
> Socrates is a human.
> Therefore Socrates is mortal.

is parodied by the fallacious

> American Indians are disappearing.
> That man is an American Indian.
> Therefore that man is disappearing.

The old riddle "Why do white sheep eat more than black ones?" turns on the confusion involved in the fallacy of division, for the answer, "Because there are more of them," treats collectively what seemed to be referred to distributively in the question.

The fallacy of division, which springs from a kind of ambiguity, resembles the fallacy of accident (discussed previously in section 4.3), which springs from unwarranted presumption. Likewise, the fallacy of composition, also flowing from ambiguity, resembles the hasty generalization we call "converse accident." But these likenesses are superficial. An explanation of the differences between the two pairs of fallacies will be helpful in grasping the errors committed in all four.

If we were to infer, from looking at one or two parts of a large machine, that because they happen to be well designed, every one of its many parts is well designed, we would commit the fallacy of converse accident, for what is true about one or two surely may not be true of all. If we were to examine every single part and find each carefully made, and from that finding infer that the entire machine is carefully made, we would also reason fallaciously, because however carefully the parts were produced, they may have been *assembled* awkwardly or carelessly. But here the fallacy is one of composition. In converse accident, one argues that some atypical members of a class have a specified attribute, and therefore that all members of the class, distributively, have that attribute; in composition, one argues that, since each and every member of the class has that attribute, the class *itself* (collectively) has that attribute. The difference is great. In converse accident, all predications are distributive, whereas in the composition fallacy, the mistaken inference is from distributive to collective predication.

Similarly, division and accident are two distinct fallacies; their superficial resemblance hides the same kind of underlying difference. In division, we argue (mistakenly) that, since the class itself has a given attribute, each of its members also has it. Thus, it is the fallacy of division to conclude that, because an army as a whole is nearly invincible, each of its units is nearly invincible. But in accident, we argue (also mistakenly) that, because some rule applies in general, there are no special circumstances in which it might not apply. Thus, we commit the fallacy of accident when we insist that a person should be fined for ignoring a "No Swimming" sign when jumping into the water to rescue someone from drowning.

Accident and converse accident are fallacies of presumption in which we assume what we have no warrant for. Composition and division are fallacies of *ambiguity,* resulting from the multiple meanings of terms. Wherever the words or phrases used may mean one thing in one part of the argument and another thing in another part, and those different meanings are deliberately or accidentally confounded, we may expect the argument to be fallacious.

| THE MAJOR INFORMAL FALLACIES |
|---|
| Fallacies of Relevance |
|     R1    Argument from Ignorance |
|     R2    Appeal to Inappropriate Authority |
|     R3    Argument *Ad Hominem:* (a) abusive and (b) circumstantial |
|     R4    Appeal to Emotion |
|     R5    Appeal to Pity |
|     R6    Appeal to Force |
|     R7    Irrelevant Conclusion |
| Fallacies of Presumption |
|     P1    Complex Question |
|     P2    False Cause |
|     P3    Begging the Question |
|     P4    Accident |
|     P5    Converse Accident |

Fallacies of Ambiguity
  A1  Equivocation
  A2  Amphiboly
  A3  Accent
  A4  Composition
  A5  Division

## Exercises

I.    Identify and explain the fallacies of ambiguity that appear in the following passages.

*1.   . . . the universe is spherical in form . . . because all the constituent parts of the universe, that is the sun, moon, and the planets, appear in this form.

—Nicolaus Copernicus, "The New Idea of the Universe"

2.   Robert Toombs is reputed to have said, just before the Civil War, "We could lick those Yankees with cornstalks." When he was asked after the war what had gone wrong, he is reputed to have said, "It's very simple. Those damyankees refused to fight with cornstalks."

—E. J. Kahn, Jr., "Profiles (Georgia)," *The New Yorker,*
13 February 1978

3.   To press forward with a properly ordered wage structure in each industry is the first condition for curbing competitive bargaining; but there is no reason why the process should stop there. What is good for each industry can hardly be bad for the economy as a whole.

—Edmond Kelly, *Twentieth Century Socialism*

4.   No man will take counsel, but every man will take money: therefore money is better than counsel.

—Jonathan Swift

*5.   I've looked everywhere in this area for an instruction book on how to play the concertina without success. (Mrs. F. M., Myrtle Beach, S.C., Charlotte Observer)
You need no instructions. Just plunge ahead boldly.

—*The New Yorker,* 21 February 1977

6.   . . . each person's happiness is a good to that person, and the general happiness, therefore, a good to the aggregate of all persons.

—John Stuart Mill, *Utilitarianism*

7.   If the man who "turnips!" cries
Cry not when his father dies,
'Tis a proof that he had rather
Have a turnip than his father.

—Mrs. Piozzi, *Anecdotes of Samuel Johnson*

8. Fallaci wrote her: "You are a bad journalist because you are a bad woman."

> —Elizabeth Peer, "The Fallaci Papers," *Newsweek*, 1 December 1980

9. A Worm-eating Warbler was discovered by Hazel Miller in Concord, while walking along the branch of a tree, singing, and in good view. *(New Hampshire Audubon Quarterly)*

   That's our Hazel—surefooted, happy, and with just a touch of the exhibitionist.

> —*The New Yorker*, 2 July 1979

*10. The basis of logic is the syllogism, consisting of a major and a minor premiss and a conclusion—thus:

> *Major Premiss:* Sixty men can do a piece of work sixty times as quickly as one man;
> *Minor Premiss:* One man can dig a post-hole in sixty seconds; therefore—
> *Conclusion:* Sixty men can dig a post-hole in one second.

   This may be called the syllogism arithmetical, in which, by combining logic and mathematics, we obtain a double certainty and are twice blessed.

> —Ambrose Bierce, *The Devil's Dictionary*

II. Each of the following passages may be plausibly criticized by some who conclude that it contains a fallacy, but each will be defended by some who deny that the argument is fallacious. Discuss the merits of the argument in each passage, and explain why you conclude that it does (or does not) contain a fallacy of ambiguity.

*1. Seeing that eye and hand and foot and every one of our members has some obvious function, must we not believe that in like manner a human being has a function over and above these particular functions?

> —Aristotle, *Nicomachean Ethics*

2. Mr. Stace says that my writings are "extremely obscure," and this is a matter as to which the author is the worst of all possible judges. I must therefore accept his opinion. As I have a very intense desire to make my meaning plain, I regret this.

> —Bertrand Russell, "Reply to Criticisms," in P. A. Schilpp, ed.,
> *The Philosophy of Bertrand Russell* (Evanston, IL:
> The Library of Living Philosophers), p. 707

3. The only proof capable of being given that an object is visible, is that people actually see it. The only proof that a sound is audible, is that people hear it: and so of the other sources of our experience. In like manner, I apprehend, the sole evidence it is possible to produce that anything is desirable, is that people actually desire it.

> —John Stuart Mill, *Utilitarianism*, ch. 4

4. Thomas Carlyle said of Walt Whitman that he thinks he is a big poet because he comes from a big country.

—Alfred Kazin, "The Haunted Chamber," *The New Republic*, 23 June 1986, p. 39

*5. Mr. Levy boasts many excellent *bona fides* for the job [of Chancellor of the New York City Public Schools]. But there is one bothersome fact: His two children attend an elite private school on Manhattan's Upper East Side. Mr. Levy . . . should put his daughter and son in the public schools. I do not begrudge any parent the right to enroll a child in a private school. My wife and I considered several private schools before sending our children to a public school in Manhattan. Mr. Levy is essentially declaring the public schools unfit for his own children.

—Samuel G. Freedman, "Public Leaders, Private Schools," *New York Times*, 15 April 2000.

6. All phenomena in the universe are saturated with moral values. And, therefore, we can come to assert that the universe for the Chinese is a moral universe.

—T. H. Fang, *The Chinese View of Life*

III. Identify and explain the fallacies of relevance, or presumption, or ambiguity as they occur in the following passages. Explain why, in the case of some, it may be plausibly argued that what appears at first to be a fallacy is not when the argument is correctly interpreted.

*1. John Angus Smith, approaching an undercover agent, offered to trade his firearm, an automatic, for two ounces of cocaine that he planned to sell at a profit. Upon being apprehended, Smith was charged with "using" a firearm "during and in relation to . . . a drug trafficking crime." Ordinarily conviction under this statute would result in a prison sentence of five years; however, if the firearm, as in this case, is "a machine gun or other automatic weapon" the mandatory sentence is 30 years. Smith was convicted and sentenced to 30 years in prison. The case was appealed to the U.S. Supreme Court.

Justice Scalia argued that, although Smith certainly did intend to trade his gun for drugs, that was not the sense of "using" intended by the statute. "In the search for statutory meaning we give nontechnical terms their ordinary meanings . . . to speak of 'using a firearm' is to speak of using it for its distinctive purpose, as a weapon." If asked whether you use a cane, he pointed out, the question asks whether you walk with a cane, not whether you display "your grandfather's silver-handled walking stick in the hall."

Justice O'Connor retorted that we may do more than walk with a cane. "The most infamous use of a cane in American history had nothing to do with walking at all—the caning (in 1856) of Senator Charles Sumner in the United States Senate."

Justice Scalia rejoined that the majority of the Court "does not appear to grasp the distinction between how a word can be used and how it is ordinarily used. . . . I think it perfectly obvious, for example, that the falsity requirement for a perjury conviction would not be satisfied if a witness answered 'No' to a prosecutor's enquiry whether he had ever 'used a firearm' even though he had once sold his grandfather's Enfield rifle to a collector."

Justice O'Connor prevailed; Smith's conviction was affirmed.

—*John Angus Smith v. United States,* 508 U.S. 223, 1 June 1993

2. After deciding to sell his home in Upland, California, novelist Whitney Stine pounded a "For Sale" sign into his front yard. But he deliberately waited to do so until 2:22 p.m. one Thursday. The house sold three days later for his asking price—$238,000. And Mr. Stine credits the quick sale to the advice of his astrologer, John Bradford, whom he has consulted for 12 years in the sale of five houses.

"He always tells me the exact time to put out the sign according to the phases of the moon, and the houses have always sold within a few months." Mr. Stine says.

—"Thinking of Buying or Selling a House? Ask Your Astrologer,"
*Wall Street Journal,* 12 October 1986

3. In the Miss Universe Contest of 1994 Miss Alabama was asked: If you could live forever, would you? And why? She answered:

> I would not live forever, because we should not live forever, because if we were supposed to live forever, then we would live forever, but we cannot live forever, which is why I would not live forever.

4. Order is indispensable to justice because justice can be achieved only by means of a social and legal order.

—Ernest Van Den Haag, *Punishing Criminals*

*5. The Inquisition must have been justified and beneficial, if whole peoples invoked and defended it, if men of the loftiest souls founded and created it severally and impartially, and its very adversaries applied it on their own account, pyre answering to pyre.

—Benedetto Croce, *Philosophy of the Practical*

6. The following advertisement for a great metropolitan newspaper appears very widely in the State of Pennsylvania:

> In Philadelphia nearly everybody reads the *Bulletin.*

7. . . . since it is impossible for an animal or plant to be indefinitely big or small, neither can its parts be such, or the whole will be the same.

—Aristotle, *Physics*

8. For the benefit of those representatives who have not been here before this year, it may be useful to explain that the item before the General Assembly is that hardy perennial called the "Soviet item." It

is purely a propaganda proposition, not introduced with a serious purpose of serious action, but solely as a peg on which to hang a number of speeches with a view to getting them into the press of the world. This is considered by some to be very clever politics. Others, among whom the present speaker wishes to be included, consider it an inadequate response to the challenge of the hour.

> —Henry Cabot Lodge, speech to the United Nations
> General Assembly, 30 November 1953

9. The war-mongering character of all this flood of propaganda in the United States is admitted even by the American press. Such provocative and slanderous aims clearly inspired today's speech by the United States Representative, consisting only of impudent slander against the Soviet Union, to answer which would be beneath our dignity. The heroic epic of Stalingrad is impervious to libel. The Soviet people in the battles at Stalingrad saved the world from the fascist plague and that great victory which decided the fate of the world is remembered with recognition and gratitude by all humanity. Only men dead to all shame could try to cast aspersions on the shining memory of the heroes of that battle.

> —Anatole M. Baranovsky, speech to the United Nations
> General Assembly, 30 November 1953

*10. Prof. Leon Kass reports a notable response to an assignment he had given students at the University of Chicago. Compose an essay, he asked, about a memorable meal you have eaten. One student wrote as follows:

> I had once eaten lunch with my uncle and my uncle's friend. His friend had once eaten lunch with Albert Einstein. Albert Einstein was once a man of great spirituality. Therefore, by the law of the syllogism, I had once eaten lunch with God.

> —Leon Kass, *The Hungry Soul: Eating and
> the Perfecting of Our Nature*, 1995

11. Clarence Darrow, renowned criminal trial lawyer, began one shrewd plea to a jury thus:

> You folks think we city people are all crooked, but we city people think you farmers are all crooked. There isn't one of you I'd trust in a horse trade, because you'd be sure to skin me. But when it comes to having sympathy with a person in trouble, I'd sooner trust you folks than city folks, because you come to know people better and get to be closer friends.

> —Irving Stone, *Clarence Darrow for the Defense*

12. The most blatant occurrence of recent years is all these knuckleheads running around protesting nuclear power—all these stupid people who do no research at all and who go out and march, pretending they care about the human race, and then go off in their automobiles and kill one another.

> —Ray Bradbury, in *Omni*, October 1979

13. When Copernicus argued that the Ptolemaic astronomy (holding that the celestial bodies all revolved around the earth) should be replaced by a theory holding that the earth (along with all the other planets) revolved around the sun, he was ridiculed by many of the scientists of his day, including one of the greatest astronomers of that time, Clavius, who wrote in 1581:

> Both [Copernicus and Ptolemy] are in agreement with the observed phenomena. But Copernicus's arguments contain a great many principles that are absurd. He assumed, for instance, that the earth is moving with a triple motion ... [but] according to the philosophers a simple body like the earth can have only a simple motion. ... Therefore it seems to me that Ptolemy's geocentric doctrine must be preferred to Copernicus's doctrine.

14. All of us cannot be famous, because all of us cannot be well known.

—Jesse Jackson, quoted in *The New Yorker*, 12 March 1984

*15. The God that holds you over the pit of hell, much as one holds a spider or some loathsome insect over the fire, abhors you, and is dreadfully provoked; his wrath towards you burns like fire; he looks upon you as worthy of nothing else but to be cast into the fire; you are ten thousand times so abominable in his eyes as the most hateful and venomous serpent is in ours. You have offended him infinitely more than a stubborn rebel did his prince; and yet it is nothing but his hand that holds you from falling into the fire every moment.

—Jonathan Edwards, "The Pit of Hell" (1741)

16. Mysticism is one of the great forces of the world's history. For religion is nearly the most important thing in the world, and religion never remains for long altogether untouched by mysticism.

—John Mctaggart Ellis Mctaggart, "Mysticism," *Philosophical Studies*

17. If science wishes to argue that we cannot know what was going on in [the gorilla] Binti's head when she acted as she did, science must also acknowledge that it cannot prove that nothing was going on. It is because of our irresolvable ignorance, as much as fellow-feeling, that we should give animals the benefit of doubt and treat them with the respect we accord ourselves.

—Martin Rowe and Mia Macdonald, "Let's Give Animals Respect They Deserve," *New York Times*, 26 August 1996.

18. If we want to know whether a state is brave we must look to its army, not because the soldiers are the only brave people in the community, but because it is only through their conduct that the courage or cowardice of the community can be manifested.

—R. L. Nettleship, *Lectures on the Republic of Plato*

19. Whether we are to live in a future state, as it is the most important question which can possibly be asked, so it is the most intelligible one which can be expressed in language.

—Joseph Butler, "Of Personal Identity"

*20. Which is more useful, the Sun or the Moon? The Moon is more useful since it gives us light during the night, when it is dark, whereas the Sun shines only in the daytime, when it is light anyway.

—George Gamow (inscribed in the entry hall of the Hayden Planetarium, New York City)

## Summary of Chapter 4

In this chapter, we have seen that **a fallacy is a type of argument that may seem to be correct, but that proves on examination not to be so.** Types of reasoning mistakes that commonly deceive have been given traditional names; three large groups of informal fallacies have been distinguished: the **fallacies of relevance,** the **fallacies of presumption,** and the **fallacies of ambiguity.**

### Fallacies of Relevance

In these, the mistaken arguments rely on premisses that may seem to be relevant to the conclusion but in fact are not. We have explained the types of reasoning mistakes in seven fallacies of relevance:

R1. **Argument from ignorance** *(ad ignorantiam):* When it is argued that a proposition is true on the ground that it has not been proved false, or when it is argued that a proposition is false because it has not been proved true.

R2. **Appeal to inappropriate authority** *(ad verecundiam):* When the premisses of an argument appeal to the judgment of some party or parties having no legitimate claim to authority in the matter at hand.

R3. **Argument against the person** *(ad hominem):* When an attack is leveled not at the claims being made or the merits of the argument, but at the person of the opponent.

Arguments *ad hominem* take two forms. When the attack is directly against persons, seeking to defame or discredit them, it is called an "**abusive** *ad hominem.*" When the attack is indirectly against persons, suggesting that they hold their views chiefly because of their special circumstances or interests, it is called a "**circumstantial** *ad hominem.*"

R4. **Appeal to emotion** *(ad populum):* When careful reasoning is replaced with devices calculated to elicit enthusiasm and emotional support for the conclusion advanced.

R5. **Appeal to pity** *(ad misericordiam):* When careful reasoning is replaced by devices calculated to elicit sympathy on the part of the hearer for the objects of the speaker's concern.

R6. **Appeal to force** *(ad baculum):* When careful reasoning is replaced with direct or insinuated threats in order to bring about the acceptance of some conclusion.

R7. **Irrelevant conclusion** *(ignoratio elenchi):* When the premisses miss the point, purporting to support one conclusion while in fact supporting or establishing another.

## Fallacies of Presumption

In these the mistaken arguments arise from reliance upon some proposition that is assumed to be true, but is in fact false, or dubious, or without warrant. We have explained the types of reasoning mistakes in five fallacies of presumption:

P1. **Complex question:** When a question is asked in such a way as to presuppose the truth of some assumption buried in that question.

P2. **False cause:** When one treats as the cause of a thing what is not really the cause of that thing, or more generally, when one blunders in reasoning that is based upon causal relations.

P3. **Begging the question** *(petitio principii):* When one assumes in the premisses of an argument the truth of what one seeks to establish in the conclusion of that argument.

P4. **Accident:** When one applies a generalization to an individual case that it does not properly govern.

P5. **Converse Accident:** When one moves carelessly or too quickly from a single case to an indefensibly broad generalization.

## Fallacies of Ambiguity

In these, the mistaken arguments are formulated in such a way as to rely on shifts in the meaning of words or phrases, from their use in the premisses to their use in the conclusion. We have explained the types of reasoning mistakes in five fallacies of ambiguity:

A1. **Equivocation:** When the same word or phrase is used with two or more meanings, deliberately or accidentally, in the formulation of an argument.

A2. **Amphiboly:** When one of the statements in an argument has more than one plausible meaning, because of the loose or awkward way in which the words in that statement have been combined.

A3. **Accent:** When a shift of meaning arises within an argument as a consequence of changes in the emphasis given to its words or parts.

A4. **Composition:** This fallacy is committed (a) when one reasons mistakenly from the attributes of a part to the attributes of the whole, or (b) when one reasons mistakenly from the attributes of an individual member of some collection to the attributes of the totality of that collection.

A5. **Division:** This fallacy is committed (a) when one reasons mistakenly from the attributes of a whole to the attributes of one of its parts, or (b) when one reasons mistakenly from the attributes of a totality of some collection of entities to the attributes of the individual entities within that collection.

# Fallacies

## Donald Nute

## More on Fallacies

Here are some additional points to remember about some of the informal fallacies.

**Appeal to authority: dogmatic.** Appeal to an inappropriate authority is a common fallacy, but there is another way in which we can commit a fallacy even when we appeal to an appropriate authority. On occasion, someone will refuse to consider evidence simply because it supports an opinion supported by some authority. It is a fallacy of criticism to refuse to consider evidence even if the authority cited is appropriate. Here is an example.

> Recent astronomical observations are claimed to support the view that there are planets orbiting stars other than our sun. But we can safely ignore this evidence. No less an authority than Copernicus, who realized that earth revolves around the sun, assures us that *all* planets revolve around the sun.

So we can give a fallacious reason for a claim by appealing to an inappropriate authority, or we can fallaciously reject a reason for a claim by clinging dogmatically to the opinion of even an appropriate authority.

**Appeal to fear.** When someone tries to get you to believe something by indicating a relation to something you fear, she *may* be committing the fallacy of appeal to fear. Whether or not a fallacy is committed depends on whether there is a proper relationship between the claim and the fearful event associated with it. Here is an example of an appeal to fear.

> Have a smoke. You don't want people to think that you are a coward.

It might be reasonable to fear being thought a coward. The person making this argument is trying to connect this fear to smoking, but being thought a coward is not a natural consequence of smoking. But consider this argument.

> You shouldn't smoke. You don't want to increase your risk of heart disease and lung cancer.

This argument also tries to link smoking with something you fear. But this is not a fallacy because we have evidence of a causal link between smoking on the one hand and heart disease and lung cancer on the other. When someone plays on your fears in an argument, you should carefully consider whether the relationship between what you fear and what the person is trying to convince you of is real or manufactured.

**Appeal to force.** Sometimes people resort to threats in an attempt to persuade us to believe something. Here is an example.

> Our government is acting in our best interest. If you don't believe that, I may have to report you to the secret police.

Now the fact that you may report me to the secret police might be a very good reason for me not to *tell* you that I think the government is oppressive. But it is hardly a reason for me to actually *believe* that the government is not oppressive. Indeed, the very existence of a secret police should be an indication that something is very wrong with the government. However, some arguments that resemble an appeal to force are not fallacies. Look at this argument.

> You should pay your rent. If you don't, I will have to evict you from your apartment.

What is this argument trying to get you to believe? That you should (it is prudent for you to) pay your rent. And what reason is being given? That if you don't, you will be put out of your apartment. That's a pretty good reason! What's the difference between these two examples? In the first example, the fact that someone may report you to the secret police is not a reason to *believe* that the government acts in your best interests even though it may be a good reason to *pretend* to believe that. But in the second example, the possibility of losing your apartment is a very good reason to believe that you should pay your rent.

**Appeal to pity.** Someone commits the fallacy of appeal to pity when she tries to convince us that we to believe something by arousing our pity in a way that is irrelevant to what she is trying to get us to believe.

> We should hire George rather than Jim. George takes rejection very badly.

Is this a good argument? Suppose the job we are talking about is as a pizza delivery person. Legitimate reasons for thinking that we should hire George rather than Jim are that George has more driving experience, a better driving record, a record of reliability, knows the neighborhood better, and so on. Here is another extreme but humorous example of the fallacy of appeal to pity.

> The defendant has been convicted of killing his parents. But we should show mercy in sentencing him. After all, he is an orphan.

This is not to say that sympathy is never relevant or a good reason for believing something. Take this example.

We should send food to Ethiopia. We have more than we need, and people are starving to death there every day.

Famine and starvation are legitimate reasons for providing help. But even starvation is not a good reason to hire someone as a brain surgeon!

**Two kinds of hasty generalization.** We commit the fallacy of hasty generalization when we base a general conclusion on specific instances where the instances are either too few or biased. The set of instances we use for our generalization is called a *sample*; so we commit the fallacy of hasty generalization when our sample is either *inadequate* or *inappropriate*.

> University of Georgia students drink too much. I talked to three students today about their drinking habits and all three admitted to being inebriated at least one occasion in the last month.

> University of Georgia students drink too much. I interviewed nearly 1000 students at local bars last semester and all of them admitted to being inebriated at least one occasion in the last month.

In the first case, three students is too small a sample to support our conclusion. So this is an example of a hasty generalization from an inadequate sample. In the second case, we are biasing our results by choosing our sample at bars. We might get quite a different result if we went to class rooms to select our 1000 interviewees. This is an example of a hasty generalization from an inappropriate sample.

**Accident.** This is also called the fallacy of reverse hasty generalization. We commit the fallacy of hasty generalization when we draw a general conclusion from specific examples. We commit the fallacy of accident when we apply a general rule to an exceptional case. Here are a couple of examples.

> We all know that birds fly. This penguin is a bird. So it can fly.

> You should keep your promises. The day your mother had her heart attack, you had promised to have lunch with me. You should have met me at the restaurant instead of rushing off to the hospital.

**Division and composition.** Both of these fallacies involve parts and wholes. We commit the fallacy of division when we claim that a part has some property because some who to which it belongs has the property. Here's an example.

> John is an American, and America is a rich nation. So John is rich.

Here, of course, John is the part and America is the whole. No doubt, America is rich. But that certainly doesn't mean that all Americans are rich.

We commit the fallacy of composition when we do the opposite: claim that something has some property because all of its parts do. Here is an example.

> People are made up of atoms. Atoms are not conscious. So neither are people. Consciousness is some sort of illusion.

**Ambiguity, Equivocation, and Amphiboly.** Our text describes two kinds of ambiguity: ambiguity of reference and grammatical ambiguity. Ambiguity of reference involves a word or phrase that has more than one meaning. A fallacy of reasoning that involves ambiguity of reference is called *equivocation*. Grammatical ambiguity involves a sentence that has a structure that can be understood in more than one way. A fallacy of reasoning that involves a grammatical ambiguity is called *amphiboly*. But we should notice that a fallacy does not occur every time there is an ambiguity. It is only when the ambiguity is used in an argument in a certain way that there is a fallacy. No argument, no fallacy. Here is a fanciful example of a fallacy of equivocation.

> Florence works in a bank. A bank is beside a body of water. So Florence works beside a body of water.

Of course, the ambiguous word here is *bank*. It could mean a financial institution or the edge of a body of water. If we read it in both premises as a financial institution, then the second premise is not true. Many banks (financial institutions) are not beside bodies of water. And if we read it in both premises as the edge of a body of water, then the first premise is in all likelihood false. So whichever way we read *bank*, one of the premises is false. However, if we read the word one way in one premise and the other way in the other premise, then both premises might well be true. But then our argument is equivalent to

> Florence works in a financial institution. The edge of a body of water is beside a body of water. So Florence works beside a body of water.

While we might accept both of these premises, we don't see why anyone would think that the conclusion follows from them. This is what happens when the fallacy of equivocation or the fallacy of amphiboly is committed. There is no single way to understand the ambiguous word, phrase, or sentence that makes all the premises true and also makes it reasonable to think the conclusion follows from the premises. But these fallacies are not always as absurd as our example. Sometimes the ambiguity is subtle and difficult to detect.

**Visit the Moons of Saturn**

How many fallacies can you identify in the following passage? I count thirteen.

You know you should spend your next vacation visiting the moons of Saturn. That's where everyone is going this year. The beauty of Saturn and its rings is unequaled. A person would have to have the aesthetic sense of a cucumber to compare it with the Martian Canals or the Rocky Mountains. The combined mass of the Saturnian moons is greater than that of earth, so you won't have to cope with light gravity while visiting the moons. The cost of a trip to Saturn is quite reasonable. People go there, spend a week, and come home with very little money. Indeed, it's the best vacation value in the solar system. You can't get more for your vacation dollar anywhere from Mercury to Pluto.

And your stay will be safe, too, despite rumors of a tourist-eating monster roaming Iapetus. There have been no eye-witness reports of such a creature. Nor is there any danger from the many picturesque volcanoes. Hundreds of visitors have returned from Saturn's moons and none of them were caught in a volcanic eruption. Recent reports that tourists have been punctured by micro-meteorites while visiting Phoebe are also unfounded. Our staff astro-physicists assure us that this could not happen. The trip to Tethys and Rhea is as safe as a trip to the grocery in your family car. The same company that makes your family car also makes the trans-Saturn space liner. Two weeks on Titan did Gertrude Higgenbotham a world of good. She went there last year and now she is healthier than she has ever been before. Don't let Ralph Vader's report, "Unsafe At Any Hyper-speed", keep you from taking the next space liner to Saturn. Vader just likes to see his name in print.

You can have the most memorable vacation of your life on the moons of Saturn or a ho-hum visit somewhere else. You should arrange a trip to Saturn today with one of our agents. They stay in close contact with the captains of all the space liners. If you make a trip to another resort planet, your name will be placed in our computer records. Don't be sorry. Come to Saturn!


**Death and Taxes**

Identify the fallacy in each of the following examples.

1. The newest tax pamphlet tells government employees about special deductions they can take. It contains information that is important to everybody from the IRS. So every tax-payer needs this pamphlet.
2. Each paragraph of the new 2000 page tax code is short and easy to understand. It's a very simple system.
3. The form 1040 is too complicated because it should be much simpler.
4. It's common practice not to report small amounts of income. You won't get burned. Everyone at my country club does it and none of them have every paid a penalty.
5. You don't have to report money you won playing cards. I never heard of such a requirement.
6. I don't think you should tell the IRS about those gifts you gave me. You wouldn't want my company to quit buying all our thingama-bobs from you, would you?
7. Death and taxes are both unavoidable. Taxes are just part of the cycle of nature.

8. Taxes killed poor Chester. He died of a heart attack right after he heard he was being audited.

9. Somebody is being audited every hour of every day. And he's getting pretty tired of it!

10. There are ways to reduce your income tax liability. Would you rather have more children or die?

11. Municipal bonds are a good way to shelter income from tax. Never mind the losses people have been suffering from investing in these bonds. Just read I. B. Rich's tax guide.

12. Here it is May 1 and that guy who got an extension from IRS just filed his tax return. He will have to pay a late penalty. Tax returns are due by April 15.

13. Doctors shouldn't have to pay taxes. Did you know that they have the highest rates of coronary and suicide of any profession?

## Practice Quiz 3

Circle the letters corresponding to the fallacies illustrated by the following examples. Note that some examples do not involve any fallacy.

1. Chrysler executives say Chrysler should be given government loans because otherwise Chrysler will go bankrupt.

**A.** appeal to authority **B.** appeal to sympathy **C.** appeal to fear **D.** none of these

2. Don't believe the reports you see in the newspapers. My doctor says only homosexuals get AIDS.

**A.** *ad populam* **B.** appeal to sympathy **C.** appeal to authority **D.** none of these

3. George must take philosophy or history next quarter. He has enrolled in philosophy. So he won't take history.

**A.** false dilemma **B.** division **C.** disjunctive fallacy **D.** none of these

4. Not long after she started using a microwave oven, Helen developed skin cancer. Those things are dangerous and should be banned!

**A.** false cause **B.** appeal to ignorance **C.** appeal to fear **D.** none of these

5. President Bush has done an excellent job of conducting the war in the Gulf. In recent polls, 85% of those responding approved his actions.

**A.** *ad populam* **B.** appeal to authority **C.** false cause **D.** none of these

6. You should have your chimney inspected and cleaned regularly. Chimney fires are the number one reason people lose their homes.

**A.** hasty generalization **B.** appeal to fear **C.** *ad populam* **D.** none of these

7. Americans dislike American beer. In a survey at the University of Georgia, 85% who drank beer usually drank imported beer.

**A.** hasty generalization **B.** appeal to fear **C.** *ad populam* **D.** none of these

8. Better red than dead!

**A.** *ad populam* **B.** *ad hominem* **C.** false dilemma **D.** none of these

9. We sterilize our pets because it is cruel to allow unwanted animals to enter the world. Can we do any less for the poor and the homeless?

**A.** appeal to sympathy **B.** false analogy **C.** hasty generalization **D.** none of these

10. Being able to type is a necessary condition for being a good secretary. Jane is a good typist; so she would make a good secretary.

**A.** hasty generalization **B.** affirming the consequent **C.** appeal to pity **D.** none of these

11. Charles couldn't have killed Henry. Charles would never hurt anyone.

**A.** question begging **B.** argument from ignorance **C.** false cause **D.** none of these

12. Either the battery is dead or the starter is broken. Since the horn works, the battery is okay. So it's the starter.

**A.** affirming the consequent **B.** disjunctive fallacy **C.** denying the antecedent **D.** none of these

13. I don't pay any attention to what the Surgeon General says about smoking. He just wants to put the tobacco companies out of business.

**A.** appeal to authority **B.** disjunctive fallacy **C.** *ad hominem* **D.** none of these

14. I doubt David's sincerity. He quotes experts who say we are headed for an ecological disaster but he drives a big gas-guzzler.

**A.** appeal to authority **B.** *ad hominem* **C.** question begging **D.** none of these

15. If Helen had made an A in math, she would be on the Dean's list. She didn't make an A in math. So she won't be on the Dean's list.

**A.** false cause **B.** false dilemma. **C.** denying the antecedent **D.** none of these

16. Mary makes an interesting case concerning the cause of her injuries. But is Mary a doctor? Of course not. So we can dismiss her argument.

**A.** appeal to authority **B.** appeal to sympathy **C.** *ad hominem* **D.** none of these

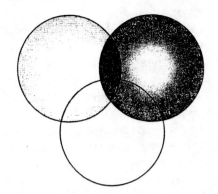

# SOLVING PROBLEMS
# USING LOGIC

*Reasoning ... is concerned with judgments about real things, and gains its essential value and vindication from its ability to yield correct judgments. For the purpose fixed by the nature of the problem, and controlling the course of reasoning, can only be attained by our finding out how, in that situation, true assertions can be made instead of false ones.*

—*Edwin Arthur Burtt*

*When we think about a problem ... we come to grips with the problem itself; we invent solutions of the problem, we pay attention to reasons for or against those possible solutions.... Effective thinking is thinking that succeeds in getting from known truths to truths that are as yet unknown.*

—*Monroe C. Beardsley*

## 3.1   PROBLEM SOLVING

Much of what we do is done as a result of *habit*. We eat, dress, and move about in habitual ways, following patterns and paths that we adopted long ago and rarely think about. This is natural and convenient, since we do not have the time to rethink every common task that we confront. But when our normal pattern is disrupted, or our normal path is blocked, we are obliged to rethink the matter. Such disruption captures our attention; at that moment we have a *problem*. Most often our problems are minor, but they are problems nevertheless if they compel us to reconsider what we ought to do. Our habits develop in a context in which many ordinary beliefs are accepted without question; normally we have no need or occasion to question them.

Problems, minor or major, mundane or abstract, arise from a conflict of some kind between the beliefs that are held and some situation to which those beliefs seem somehow inappropriate. This collision between situations and beliefs that do not "fit" them gives rise to uncertainty, to doubt. Not being sure of our next appropriate step provokes inquiry. Charles Sanders Pierce wrote: "The irritation of doubt causes a struggle to attain a state of belief. I shall term this struggle *Inquiry*."[1]

Of all forms of inquiry, the most fruitful and most dependable is the application of reason to the problematic situation. We examine and reexamine the problem from every point of view that occurs to us; we marshal the relevant information that is available to us; we seek some new insight into the situation, or try to construct some new set of beliefs that will enable us to overcome the problematic doubt and its discomforts. John Dewey put the matter this way:

> . . . thinking takes its departure from specific conflicts in experience that occasion perplexity and trouble. Men do not, in their natural estate, think when they have no troubles to cope with, no difficulties to overcome. A life of ease, of success without effort, would be a thoughtless life, and so also would a life of ready omnipotence.[2]

Of all the problems we encounter, the most serious, broadly speaking, have to do with the avoidance of suffering, the fulfillment of duty, and the achievement of happiness. These goals are not easily attained; to advance them we need to increase, as far as we are able, our ability to control ourselves and the world about us. And this, in turn, makes it essential for us to learn as much as we can about causes and effects.

Medical investigators, for example, traditionally have sought to discover the causes of specific diseases so that patients might be cured, returned to health by the elimination of the cause of their disorders. More recently there has been greater emphasis put upon health maintenance and promotion, investigators seeking to identify those aspects of diet, exercise, and environment that produce physical vigor and mental stability. Similarly, in all the fields of study that bear upon serious human problems, science and technology have advanced our control of the world around us by increasing our understanding of it. Scientific theories devised and confirmed, scientific laws discovered, instruments invented and machinery designed—all these represent so many problems solved, so much effective thinking and productive reasoning.

It is the mark of the educated mind, as John Dewey observed, to search for what is doubtful, and to derive pleasure from the resolution of those doubts. Where problems do not arise because of some disruption of our

---

[1] Charles Sanders Pierce, "The Fixation of Belief," (1877); reprinted in Irving M. Copi and James A. Gould, eds., *Readings on Logic*, 2d ed. (New York: Macmillan, 1972.

[2] John Dewey, *Reconstruction in Philosophy* (Boston: Beacon Press, 1957), 138–139.

habits, we are likely to *seek out* what is puzzling or problematic for the satisfaction we derive from inquiry. In mathematics and some other fields of study, the solving of problems becomes the central focus of activity, each problem solved opening the door to new problems, with new challenges for the inquiring intellect. The role of the problematic situation, as the first phase in the general pattern of scientific inquiry, is discussed at greater length in Chapter 15 of this book.

## 3.2 PROBLEMS IN REASONING

Up to this point we have been discussing problems encountered by others. We turn now to problems that confront *us*, problems whose solution requires arguments that we must construct, setting forth our own premises, drawing our own inferences. If, as we go forward, the data at hand seem insufficient, it is we who must seek the additional information needed for the solution; and if the situation appears to have been misdescribed, it is we who must turn back to organize the problem afresh, devising a more fruitful plan of attack. In this, as in the development of most skills, experience is critical, and as the old saying goes, practice makes perfect.

For such practice we need problems arising in a context understood equally by us all, problems designed to exercise our reasoning powers. Games, such as chess and Mastermind, are excellent for this purpose—but usually they require some physical props in the form of a playing board and pieces, as well as knowledge of the rules of the game. It is more convenient here to work mainly with a set of purely logical puzzles, problems of reasoning whose solutions are attainable by anyone with the ability to construct, from the premisses given, the arguments needed to reach them. "Brainteasers," such problems are called—contrived but often delightful exercises in which a problem situation is presented as a mass of more-or-less unrelated data, or propositions given as true in the statement of the puzzle, and a specific question or group of questions is then posed, the answers to which constitute the solution to the problem.

Brainteasers are not altogether removed from the problems of real life. Members of a jury may have to sort out the evidence presented to them, and from that evidence reconstruct events in dispute so as to come to a rational verdict in a courtroom trial. Journalists may be required to collect, analyze, and rearrange data so as to produce an intelligible and therefore publishable account of some developing news event. And of course scientists are continually seeking to explain apparently unrelated data by appealing to scientific laws and theories from which just those data may have been predicted to emerge, in the situations that gave rise to them.

The brainteaser generally is much easier to solve than these real-world problems, because in it all the information needed to obtain a solution has been provided. Nevertheless some such problems can be quite challenging.

Many subconclusions are likely to be needed, and the required chain of reasoning may take unforeseen twists. Consider this relatively simple brainteaser, as an example:

> In a certain flight crew, the positions of pilot, copilot, and flight engineer are held by three women, Allen, Brown, and Carr, though not necessarily in that order.
> The copilot, who is an only child, earns the least.
> Carr, who married Brown's sister, earns more than the pilot.
> What position does each of the three persons hold?

How does one attack such a problem? Some organization of the information is required that will facilitate inferences, provide direction for our analysis. In this case we are given more information about one of the three persons mentioned than about the others—Carr, whom we know to be male because he married Brown's sister. What can we deduce from the given premises about his position? He earns more than the pilot, so he is not the pilot. And since the pilot earns less than he does, and the copilot earns the least, Carr is not the copilot. So, by elimination, Carr must be the flight engineer.

With that subconclusion, added to what had been given as true, we can determine Brown's position. Brown is not the copilot, because Brown has a sister and the copilot is an only child. And since Brown is not the flight engineer (since Carr is) we can conclude, again by elimination, that Brown must be the pilot. Only Allen is left; again by elimination we can deduce that Allen must be the copilot.

In grappling with puzzles of this kind there is no fixed pattern of inference or argument that will lead to solution. But when we are asked in a brainteaser to match a set of names with items in some other category (positions, or places of residence, or the like) it is useful to construct a graphic display of the alternatives, called a *matrix,* which we can fill in as we accumulate new information. To appreciate the usefulness of a matrix, consider the following puzzle:

> Alonzo, Kurt, Rudolf, and Willard are four creative artists of great talent. One is a dancer, one is a painter, one is a singer, and one is a writer, though not necessarily in that order.
> (1) Alonzo and Rudolf were in the audience the night the singer made his debut on the concert stage.
> (2) Both Kurt and the writer have had their portraits painted from life by the painter.
> (3) The writer, whose biography of Willard was a best-seller, is planning to write a biography of Alonzo.
> (4) Alonzo has never heard of Rudolf.
> What is each man's artistic field?

To keep the many facts asserted in these premises in mind, and also to remember the several subconclusions that may have been inferred from them, would be a demanding task. Writing our inferences down in the form of notes might prove helpful, but could also result in a confusing clutter. We need a method by which the information given and the intermediate conclusions drawn can be efficiently stored, a method that will keep what is known and what is inferred in order and available for use, as the number of our inferences increases and the chain of argument lengthens. In the matrix we construct there will be room to represent all the relevant possibilities, and to record each inference drawn.

The matrix for this problem must display an array of the four persons (in four rows) and the four artistic professions (in four columns) that they hold. It would look like this:

| | DANCER | PAINTER | SINGER | WRITER |
|---|---|---|---|---|
| ALONZO | | | | |
| KURT | | | | |
| RUDOLF | | | | |
| WILLARD | | | | |

When we conclude that the individual whose name is at the left of one of the rows cannot be the artist whose field heads one of the columns, we write an N (for "no," or a "–") in the box to the right of that person's name and in the column headed by that field. We can infer immediately (from premiss 1) that neither Alonzo nor Rudolph is the singer, so we place an N to the right of their names, in the third (singer) column. Similarly, we can infer from premiss 2 that Kurt is neither the painter nor the writer, so we enter an N to the right of his name in the second (painter) and fourth (writer) columns. From premiss 3 we see that the writer is neither Alonzo nor Willard, so we enter N to the right of their names in the fourth column. The entries we have made thus far are all justified by the information originally given, and our matrix now looks like this:

| | DANCER | PAINTER | SINGER | WRITER |
|---|---|---|---|---|
| ALONZO | | | N | N |
| KURT | | N | | N |
| RUDOLF | | | N | |
| WILLARD | | | | N |

From the information now at hand we can conclude by elimination that Rudolf must be the writer, so we enter a Y (for "yes," or a "+") in the box to the right of Rudolf's name in the fourth (writer) column, and we place an N in the other boxes to the right of his name. The array now makes it evident that the painter must be either Alonzo or Willard, and we can eliminate Alonzo in this way: Rudolf had his portrait painted by the painter (from premiss 2), and Alonzo has never heard of Rudolf (from premiss 4)—therefore it must be that Alonzo is not the painter. Thus we enter N to the right of Alonzo's name under column two (painter). We next conclude that Alonzo must be the dancer, so we enter Y to the right of Alonzo's name in the first (dancer) column. Now we can enter an N in the dancer column for both Kurt and Willard. The only possible category remaining for Kurt is singer, and therefore we enter a Y in that box, and an N in the singer column to the right of Willard's name. Again by elimination we conclude that Willard must be the painter, put a Y in the last empty box in the matrix, and our completed graphic display now looks like this:

|  | DANCER | PAINTER | SINGER | WRITER |
|---|---|---|---|---|
| ALONZO | Y | N | N | N |
| KURT | N | N | Y | N |
| RUDOLF | N | N | N | Y |
| WILLARD | N | Y | N | N |

From the filled-in matrix we can read off the solution: Alonzo is the dancer; Kurt is the singer; Rudolf is the writer; Willard is the painter.

Brainteasers of this general kind become more complicated when there is an increase in the number of dimensions required for solution, and some such problems introduce several such dimensions, presenting very challenging problems whose solutions are hardly possible without the use of a matrix.[3]

Some problems in reasoning must be approached in a different way, because the needed subconclusions can be established only by means of more complex arguments. Relations (such as "father" and "son") or the meanings of terms used (such as "twin") may have to be relied upon in order to formulate the premises from which those subconclusions can be derived. The following problem is a good example. Before you turn to its solution, which appears on page 77, try to construct for yourself the chain of reasoning that leads to the answer of the question it asks. The solution is not an easy one.

THE PROBLEM: Mr. Short, his sister, his son, and his daughter are fond of golf and often play together. The following statements are true of their foursome:

(1) The best player's twin and the worst player are of the opposite sex.
(2) The best player and the worst player are the same age.
Which one of the foursome is the best player?

---

[3] Readers who find logical problems of this kind enjoyable will encounter a feast of such delights in a continuing series of collections of them, entitled *Original Logic Problems*, and published by The Penny Press, Norwalk, CT.

*The solution:* A series of arguments will lead to the answer. We begin by focusing on the ages of the players, since on that topic we are given a considerable amount of information. Combining what we are told in the two premises, we can reliably conclude that three of the four golfers are of the same age.

First, the best player and the worst player are of the same age, from (2). Second, the best player and the best player's twin are the same age, from the meaning of the word "twin." Third, we know that the best player's twin and the worst player are different players, because we are told (in 1) that they are of opposite sex. So we can reliably infer that there are three players of the same age: the best player, the best player's twin, and the worst player.

The remaining player must be Mr. Short, since he must be older than his son and daughter. So the three players of the same age are Mr. Short's son, and his daughter, and his sister. Therefore it must be that the twins mentioned in statement (1) are Mr. Short's son and daughter. One of these two must be the best player.

But it cannot be his son, as the following argument shows:

If the best player were Mr. Short's son, then the son's twin (Mr. Short's daughter) would be of the opposite sex from the worst player, from (1). In that case the worst player must be a male and therefore cannot be Mr. Short's sister. Nor (in that case) can the worst player be Mr. Short's son, who has been assumed to be the best player. So if the son were the best player, the worst player would have to be Mr. Short himself.

But this cannot be, because the best player and the worst player are the same age, as we know from (2), and a man cannot be the same age as his own son. Therefore the best player cannot be Mr. Short's son. Therefore the best player must be Mr. Short's daughter.

## 3.3 RETROGRADE REASONING

Sometimes we must reason backward from what is to what was. Reasoning problems of this form are of great interest because they mirror, in some ways, the logical challenges often presented by situations in real life. Many scientists—archeologists, or geologists, and others—commonly confront states of affairs whose reality is undoubted, but whose causes are highly problematic: How did this state of affairs come to pass? Similarly, the police detective is presented with the brute facts of a crime and must try to deduce the circumstances that led to its commission, and thereby to identify the criminal. The problem, in such cases, is not what *will* happen but what *did* happen. What was the chain of events that led to the facts now confronted? Such reasoning is sometimes called *retrograde* analysis.

Accurate medical diagnosis—especially if the patient's condition is rare, and his symptoms easily confused with those of other disorders—presents many challenges of this kind. For astronomers, whose data consist largely of observations of extraterrestrial phenomena, their task often is retrograde:

What caused that? Comet Hyakutake, streaking by the earth in 1996, was found, to the amazement of astronomers and for reasons unknown, to be emitting variable X-rays 100 times stronger than anyone had ever predicted a comet might emit. One of the comet experts at the Max Planck Institute in Germany remarked: "Now we have our work cut out for us in explaining these data—but that's the kind of problem you love to have."

Because we do love to have them, we sometimes construct them artificially. Deliberately devising problems for purposes of retrograde analysis presents a special difficulty: The setting of the problem must supply the logical framework which, in the real world, is supplied by the historical or scientific background of the phenomena under investigation. Contrived problems in retrograde analysis can be enjoyable and instructive; what appears simple turns out not to be so, and the solution (as in real science) may require some insight into the situation not elicited by its superficial examination. But we must provide some set of rules or laws, within which the logical analysis can take place.

Here we use the rules of chess; those who are not familiar with these rules may skip the following illustration. No skill at playing chess is required to solve these problems, however; only the rules of the game (to provide a theoretical context) need be understood. Retrograde problems in chess commonly take this form: An arrangement of pieces on the chessboard is given; it was reached in a game of chess in which all the rules of the game were strictly obeyed. What move, or series of moves, we are asked, has just been completed? Only reason and the rules of chess are needed for the solution. Here is an example of such a problem. The diagram below presents a position reached in an actual game of chess, all moves having been made in accordance with the rules of chess.

Figure 3-1

For the purpose of analysis the rows are numbered from bottom to top, 1 to 8, and the columns are lettered from left to right, a to h. Each square on the board is then uniquely identifiable; thus the black king is on a8, the white pawn is on h2, and so on. The problem is this: The last completed move was just made by black. What was that move? And what was white's last move just before that? Can you reason out the solution before turning to the paragraph that follows?

The black king just moved; it could not have moved to its present position from b7, or from b8, since the two kings may never rest on adjacent squares; therefore we may be certain that the black king has just moved from a7, where it was in check.

That much is easily deduced. But with what preceding white move could the black king have thus been put in check? No move by the white bishop (on g1) could have done it, because there would have been no way for that bishop to move to that square, g1, without the black king having been in check, with white to move! Therefore it must be that the check was *discovered* by the movement of a white piece that had been blocking the bishop's attack, and was then captured by the black king on its move to a8. What white piece could have been on that black diagonal and from there moved to the white square in the corner? It could only have been a knight that had been on b6. We may therefore be certain that before black's last move (the black king from a7 to a8) white's last move was that of a white knight from b6 to a8.[4]

The problems of reasoning that confront us in the real world are rarely as tidy as the contrived logical puzzles being discussed in this chapter, of course. Many real problems are not accurately described in the first instance, and their misdescription may prove so misleading that, if we decide to rely upon it, no solution can be reached. In cases of this kind, some part or parts of the initial description of the problem need to be rejected or replaced. But such rejection or replacement is not permitted when we are seeking to solve logical puzzles of the sort presented in this chapter.

Some problems in the real world, moreover, even when accurately described, may be incomplete, in the sense that something not originally available may be essential for the solution. The solution may depend upon some additional scientific discovery, or the invention of some previously unimagined invention or equipment, or the search of some as-yet-unexplored territory. But in the statement of a logical puzzle, as in the writing of a good murder mystery, all the information that is sufficient for the solution must be given; otherwise we feel that the mystery writer, or the problem-maker, has misled and unfairly deceived us.

And finally, while the logical puzzle presents an explicitly formulated

---

[4] Readers who find retrograde analysis enjoyable will take delight in a collection of such problems, compiled by the logician Raymond Smullyan and entitled *The Chess Mysteries of Sherlock Holmes* (New York: Alfred A. Knopf, 1979).

question (*e.g.,* which one of the foursome is the best golfer? What were black and white's last moves?) whose answer, if given and proved, certifies that the problem has been solved, that is not the form in which many real-world problems arise. Often they are identified, initially at least, only by the recognition of some inconsistency, or by our feeling that something is out of place or somehow doesn't "seem right"—rather than by an explicit question with an explicit answer to be supplied.

Yet in spite of all these differences, contrived exercises are similar enough to reasoning problems in the real world to justify their use in the study of logic.

## Exercises

The following problems require reasoning for their solution. To prove that an answer is correct requires an argument (often containing subsidiary arguments) whose premises are contained in the statement of the problem—and whose final conclusion is the answer to it. If the answer is correct, a valid argument proving it can be constructed. In working at these problems, readers are urged to concern themselves not merely with discovering the answers, but also with formulating arguments to prove those answers correct.

*1.  In a certain mythical community, politicians never tell the truth, and nonpoliticians always tell the truth. A stranger meets three natives and asks the first of them, "Are you a politician?" The first native answers the question. The second native then reports that the first native denied being a politician. The third native says that the first native *is* a politician.

How many of these three natives are politicians?

2.  Of three prisoners in a certain jail, one had normal vision, the second had only one eye, and the third was totally blind. The jailor told the prisoners that, from three white hats and two red hats, he would select three and put them on the prisoners' heads. None could see what color hat he wore. The jailor offered freedom to the prisoner with normal vision if he could tell what color hat he wore. To prevent a lucky guess, the jailor threatened execution for any incorrect answer. The first prisoner could not tell what hat he wore. Next the jailor made the same offer to the one-eyed prisoner. The second prisoner could not tell what hat he wore either. The jailor did not bother making the offer to the blind prisoner, but he agreed to extend the same terms to that prisoner when he made the request. The blind prisoner said:

> I do not need to have my sight;
> From what my friends with eyes have said,
> I clearly see my hat is _____!

How did he know?

3. On a certain train, the crew consists of the brakeman, the fireman, and the engineer. Their names listed alphabetically are Jones, Robinson, and Smith. On the train are also three passengers with corresponding names, Mr. Jones, Mr. Robinson, and Mr. Smith. The following facts are known:

   a. Mr. Robinson lives in Detroit.
   b. The brakeman lives halfway between Detroit and Chicago.
   c. Mr. Jones earns exactly $20,000 a year.
   d. Smith once beat the fireman at billiards.
   e. The brakeman's next-door neighbor, one of the three passengers mentioned, earns exactly three times as much as the brakeman.
   f. The passenger living in Chicago has the same name as the brakeman.

   What is the engineer's name?

4. The employees of a small loan company are Mr. Black, Mr. White, Mrs. Coffee, Miss Ambrose, Mr. Kelly, and Miss Earnshaw. The positions they occupy are manager, assistant manager, cashier, stenographer, teller, and clerk, though not necessarily in that order. The assistant manager is the manager's grandson, the cashier is the stenographer's son-in-law, Mr. Black is a bachelor, Mr. White is twenty-two years old, Miss Ambrose is the teller's step-sister, and Mr. Kelly is the manager's neighbor.
   Who holds each position?

*5. Benno Torelli, genial host at Hamtramck's most exclusive nightclub, was shot and killed by a racketeer gang because he fell behind in his protection payments. After considerable effort on the part of the police, five suspects were brought before the district attorney, who asked them what they had to say for themselves. Each of them made three statements, two true and one false. Their statements were

LEFTY:   I did not kill Torelli. I never owned a revolver in all my life. Spike did it.

RED:   I did not kill Torelli. I never owned a revolver. The others are all passing the buck.

DOPEY:   I am innocent. I never saw Butch before. Spike is guilty.

SPIKE:   I am innocent. Butch is the guilty one. Lefty did not tell the truth when he said I did it.

BUTCH:   I did not kill Torelli. Red is the guilty one. Dopey and I are old pals.

Whodunnit?

6.  Five men who were buddies in the last war are having a reunion. They are White, Brown, Peters, Harper, and Nash, who by occupation are printer, writer, barber, neurologist, and heating contractor. By coincidence, they live in the cities of White Plains, Brownsville, Petersburg, Harper's Ferry, and Nashville, but no man lives in the city having a name similar to his, nor does the name of his occupation have the same initial as his name or the name of the city in which he lives.

    The barber doesn't live in Petersburg, and Brown is neither a heating contractor nor a printer—nor does he live in Petersburg or Harper's Ferry. Mr. Harper lives in Nashville and is neither barber nor writer. White is not a resident of Brownsville, nor is Nash, who is not a barber or a heating contractor.

    With only the information given, determine the name of the city in which Nash resides.

7.  Daniel Kilraine was killed on a lonely road, two miles from Pontiac, Michigan, at 3:30 A.M. on March 17 of last year. Otto, Curly, Slim, Mickey, and the Kid were arrested a week later in Detroit and questioned. Each of the five made four statements, three of which were true and one of which was false. One of these persons killed Kilraine.

    Their statements were

    OTTO:  I was in Chicago when Kilraine was murdered. I never killed anyone. The Kid is the guilty one. Mickey and I are pals.

    CURLY:  I did not kill Kilraine. I never owned a revolver in my life. The Kid knows me. I was in Detroit the night of March 17.

    SLIM:  Curly lied when he said he never owned a revolver. The murder was committed on St. Patrick's Day. Otto was in Chicago at this time. One of us is guilty.

    MICKEY:  I did not kill Kilraine. The Kid has never been in Pontiac. I never saw Otto before. Curly was in Detroit with me on the night of March 17.

    THE KID:  I did not kill Kilraine. I have never been in Pontiac. I never saw Curly before. Otto erred when he said I am guilty.

    Whodunnit?

8.  A woman recently hosted a political meeting to which she invited five guests. The names of the six people who sat down at the circular table were Abrams, Banjo, Clive, Dumont, Ekwall, and Fish. One of them was deaf, one was very talkative, one was terribly fat, one simply hated Dumont, one had a vitamin deficiency, and one was the hostess. The person who hated Dumont sat directly opposite Banjo. The deaf one sat opposite Clive, who sat between the one who had a vitamin deficiency and the one

who hated Dumont. The fat one sat opposite Abrams, next to the deaf person and to the left of the one who hated Dumont. The person who had a vitamin deficiency sat between Clive and the one who sat opposite the person who hated Dumont. Fish, who was a good friend of everyone, sat next to the fat person and opposite the hostess.

Identify each of these people, matching name and description.

9. Three people went into a hotel and rented a room for $30, each paying $10 as his share. Later, the clerk discovered that the price of the room was only $25. He handed the bellman five $1 bills and asked him to return them to the three people. The bellman, not knowing how to divide $5 among three people, instead gave each person $1 and the rest to charity.

The three people originally paid $10 each, but each received $1 back, so they had now paid a total of $27 for the room. Add to that the $2 that the bellman gave away, and you have a total expenditure of $29 instead of $30. What happened to the other dollar?

*10. A jeweler has ten diamonds, nine of them exactly the same weight, the tenth slightly different. They are all mixed together, and his problem is to select the one that is different and to tell whether it is lighter or heavier than the others. How can he do this by making only three uses of his balance scale?

11. Imagine a room with four walls, a nail placed in the center of each wall, as well as in the ceiling and floor, six nails in all. The nails are connected to each other by strings, each nail connected to every other nail by a separate string. These strings are of two colors, red and blue, and of no other color. All these strings obviously make many triangles, since any three nails may be considered the apexes of a triangle.

Can the colors of the strings be distributed so that no one triangle has all three sides (strings) of the same color? If so, how? And if not, why not?

12. In a certain bank there are eleven distinct positions, namely, in decreasing rank, President, First Vice-President, Second Vice-President, Third Vice-President, Cashier, Teller, Assistant Teller, Bookkeeper, First Stenographer, Second Stenographer, and Janitor. These eleven positions are occupied by the following, listed alphabetically: Mr. Adams, Mrs. Brown, Mr. Camp, Miss Dale, Mr. Evans, Mrs. Ford, Mr. Grant, Miss Hill, Mr. Jones, Mrs. Kane, and Mr. Long. Concerning them, only the following facts are known:

a. The Third Vice-President is the pampered grandson of the President and is disliked by both Mrs. Brown and the Assistant Teller.

b. The Assistant Teller and the Second Stenographer shared equally in their father's estate.

c. The Second Vice-President and the Assistant Teller wear the same style of hat.

d. Mr. Grant told Miss Hill to send him a stenographer at once.

e. The President's nearest neighbors are Mrs. Kane, Mr. Grant, and Mr. Long.

f. The First Vice-President and the Cashier live at the exclusive Bachelor's Club.

g. The janitor, a miser, has occupied the same garret room since boyhood.

h. Mr. Adams and the Second Stenographer are leaders in the social life of the younger unmarried set.

i. The Second Vice-President and the Bookkeeper were once engaged to be married to each other.

j. The fashionable Teller is the son-in-law of the First Stenographer.

k. Mr. Jones regularly gives Mr. Evans his discarded clothing to wear, without the elderly Bookkeeper knowing about the gift.

Show how to match correctly the eleven names against the eleven positions occupied.

13. Picture a checkerboard (or chessboard) having eight rows and eight columns of squares, alternately colored red and black. We are given a package of oblong dominoes, each one covering two of the squares of the chessboard, and the task of covering the chessboard completely. Obviously 32 dominoes are needed to cover the entire board.

But suppose we are given only 31 dominoes, so that, seeking to cover the chessboard, we must leave two squares empty. Suppose also that the upper-left-hand corner of the chessboard is left empty, so that one other square will also have to be left uncovered. Can the 31 dominoes be placed in such a way as to leave, as the other empty square, the square in the lower-right-hand corner? If so, how? And if not, why not?

14. In the same mythical community described in Exercise 1, a stranger meets three other natives and asks them, "How many of you are politicians?" The first native replies, "We are all

politicians." The second native says, "No, just two of us are politicians." The third native then says, "That isn't true either."

Is the third native a politician?

## Challenge to the Reader

Here is a final problem in reasoning whose solution will require the construction of a set of sustained arguments. It isn't easy—but solving it is well within your power and will give you great pleasure.

15. You are presented with a set of twelve metal balls, apparently identical in every respect: size, color, and so on. In fact, eleven of them are identical, but one of them is "odd": It differs from all the rest in weight only; it is either heavier, or lighter, than all the others. You are given a balance scale, on which the balls can be weighed against one another. If the same number of balls are put on each side of the balance, and the "odd" ball is on one side, that side will go down if the odd ball is heavier, or up if the odd ball is lighter; the two sides will balance if the odd ball is not among those weighed and the same number of balls are placed on each side. You are allowed three weighings only; any removal or addition of a ball constitutes a separate weighing.

    Your challenge is this: Devise a set of three weighings that will enable you to identify the odd ball wherever it may lie in a random mixing of the twelve balls, *and* that will enable you to determine whether the odd ball is heavier or lighter than the rest.

## Summary of Chapter 3

In this chapter we have explained the central role of **the problematic situation** in stimulating inquiry, and **the power of reasoning** in alleviating the uncertainties such problems can create, in science and in everyday life. We have exhibited the ways in which logic may be used to resolve some such problematic situations, by illustrating the process of reasoning as it may be applied to various kinds of contrived problems, commonly known as brainteasers. We emphasize here the intellectual pleasure that is offered by the exercise of reason.

# Constraint Satisfaction Problems and Logic Puzzles

**Donald Nute**

Logic puzzles and many games belong to a class of problems that require the problem-solver to simultaneously satisfy a set of constraints. Here are other examples of constraint satisfaction problems.

1. Scheduling
2. Resource allocation
3. Solving sets of equations
4. Assembly

Here are some exercises to help develop your skills at solving constraint satisfaction problems.

1. Classes are offered periods 1-8 with 1-4 in the morning and 5-8 in the afternoon. You need three classes and you can use MAT, CHM, PHY, or HIS. CHM is offered odd periods and MAT is offered all periods. HIS is offered periods 2 and 4. PHY is offered periods 5 and 7. CHM and MAT are taught on south campus. HIS and PHY are taught on north campus. You can't schedule back-to-back classes on opposite ends of campus. You have to work mornings or afternoons and you don't want a first period class. Can you satisfy all these constraints? If so, do you tell your boss you will work in the mornings or in the afternoons?

2. Mr. Adams, Mrs. Barber, Mr. Cox, Miss Duke, and Miss Evans live in a row of houses in the same block. Each owns a dog. The dogs they own are a beagle, a collie, a dschshund, a poodle, and a retriever. Mr. Cox and Miss Duke live at the ends of the row of houses. A woman owns the retriever. The collie lives in the middle house. Miss Duke does not own thepoodle. The dachshund was a gift from the owner's husband. The retriever lives between the collie and the beagle. Which breed of dog does each person own?

3. Skeletons of Eucentrosaurus, Hadrosaurus, Herrerasaurus, Megasaurus, and Nuoerosaurus have been found in Argentina, Canada, China, England, and the U.S. None of these dinosaurs has been found in more than one of these countries. The dinosaur from China is the largest of the bunch, Herrerasaurus was the smallest, and Megasaurus was larger than Hadrosaurus or Eucentrosaurus. The dinosaurs from China and North America were plant-eaters but Megasaurus ate meat. Eucentrosaurus lived in North America. The dinosaurs from North America and England lived later than Herrerasaurus. Hadrosaurus lived in Argentina or the U.S. Which dinosaur lived in which country?

To make a widget using a widget-maker, you must put a metal blank in the slot, push the button, turn the crank, pull the lever, and turn the key, but these actions must be done in a certain order. The first thing you do is either pull the lever or turn the key. You can't put the blank in the slot until after you push the button and turn the crank, and you have to do something after you put in the blank. The key won't turn when there is no blank in the slot. You must push the button immediately after you pull the lever. How do you make a widget?

4. (From John and Sally Quinn, *Logic Puzzles for Students*, http://members.home.net/sallycquinn/) Jack has a high school crush on Jill. During study hall, he finally gathers all of his courage and writes her a note asking her out on Saturday night. The note passes to five students (who all read it) before it gets to Jill. Just as Jill gets the note, Mrs. Wilson the teacher confiscates it. After reading the note, she wants to know all who were involved in the note passing incident. She questions her students, and receives the following responses.
   o The girl studying English passed it to Paul who passed it to the girl in green.
   o Josephine passed it to the boy in blue who gave it to Alexis who was reading.
   o The girl in black gave it to Jill.
   o Jack first gave it to Mary who was studying English.
   o The girl in black who was reading got the note from Derrick.

   Mrs. Wilson remembers the following facts from study hall.

   o Paul was wearing yellow.
   o Derrick was studying French.
   o The girl in green was studying science.
   o One of the students other than Jack or Jill was wearing red, and one was studying history.

   From the information given by the students, can you determine what color each culprit was wearing, the subject they were studying and the order that they received the note?

5. (Modified from Sally Quinn's Puzzle Spot, http://www.norfacad.pvt.k12.va.us/puzzles/sallys.htm.)


   Dear Mom and Dad,

   I am having a great time at camp. There are five guys in my cabin and our beds are all lined up in a row. My bed is up against a wall with a window, and when I sleep on my left side I can look out at the moonlight. The boy whose bed is next to mine is from Maine and Sam is next to him. The kids in my cabin come from all over the USA. Mac and the Franklin boy are from neighboring states. John

Smith is the only boy from west of the Mississippi River. Fred is from the most southern state and the Thomas kid is from the most northern state. Tim and Sam took a plane to camp, but Mac got to ride in a train. When Mr. Miller came to visit his son, he took Sam, Fred, Tim, and me out to dinner with them. When Sam's mom writes to him from North Carolina, she always sends him cookies. He shares them with Mac and Tim whose beds are next to his. After lights out, I can whisper to the guys whose beds are close. I don't get to talk to the Smith boy much because his bed is the farthest away from mine.

Love, Mort

Can you determine who sleeps where in the cabin and where each boy is from?

6. (Modified from Sally Quinn's Puzzle Spot, http://www.norfacad.pvt.k12.va.us/puzzles/sallys.htm)

"You'll be late for your own funeral." Her mother's words kept repeating in Alex's head as she approached the fair grounds-late again! It was a curse, no matter how hard she tried, she was always late. This time she had missed the first class of the local horse show. Not really a major crisis, but she had to report the results to the local paper. She couldn't let her boss know that she had arrived late. His last words were, "If you are late one more time, you're fired!" She needed to figure out another way to write her article accurately for the paper. As Alex entered the show grounds, she overheard bits of conversation which she jotted down.

- o No horse and rider had the same name.
- o Danny rode his white mare.
- o The horse named April finished behind the rider named Sue and ahead of the black mare.
- o April rode the Chestnut gelding and finished one place ahead of the bay horse.
- o The Gray horse named Gopher was not first or last place.
- o The horse named Doc was first, and the rider named Doc was third.

By looking at a program, Alex discovered that the horses and riders names were Doc, April, Sue, Danny, and Gopher. She knew that April and Sue were the only mares. Does Alex have enough information to fool her boss and write the article accurately?

7. There are three gentlemen in a meeting: Mr. Yellow, Mr. Green and Mr. Brown. They are wearing yellow, green and brown ties. Mr. Yellow says: "Did you notice that the color of our ties are different from our names?" The person who is wearing the green tie says, "Yes, you are right!" Do you know who is wearing what color of tie?

8. When the Titanic sank in the ocean, four gentlemen and four young ladies floated on to an island. After a while, all of them fell in love with each other. Each person loved one and only one. The girl that John loved fell in love with Jim. The girl that Allan loved fell in love with Bill. The gentleman that Rose loved fell in love with Mary. Gloria loved the gentleman who loved rose. Gloria did not like Jim and John. Bill did not like Mary. Jill did not like the gentleman who loved her. The question is: Whom did Allan love?

9. There are five houses in a row and in five different colors. In each house lives a person from a different country. Each person drinks a certain drink, smokes a certain cigar and keeps a certain pet. No two people drink the same drink, smoke the same cigar or keep the same pet.   The Brit lives in a red house. The Swede keeps dogs. The Dane drinks tea. The green house is on the left of the white house. The green house owner drinks coffee. The person who smokes Pall Mall rears birds. The owner of the yellow house smokes Dunhill. The man living in the house right in the centre drinks milk. The Norwegian lives in the first house. The man who smokes Blends lives next to the man who keeps cats. The man who keeps horses lives next to the one who smokes Dunhill. The man who smokes Bluemaster drinks beer. The German smokes Prince. The Norwegian lives next to the blue house. The man who smokes Blend has a neighbur who drinks water. Who owns the fish?

10. (From John and Sally Quinn, *Logic Puzzles for Students*, http://members.home.net/sallycquinn/) Jack's parents are going to his school for parents' night. They are supposed to visit his classes, but Jack forgot to give them a copy of his schedule. They each remember a few things that Jack has told them about his classes. By piecing together these facts, they are able to determine who teaches each class and when it meets during the five bells.

Jack's father remembers these facts.

- o  Math is Jack's hardest subject, and he is glad that is first everyday.
- o  Mr. James' class is before science and history and none of these three is last.
- o  A woman teaches P.E. and a man teaches English.

Jack's mother remembers these facts.

- o  A man teaches history.
- o  Mrs. Jack teaches science third bell.
- o  Mrs. Jarvis' class is the last class of the day.

What is Jack's schedule, including the instructors?

# SOLUTIONS TO SELECTED EXERCISES

## SECTION 1.3

*Exercises on pp. 10-13*

5.     PREMISS:   We are all sinners.
    CONCLUSION:   We ought to forbear to judge.

10.    PREMISS:   Light moves at a finite speed.
    CONCLUSION:   Looking at objects that are millions of miles away is actually looking at light that was emitted many years ago.

15.    PREMISSES:   The more poorly students perform, the more money public education asks for and gets.
    CONCLUSION:   The institution of public education thrives on its own failures.

20.    PREMISSES:   In 1998 AIDS was the infectious disease that killed most people around the world.
    The AIDS epidemic is not abating.
    CONCLUSION:   Unquestionably, no more important goal exists in medical research today than the development of an AIDS vaccine.

## SECTION 1.4

*Exercises on pp. 21-23*

5.     PREMISS:   The divorce rate is very low where marriage is prearranged.
    CONCLUSION:   If you marry without love you may later come to love the person you marry.
    PREMISS:   The divorce rate is very high where marriage decisions are based on love.
    CONCLUSION:   If you marry the person you love you may not have a successful marriage.

10.    PREMISSES:   Petitioner argues that Congress may regulate gender-motivated crime because of its substantial economic effects. Gender-motivated violence is a subset of all violent crime, and is certain to have lesser nationwide economic impact than does the total of violent crimes.
    CONCLUSION:   Petitioner's reasoning would allow Congress to regulate murder or any other type of violence.

11.    DISCUSSION:   Variants of the following arguments were presented by several Supreme Court justices.
    To support the conclusion that the death sentence should be nullified in this case, premisses such as these were employed:
        The question asked by the jury on their return indicates that they were confused or uncertain about their duty with respect to the imposition of the death penalty.

The agitation of the jurors further supports the belief that they were confused.

A death sentence imposed by a jury confused or uncertain about its duty ought not be sustained.

To support the conclusion that the death sentence should not be nullified, premisses such as these were employed:

The judge's instructions—that the jury "may" impose the death penalty—were clear.

The question asked by the jury was answered by directing their attention to this clear instruction.

A jury is presumed to understand a judge's answer to its questions.

(The case was *Weeks v. Angelone*, decided 19 January 2000. The death sentence was upheld in a 5–4 decision of the Court.)

## SECTION 1.5

*Exercises on pp. 30-36*

**I.**

5.    PREMISSES:    If future scientists find a way to signal back in time, their signals would have reached us already.
But such signals have not reached us.
       CONCLUSION:    Future scientists never will find a way to signal back in time.

10.    PREMISSES:    The IRS code is inordinately complex, imposes an enormous burden on taxpayers, and thus undermines compliance with the law.
Repeated efforts to simplify and reform the law have failed.
Further patchwork will only compound the problem.
       CONCLUSION:    It is time to repeal the IRS code and start over.
(The first premiss of this argument may be analyzed as containing an argument that has two premisses and the conclusion is that the IRS code undermines compliance with the law.)

**II.**

5.    PREMISS:    Vacuum cleaners to insure clean houses are essential.
       CONCLUSION:    Our houses are generally clean.
       PREMISS:    Street cleaners to clean streets are an unfortunate expense.
       CONCLUSION:    Our streets are generally filthy.

10.    DIAGRAMED:    ① [This dichotomy between the "best" and the "best black" is not something manufactured by racists to denigrate the abilities of professionals who are not white.] ② [On the contrary, it is reinforced from time to time by those students who demand that universities commit to hiring some preset number of minority faculty members . . . saying (in effect), "Go out and hire the best blacks."] ③ [And it is further reinforced by faculty members who see these demands as nothing more than claims for simple justice.]

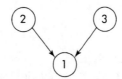

15.    PREMISSES:   Because I like Nolan Myers I heard toughness and confidence in his answers.
                         If I hadn't liked him I would have heard arrogance and bluster.
      CONCLUSION:   (and the premiss of a succeeding argument): The first impression becomes a self-fulfilling prophesy: We hear what we expect to hear.
      CONCLUSION:   The interview is biased in favor of the nice.
                         (Each of the first two premisses may be analyzed as an argument as well.)

20.    PREMISSES:   Native American beliefs about the past and the dead should not be allowed to dictate government policy on the investigation and interpretation of early American prehistory.
                         Only theories built on empirical evidence and capable of adjustment are scientific.
      CONCLUSION:   If a choice must be made between Native American theories and scientific theories, primacy should be given to scientific theories.

## SECTION 1.6

*Exercises on pp. 39-44*

5. This is not an argument, but a brief account of what black holes are, and an explanation of why they appear black.

10. This is an explanation of why traditionally Cupid is painted blind, and thus an explanation of why it is that so much conduct, under the influence of love, is not rational.

15. On the surface, this may be taken as an explanation of why it is that girls become afraid of science and find it less interesting than do boys. But it also serves as an argument supporting the claim that, since these outcomes are learned, parents and teachers can and should do more to encourage girls' interests in science.

20. Although this passage may be taken to explain some of what goes on in the schools, it is essentially an argument whose conclusion, stated first, is the controversial claim that Americans are simply not learning science—a conclusion supported by the five premisses that follow.

25. This is essentially an explanation, an account of the unacknowledged social and political circumstances that account for the fact that "black boys tend to shoot." It may also serve indirectly as an argument in support of policies that would alter those circumstances.

## Section 1.10

*Exercises on pp. 56-60*

1. ① [Democratic laws generally tend to promote the welfare of the greatest possible number] for ② [they emanate from the majority of the citizens, who are subject to error, but who cannot have an interest opposed to their own advantage.] ③ [The laws of an aristocracy tend, on the contrary, to concentrate wealth and power in the hands of the minority;] because ④ [an aristocracy, by its very nature, constitutes a minority.] It may therefore be asserted as a general proposition, that ⑤ [the purpose of a democracy in its legislation is more useful to humanity than that of an aristocracy.]

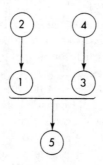

5.   "... You appeared to be surprised when I told you, on our first meeting, that you had come from Afghanistan."

"You were told, no doubt."

"Nothing of the sort. I *knew* you came from Afghanistan. From long habit the train of thoughts ran so swiftly through my mind that I arrived at the conclusion without being conscious of intermediate steps. There were such steps, however. The train of reasoning ran, ' ① [Here is a gentleman of a medical type,] but ② [with the air of a military man.] Clearly ③ [an army doctor,] then. ④ [He has just come from the tropics,] for ⑤ [his face is dark,] and ⑥ [that is not the natural tint of his skin,] for ⑦ [his wrists are fair.] ⑧ [He has undergone hardship and sickness], as ⑨ [his haggard face says clearly.] ⑩ [His left arm has been injured.] ⑪ [He holds it in a stiff and unnatural manner.] ⑫ [Where in the tropics could an English army doctor have seen much hardship and got his arm wounded? Clearly in Afghanistan.]' The whole train of thought did not occupy a second. I then remarked that you came from Afghanistan, and you were astonished."

"It is simple enough as you explain it," I said, smiling.

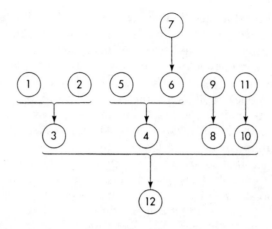

**10.** ① [Nothing is demonstrable unless the contrary implies a contradiction.]
② [Nothing that is distinctly conceivable implies a contradiction.]
③ [Whatever we conceive as existent, we can also conceive as nonexistent.]
Therefore, ④ [there is no being whose nonexistence implies a contradiction.]
Consequently ⑤ [there is no being whose existence is demonstrable.]

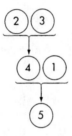

## SECTION 1.11

*Exercises on pp. 67-69*

1. If the first native is a politician, then he lies and denies being a politician. If the first native is not a politician, then he tells the truth and denies being a politician. In either case, then, the first native denies being a politician.

   Since the second native reports that the first native denies being a politician, he tells the truth, and is, therefore, a nonpolitician.

   The third native asserts that the first native is a politician. If the first native is a politician, then the third native speaks the truth and is, therefore, a nonpolitician. If the first native is a nonpolitician, then the third native lies and is, therefore, a politician. Hence only one of the first and third natives is a politician, and since the second is a nonpolitician, there is only one politician among the three natives.

5. Since Lefty said that Spike did it, Spike's first and third statements are equivalent in meaning and therefore either both true or both false. Since only one statement is false, they are both true.

Dopey's third statement is, therefore, false, and so his first two are true. Therefore Butch's third statement is false and so his first two are true, of which the second reveals that Red is the guilty man.

(An alternative method of solving this problem is suggested by Peter M. Longley of the University of Alaska. All but Red both assert their innocence *and* accuse someone else. If their professions of innocence are false, so are their accusations of other persons. But no one makes two false statements, so their statements that they are innocent must be true. Hence Red is the guilty one. This solution, however, presupposes that only one of the men is guilty.)

(Still another method of solving this problem comes from James I. Campbell of Eisenhower College and Walter Charen of Rutgers College. Dopey's second statement and Butch's third statement are contradictory, so at least one must be false. But if Dopey's second statement were false, his third statement would be true and Spike would be guilty. However, if Spike were guilty, his first and third statements would both be false, so he cannot be guilty and hence Dopey's second statement cannot be false. Therefore, Butch's third statement must be false, whence his second statement is true and Red is the guilty man.)

10. It is not possible to distribute the strings so that no one triangle has all three sides (strings) of the same color; at least one triangle must have three sides of the same color.

    Consider any one nail, say the one on a wall we call A. From it stretch five strings, and of these five at least three must be of the same color, since only two colors (red and blue) are available. Suppose that three of the strings from the nail in wall A are red, and that they go to the other three walls, B, C, and D. Now consider the triangle formed by the nails on these three other walls, B, C, and D. They must not all be of the same color, so they cannot all be blue, so at least one of them must be red. But if any one of the strings connecting B, C, and D is red, it must complete a triangle of three red strings. (Suppose the string connecting B and D is the red one. Then there will be a triangle of three red strings connecting A, B and D, etc.) No matter which nail we begin with, there is no way to avoid at least one triangle all of whose sides are strings of the same color.

11. Challenge to the reader:

    Presenting the solution to this lovely problem would rob our readers of too much pleasure. One hint will be enough: Every correct solution (there are several!) must begin with a weighing in which four balls are weighed against four. From this point, the solution is straightforward!

## Section 8.2

*Exercises on pp. 83-86*

I. **1.** True. **5.** True. **10.** True. **15.** False. **20.** True. **25.** False.

II. **1.** True. **5.** False. **10.** True. **15.** True. **20.** False. **25.** False.

III. **1.** True. **5.** True. **10.** False. **15.** False. **20.** True. **25.** False.

IV. **1.** $I \bullet \sim L$ **5.** $\sim I \bullet \sim L$ **10.** $\sim(E \vee J)$
**15.** $\sim I \vee L$ **20.** $(I \bullet E) \vee \sim(J \bullet S)$ **25.** $(L \bullet E) \bullet (S \bullet J)$

## Section 8.3

*Exercises on pp. 93-95*

I. 1. True. **5.** False. **10.** True. **15.** False. **20.** False. **25.** True.

II. **1.** True. **5.** False. **10.** False. **15.** True. **20.** False. **25.** True.

III. **1.** $A \supset (B \supset C)$ **5.** $(A \bullet B) \supset C$ **10.** $\sim[A \supset (B \bullet C)]$
**15.** $B \supset (A \vee C)$ **20.** $B \vee C$ **25.** $(\sim C \bullet \sim D) \supset (\sim B \vee A)$

## Section 8.4

*Exercises on pp. 106-109*

I. pp. 331–333
e. 10 is the specific form of *e*.
o. 3 has *o* as a substitution instance, and 24 is the specific form of *o*.

**II.** p. *107*

**1.**

| *p* | *q* | *p ⊃ q* | *~q* | *~p* | *~q ⊃ ~p* |
|---|---|---|---|---|---|
| T | T | T | F | F | T |
| T | F | F | T | F | F |
| F | T | T | F | T | T |
| F | F | T | T | T | T |
| valid | | | | | |

**5.**

| *p* | *q* | *p ⊃ q* |
|---|---|---|
| T | T | T |
| T | F | F |
| F | T | T |
| F | F | T |
| invalid (shown by second row) | | |

**10.**

| *p* | *q* | *p • q* |
|---|---|---|
| T | T | T |
| T | F | F |
| F | T | F |
| F | F | F |
| valid | | |

**15.**

| *p* | *q* | *r* | *q ⊃ r* | *p ⊃ (q ⊃ r)* | *p ⊃ r* | *q ⊃ (p ⊃ r)* | *p ∨ q* | *(p ∨ q) ⊃ r* |
|---|---|---|---|---|---|---|---|---|
| T | T | T | T | T | T | T | T | T |
| T | T | F | F | F | F | F | T | F |
| T | F | T | T | T | T | T | T | T |
| T | F | F | T | T | F | T | T | F |
| F | T | T | T | T | T | T | T | T |
| F | T | F | F | T | T | T | T | F |
| F | F | T | T | T | T | T | F | T |
| F | F | F | T | T | T | T | F | T |
| invalid (shown by fourth and sixth row) | | | | | | | | |

**20.**

| p | q | r | s | p • q | p ⊃ q | (p • q) ⊃ r | r ⊃ s | p ⊃ (r ⊃ s) | (p ⊃ q) • [(p • q) ⊃ r] | p ⊃ s |
|---|---|---|---|---|---|---|---|---|---|---|
| T | T | T | T | T | T | T | T | T | T | T |
| T | T | T | F | T | T | T | F | F | T | F |
| T | T | F | T | T | T | F | T | T | F | T |
| T | T | F | F | T | T | F | T | T | F | F |
| T | F | T | T | F | F | T | T | T | F | T |
| T | F | T | F | F | F | T | F | F | F | F |
| T | F | F | T | F | F | T | T | T | F | T |
| T | F | F | F | F | F | T | T | T | F | T |
| F | T | T | T | F | T | T | T | T | T | T |
| F | T | T | F | F | T | T | F | T | T | T |
| F | T | F | T | F | T | T | T | T | T | T |
| F | T | F | F | F | T | T | T | T | T | T |
| F | F | T | T | F | T | T | T | T | T | T |
| F | F | T | F | F | T | T | F | T | T | T |
| F | F | F | T | F | T | T | T | T | T | T |
| F | F | F | F | F | T | T | T | T | T | T |

valid

## III. p. 107

**1.** $(A \lor B) \supset (A \bullet B)$     $(p \lor q) \supset (p \bullet q)$
  $A \lor B$     has the specific   $p \lor q$
  $\therefore A \bullet B$     form     $\therefore p \bullet q$

| p | q | p ∨ q | p • q | (p ∨ q) ⊃ (p • q) |
|---|---|---|---|---|
| T | T | T | T | T |
| T | F | T | F | F |
| F | T | T | F | F |
| F | F | F | F | T |

valid

**5.** $(I \lor J) \supset (I \bullet J)$     $(p \lor q) \supset (p \bullet q)$
  $\sim(I \lor J)$     has the specific   $\sim(p \lor q)$
  $\therefore \sim(I \bullet J)$     form     $\therefore \sim(p \bullet q)$

| p | q | p ∨ q | p • q | (p ∨ q) ⊃ (p • q) | ~(p ∨ q) | ~(p • q) |
|---|---|---|---|---|---|---|
| T | T | T | T | T | F | F |
| T | F | T | F | F | F | T |
| F | T | T | F | F | F | T |
| F | F | F | F | T | T | T |

valid (Note: Fallacy of denying the antecedent is *not* committed here!)

**10.** $U \supset (V \lor W)$                    $p \supset (q \lor r)$
    $(V \bullet W) \supset {\sim}U$    has the specific    $(q \bullet r) \supset {\sim}p$
    $\therefore {\sim}U$                    form            $\therefore {\sim}p$

| $p$ | $q$ | $r$ | $q \lor r$ | $p \supset (q \lor r)$ | $q \bullet r$ | ${\sim}p$ | $(q \bullet r) \supset {\sim}p$ |
|---|---|---|---|---|---|---|---|
| T | T | T | T | T | T | F | F |
| T | T | F | T | T | F | F | T |
| T | F | T | T | T | F | F | T |
| T | F | F | F | F | F | F | T |
| F | T | T | T | T | T | T | T |
| F | T | F | T | T | F | T | T |
| F | F | T | T | T | F | T | T |
| F | F | F | F | T | F | T | T |
| Invalid (shown by second and third row) | | | | | | | |

## IV. pp. *108-109*

**1.** $A \supset (B \bullet C)$                    $p \supset (q \bullet r)$
    ${\sim}B$            has the specific    ${\sim}q$
    $\therefore {\sim}A$            form            $\therefore {\sim}p$

| $p$ | $q$ | $r$ | $q \bullet r$ | $p \supset (q \bullet r)$ | ${\sim}q$ | ${\sim}p$ |
|---|---|---|---|---|---|---|
| T | T | T | T | T | F | F |
| T | T | F | F | F | F | F |
| T | F | T | F | F | T | F |
| T | F | F | F | F | T | F |
| F | T | T | T | T | F | T |
| F | T | F | F | T | F | T |
| F | F | T | F | T | T | T |
| F | F | F | F | T | T | T |
| valid | | | | | | |

**5.** $M \supset (N \supset O)$                    $p \supset (q \supset r)$
    $N$            has the specific    $q$
    $\therefore O \supset M$    form            $\therefore r \supset p$

| $p$ | $q$ | $r$ | $q \supset r$ | $p \supset (q \supset r)$ | $r \supset p$ |
|---|---|---|---|---|---|
| T | T | T | T | T | T |
| T | T | F | F | F | T |
| T | F | T | T | T | T |
| T | F | F | T | T | T |
| F | T | T | T | T | F |
| F | T | F | F | T | T |
| F | F | T | T | T | F |
| F | F | F | T | T | T |
| invalid (shown by fifth row) | | | | | |

**10.** symbolized    specific form
$C \supset (I \bullet D)$    $p \supset (q \bullet r)$    valid
$(I \vee D) \supset B$    $(q \vee r) \supset s$
$\therefore C \supset B$    $\therefore p \supset s$

## SECTION 8.5

*Exercises on pp. 113-114*

I.

**1.** *c* is the specific form of 1.
**5.** *c* has 5 as a substitution instance, and *i* is the specific form of 5.
**10.** *e* has 10 as a substitution instance.

II.
**1.**

| $p$ | $q$ | $p \supset q$ | $p \supset (p \supset q)$ | $[p \supset (p \supset q)] \supset q$ |
|---|---|---|---|---|
| T | T | T | T | T |
| T | F | F | F | T |
| F | T | T | T | T |
| F | F | T | T | F |
| contingent | | | | |

**5.**

| $p$ | $q$ | $\sim q$ | $q \bullet \sim q$ | $p \supset$ $(q \bullet \sim q)$ | $p \supset$ $[p \supset (q \bullet \sim q)]$ |
|---|---|---|---|---|---|
| T | T | F | F | F | F |
| T | F | T | F | F | F |
| F | T | F | F | T | T |
| F | F | T | F | T | T |
| contingent | | | | | |

**10.** Contingent.    Final column:    T T T T T T T T T F F T T F T

III.
**1.**

| $p$ | $q$ | $p \supset q$ | $\sim q$ | $\sim p$ | $\sim q \supset \sim p$ | $(p \supset q) \equiv$ $(\sim q \supset \sim p)$ |
|---|---|---|---|---|---|---|
| T | T | T | F | F | T | T |
| T | F | F | T | F | F | T |
| F | T | T | F | T | T | T |
| F | F | T | T | T | T | T |
| tautology | | | | | | |

**5.**

| $p$ | $q$ | $p \lor q$ | $p \cdot (p \lor q)$ | $p \equiv [p \cdot (p \lor q)]$ |
|---|---|---|---|---|
| T | T | T | T | T |
| T | F | T | T | T |
| F | T | T | F | T |
| F | F | F | F | T |

tautology

**10.**

| $p$ | $q$ | $p \supset q$ | $p \lor q$ | $(p \lor q) \equiv q$ | $(p \supset q) \equiv [(p \lor q) \equiv q]$ |
|---|---|---|---|---|---|
| T | T | T | T | T | T |
| T | F | F | T | F | T |
| F | T | T | T | T | T |
| F | F | T | F | T | T |

tautology

**15.**

| $p$ | $q$ | $r$ | $q \lor r$ | $p \cdot (q \lor r)$ | $p \cdot q$ | $p \cdot r$ | $(p \cdot q) \lor (p \cdot r)$ | $[p \cdot (q \lor r)] \equiv [(p \cdot q) \lor (p \cdot r)]$ |
|---|---|---|---|---|---|---|---|---|
| T | T | T | T | T | T | T | T | T |
| T | T | F | T | T | T | F | T | T |
| T | F | T | T | T | F | T | T | T |
| T | F | F | F | F | F | F | F | T |
| F | T | T | T | F | F | F | F | T |
| F | T | F | T | F | F | F | F | T |
| F | F | T | T | F | F | F | F | T |
| F | F | F | F | F | F | F | F | T |

tautology

**20.** tautology    Final column:  T T T T

## SECTION 11.1

*Exercises on pp. 148-152*

5. Analogical argument.
15. Nonargumentative use of analogy.

10. Analogical argument.
20. Analogical argument.


## SECTION 11.2

*Exercises on pp. 156-162*

I. **pp. 157-158**

5. (a) more, criterion 2; (b) less, criterion 5; (c) more, criterion 3; (d) neither, criterion 4; (e) more, criterion 6; (f) more, criterion 1.

II. **pp. 159-162**

1. Large diamonds, armies, great intellects all have the attributes of greatness [of value for diamonds, of military strength for armies, of mental superiority for intellects], and of divisibility [through cutting for diamonds; dispersion for armies; interruption, disturbance, and distraction for intellects].

   Large diamonds and armies all have the attribute of having their greatness diminish when they are divided.

   Therefore great intellects also have the attribute of having their greatness diminish when they are divided.

   (1) There are only three kinds of instances among which the analogies are said to hold, which is not very many. On the other hand, there are many, many instances of these kinds. By our first criterion the argument is fairly cogent.

   (2) There are but two kinds of instances in the premises with which the conclusion's instances are compared. Armies and large diamonds are, however, quite dissimilar to each other, so from the point of view of our second criterion, the argument is moderately cogent.

   (3) There are only three respects in which the things involved are said to be analogous. This is not many and the argument is accordingly rather weak.

   (4) Schopenhauer recognizes that the question of relevance is important, for he introduces a separate little discussion on this point. He urges that the superiority (the "greatness") of a great intellect "depends upon" its concentration or undividedness. Here he invokes the illustrative or explanatory (nonargumentative) analogy of the concave mirror, which focuses all its available light upon one point. There is indeed some merit in this claim, and by our fourth criterion the argument has a fairly high degree of cogency.

   (5) The instances with which the conclusion deals are enormously different from the instances mentioned in the premises. There are so many disanalogies between intellects, on the one hand, and large diamonds and armies, on the other, that by our fifth criterion Schopenhauer's argument is almost totally lacking in probative force.

(6) The conclusion states only that, when "divided," a great intellect will sink to the level of an ordinary one. This is not a terribly bold conclusion relative to the premises, and so by our sixth criterion the argument is fairly cogent.

Finally, however, it must be admitted that the whole passage might plausibly be analyzed as invoking large diamonds and armies for illustrative and explanatory rather than argumentative purposes. The plausibility of this alternative analysis, however, derives more from the weakness of the analogical argument than from what is explicitly stated in the passage in question.

5. This passage can be analyzed in two different ways. In both ways the analogical argument is presented primarily as an illustration of the biologist's reasoning.

(I) Porpoises and men all have lungs, warm blood, and hair.
Men are mammals.
Therefore porpoises also are mammals.

(1) There are many instances examined, which makes the conclusion probable.

(2) There are very few dissimilarities among men—biologically speaking—and by our second criterion this tends to weaken the argument.

(3) There are only three respects noted in the premises in which porpoises and men resemble each other. In terms of their sheer number, this is not many: not enough to make the argument plausible.

(4) But in terms of relevance the argument is superlatively good, because biologists have found the three attributes noted in the premises to be such remarkably dependable indicators of other mammalian characteristics.

(5) There are many disanalogies between men and porpoises: porpoises are aquatic, men are terrestrial; porpoises have tails, men do not; porpoises do not have the well-developed, highly differentiated limbs characteristic of men; and so on. These tend to weaken the argument.

(6) The conclusion is very bold relative to the premises, because so many attributes are summarized in the term "mammal" (shown by the variety of other, specific attributes confidently predicted by the zoologist). This tends, of course, to weaken the argument.

**Alternative analysis:**

(II) Porpoises and humans all have lungs, warm blood, and hair.
Humans also nurse their young with milk, have a four-chambered heart, bones of a particular type, a certain general pattern of nerves and blood vessels, and red blood cells that lack nuclei.
Therefore porpoises also nurse their young with milk, have a four-chambered heart, bones of the same particular type, the same general pattern of nerves and blood vessels, and red blood cells that lack nuclei.

This version of the analogical argument contained in the given passage is evaluated in much the same way as the first one discussed. It is somewhat stronger an argument than the first one according to the sixth criterion, because in spite of the apparently greater detail in the second version's conclusion, it is more modest than that of the first version, since being a mammal entails all of these anatomical details plus many more.

Nature has a way of reminding us that such arguments are only probable, however, and never demonstrative. For the platypus resembles all other mammals in having lungs, warm blood, hair, nursing their young with milk, and so on. Other mammals are viviparous (bearing their young alive). Therefore the platypus. . .? No, the platypus lays eggs.

10. This is an example of a very strong analogical argument. Using all of the six criteria for appraisal, we are not likely to find the argument deficient. The number of instances (our past visits to the dentist) probably is considerable. The variety of work done on our teeth during these visits (variety within the cases used in the premises) is likely to be substantial. The respects in which our dental visits and the dental visit in question are similar are likely to be many and significant: the same kind of treatment, on the same bodily organs, using the same kind of dental instruments, and so on. This is a case very much like those with which we have direct experience. The causal relevance of the treatments is undoubted. The claim made in the conclusion (merely that the extraction hurt him) is modest and entirely reasonable. If the argument proves in some degree vulnerable, that is likely to be because the person whose treatment is in question differs importantly from me with respect to his or her tolerance for pain. On this fifth criterion—the identification of some significant disanalogies—the argument may be attacked, but that attack is not likely to succeed in persuading us that his tooth extraction without anesthetic did not hurt him.

15. A watch and other human artifacts display an intricacy that justifies our inference that they have been designed by their maker. Natural mechanisms also are intricate, as are the processes of the universe; hence we are justified in concluding that they also are designed by some Maker.

    (1) There is an unlimited number of manufactured mechanisms that we know to have been designed and made. On the first criterion, the argument has much support.

    (2) There are many great dissimilarities among the cases in the premises, which strengthen the argument, but these dissimilarities do not block the major disanalogies noted under (5), so the argument cannot be said to gain very much from its strength on this criterion.

    (3) There is only one respect in which the products of human design are claimed to be like the products of the divine Maker, namely, the intricacy and complexity of the designs encountered—the "curious adapting of means to ends," as Hume put it in the *Dialogues Concerning Natural Religion*. Although this is only one respect, it is a respect of great importance if established. This single (but disputable) respect leaves the argument in problematic circumstances.

    (4) Whether the analogy is relevant is difficult to say. For those who doubt the applicability of cause-and-effect reasoning beyond the range of experienced phenomena, it would not be relevant and would be held to fail on that ground. For those who accept the universal applicability of

causal analysis, going beyond human experience even to the universe itself, the analogy is indeed relevant.

(5) There are many great disanalogies between the human artifacts mentioned in the premisses and the natural mechanisms we encounter. The size, duration, and general character of the universe render it greatly and importantly different from any watch or other humanly designed machine. From this point of view also, the conclusion has only little probability.

(6) How modest this conclusion is, relative to the premisses, depends on what is included in the claim that there is a divine Maker of the natural universe. If implicit in this conclusion is the singularity, perfection, infinity, and incorporeality of a supernatural Maker (as commonly intended by such arguments), the conclusion is very bold relative to the premisses, rendering the argument weak. If the qualities normally attributed to God are not part of the conclusion, the mere claim that there is a "Maker" may be modest enough to be well supported by the premisses.

All things considered, the argument is neither worthless nor compelling. The degree of probability with which it warrants its conclusion decreases, however, as the similarity of the Maker in that conclusion to the God of traditional Western theism increases. The truth of such theism, of course, is not affected by the weakness of an argument designed to establish it.

## SECTION 11.3

*Exercises on pp. 165-168*

5. The argument being refuted is the following:

> Trees are cut down in very great numbers to make paper.
> Using recycled paper would make it unnecessary to cut down many of those trees.
> Therefore, we ought to use recycled paper to reduce the slaughter of trees.

The refuting analogy is:

> Cornstalks are cut down in very great number to harvest corn.
> Cutting back on corn consumption would make it unnecessary to cut down many of those cornstalks.
> Therefore we ought to cut down on corn consumption in order to reduce the slaughter of cornstalks.

The refuting analogy does have the same form as the argument under attack. Moreover, its premisses are true and its conclusion surely is false. These considerations make this an effective counterargument. However, the refuting analogy supposes that the environmental status of cornstalks is essentially akin to that of trees. That plainly is disputable, and if a substantial disanalogy can be exhibited here, that would greatly weaken the purportedly refuting analogical argument.

## SECTION 4.2

*Exercises on pp. 194-199*

**I.**

1. *Ignoratio elenchi*—concern for the homeless is admirable, but not relevant to the pains allegedly felt by lobsters.
5. *Ignoratio elenchi.*
10. *Ad hominem* (abusive).
15. *Ad baculum*—plainly an appeal to the threat of force.

**II.**

1. Mr. Welch honestly believed that this attack against General Electric was based upon a false premiss, and his response may be taken as his very emphatic way of insisting that it was false. On the other hand, since his response is aimed at the speaker in her capacity as a nun, it is also in the form of an argument *ad hominem* (circumstantial).
5. Here again the attack is leveled against the claims of the NEA on the supposition that what is contained in the press release is no more than material designed to serve the interests of its members—an argument *ad hominem* (circumstantial). It is indeed wise practice to consider the interests of organizations that issue press releases, the better to interpret the claims made; but it is unfair to suppose that the claims made are mistaken, or the facts announced are false, just because they serve the purposes of the organizations issuing the press release.
10. The writer correctly contends that one who takes a revolutionary point of view need not sustain the obligation to provide a detailed account of the changes sought, and thus (although the context is not clear) the "interrogator" referred to may be addressing a matter that is not relevant. But the writer, in questioning the sincerity of the interrogator, commits an *ad hominem* (abusive).

## SECTION 4.3

*Exercises on pp. 205-207*

1. False Cause (*post hoc ergo propter hoc*)
5. *Petitio principii*
10. False Cause

## Section 4.4

*Exercises on pp. 215-221*

**I.**

1. Composition. It cannot be inferred from the fact that the parts have a specified shape that the whole has that same shape.
5. This is only a joke, of course. The argument of the joke is that, since you need
   no instruction on how to play the concertina without success, you need no
   instruction on how to play the concertina at all. If one were thus to interpret
   the phrase "without success" as though it modified the phrase "how to play
   the concertina," when in fact it was intended to modify "looked
   everywhere," this silly argument would commit the fallacy of amphiboly.
   Our recognition of the inadvertent amphiboly gives some amusement.
10. Composition.

**II.**

1. It may be argued that although the parts have functions, this does not permit
   the inference that the whole has functions. On this view, Aristotle here commits the fallacy of composition. On the other hand, many will argue that we
   may reasonably infer from the patterns found in some natural objects that
   similar patterns may be expected in other natural objects, in which case the
   passage would commit no fallacy.
5. It may be argued that the passage commits an *ad hominem* (circumstantial)
   fallacy in supposing that the competence of the school's chancellor is suspect
   in view of the school placement of his own children. On the other hand,
   many will argue that in placing his own children in private schools, the chancellor does unavoidably undermine public confidence in his support of the
   public schools, and that this conclusion is not fallacious.

**III.**

1. Equivocation, or alleged equivocation, is the nub of this dispute. If Justice
   Scalia were correct, the statute that increases the severity of punishment for
   "using" a firearm was not meant to impose that additional sanction on one
   who *traded* his firearm in the commission of the crime. Justice O'Connor, on
   the other hand, treats the terms "using" in the statute very broadly, so that
   any role the firearm may have played would satisfy the condition of being
   "used." Justice Scalia insists that her argument commits an equivocation
   because it treats "use" as meaning "use in any way whatever," while statutes
   ought to be read so that their words carry *ordinary* meanings. There is no
   obvious resolution of the logical issue; the legal issue was resolved by a vote
   of the Court.
5. An argument *ad populum* is plainly involved here, insofar as it is believed that
   a conclusion may be held acceptable because it was so widely approved. But
   it is probable that the author (Croce) is doing no more than calling attention
   to widespread irrationality at the time of the Inquisition.

10. This passage plays with false cause—but mixes with that fallacy an appeal to inappropriate authority. On the other hand the author, in jesting, is also ridiculing such an argument.

15. This argument may be construed to contain no fallacy, or to contain a blatant argument *ad baculum*, a resort to the threat of force. If construed to mean that congregants ought to behave in certain ways lest they be severely punished by an angry God, the argument contains no fallacy—although its factual supposition may be questioned, of course. If construed to mean also that, because those punishments are so fearfully threatening, some propositions (having nothing directly to do with God's anger) are *true*, and should be believed, the argument is fallacious, since the threats would not be relevant to the truth or falsity of those propositions. Probably the argument was intended in both ways.

20. A fallacy of false cause lies behind the humor in this passage. The answer to the query supposes, mistakenly, that the light in the daytime is caused by something other than the sun!

SECTION 3.3

*Exercises pp. 240-245*

**1.** If the first native is a politician, then he lies and denies being a politician. If the first native is not a politician, then he tells the truth and denies being a politician. In either case, then, the first native denies being a politician.

Since the second native reports that the first native denies being a politician, he tells the truth, and is, therefore, a nonpolitician.

The third native asserts that the first native is a politician. If the first native is a politician, then the third native speaks the truth and is, therefore, a nonpolitician. If the first native is a nonpolitician, then the third native lies and is, therefore, a politician. Hence only one of the first and third natives is a politician, and since the second is a nonpolitician, there is only one politician among the three natives.

**5.** Since Lefty said that Spike did it, Spike's first and third statements are equivalent in meaning and therefore either both true or both false. Since only one statement is false, they are both true.

Dopey's third statement is, therefore, false, and so his first two are true. Therefore Butch's third statement is false and so his first two are true, of which the second reveals that Red is the guilty man.

(An alternative method of solving this problem is suggested by Peter M. Longley of the University of Alaska. All but Red both assert their innocence *and* accuse someone else. If their professions of innocence are false, so are their accusations of other persons. But no one makes two false statements, so their statements that they are innocent must be true. Hence Red is the guilty one. This solution, however, presupposes that only one of the men is guilty.)

(Still another method of solving this problem comes from James I. Campbell of Eisenhower College and Walter Charen of Rutgers College. Dopey's second statement and Butch's third statement are contradictory, so at least one must be false. But if Dopey's second statement were false, his third statement would be true and Spike would be guilty. However, if Spike were guilty, his first and third statements would both be false, so he cannot be guilty and hence Dopey's second statement cannot be false. Therefore, Butch's third statement must be false, whence his second statement is true and Red is the guilty man.)

**10.** Number the diamonds, 1 to 10, and proceed as follows:

First weighing: 1, 2, 3, 4 against 5, 6, 7, 8

A. If they balance: The odd diamond must be 9 or 10.

Weigh 9 against 1; if 9 goes up, it is the odd diamond and light; if 9 goes down, it is the odd diamond and heavy; if they balance, the odd diamond must be 10. Then weigh 10 against 1; if 10 goes up, it is light; if it goes down, it is heavy.

B. If the eight diamonds in the first trial do not balance:

Suppose that 1, 2, 3, 4 go down, while 5, 6, 7, 8 go up.

Then weigh 1, 2, 8, 9 against 3, 4, 7, 10. If 1, 2, 8, 9 go down, the odd diamond must be either 1 or 2 and heavy, or 7 and light. Then weigh 1 against 2; if either goes down, it is the odd diamond and heavy. If they balance, the odd diamond is 7 and light. If, on the second weighing, 3, 4, 7, 10 go down, the odd diamond must be either 3 or 4 and heavy, or 8 and light. Weigh 3 against 4; if either goes down, it is the odd diamond and heavy; if they balance, the odd diamond is 8 and light.

Here is another solution for Exercise 10:

Number the diamonds, 1 to 10; then proceed as follows:

First weighing: Put the diamonds numbered 1, 2, and 3 on one side of the scale, and those number 4, 5, and 6 on the other side. If the two sides balance, we know the odd diamond is either 7, 8, 9, or 10. In that case, as a second weighing, put numbers 7 and 8 on one side of the scale, and numbers 9 and 2 (or any other number 1–6) on the other side. If these balance, the odd diamond must be 10; weigh it against any one of diamonds 1–6; if it goes down, it is heavy, and if it goes up, it is light. If on the second weighing, 7 and 8 go down and 9 and 2 go up, the odd diamond is heavy if it is seven or eight, and it is 9 if it is light. Then weigh 7 against 8; if either goes down, it is the odd diamond and heavy. If 7 and 8 balance, the odd diamond is 9 and light.

If, on the first weighing (1, 2, 3 against 4, 5, 6) one side (say, 1, 2, 3) goes down, then as a second trial put 1, 2, 4, 5 on one side of the scale, and 7, 8, 9, 10 on the other. If these balance the odd diamond must be either 3 and heavy, or 6 and light. Then put 3 on one side of the scale, 7 on the other. If these two balance, the odd diamond is 6 and light. If, on this second weighing (1, 2, 4, 5 against 7, 8, 9, 10) the side with 1, 2, 4, 5 goes down, we know the odd diamond must be 1 or 2 and must be heavy. Then we weigh 1 against 2 and the one that goes down is the odd diamond and is heavy. If on the second weighing the side with 1, 2, 4, 5 goes up, we know that the odd diamond must be either 4 or 5 and must be light. Weigh 4 against 5, and the diamond that goes up is the odd diamond and is light.

There are other solutions, all of which are variations on one of the two given above.